Under the Shade Tree

Praise for *Under the Shade Tree*

"Joseph Ogbonnaya's *Under the Shade Tree* is an insightful, honest, and critical narrative of the pivotal role of the Bible in the development of African Christianity. With a broad and incisive sweep of history, events, people, and places, he offers a compelling account of African Christianity and its culturally contextualized reading of the Bible, highlighting its distinctiveness, flaws, vibrancy, and relevance for global Christianity. This work is a tremendous contribution to biblical hermeneutics."

  Agbonkhianmeghe E. Orobator, SJ, dean of the Jesuit School of Theology of Santa Clara University and author of *Theology Brewed in an African Pot*

"*Under the Shade Tree* is a theological solution to the recuring problem of ahistorical reading of the Bible in general and in Africa in particular. Joseph Ogbonnaya's work brings a freshness that bridges existing gaps between systematic theology and biblical hermeneutics. Common folks will flock to it because it offers the non-specialist some sensible guides for reading Scripture in the twenty-first century. Scholars will embrace it because it draws from the richness of the Christian tradition and is grounded in the ecclesial practices of the Catholic Church."

  Cyril Orji, professor of systematic theology, University of Dayton and author of *Unmasking the African Ghost: Theology, Politics, and the Nightmare of Failed States*

"Joseph Ogbonnaya's *Under the Shade Tree* is an erudite and even-handed tour through the problems and promises, past and present, of African biblical hermeneutics. At once broadly ecumenical, but also recognizably Catholic in its approach, *Under the Shade Tree* evinces an unwavering commitment to the 'autochthonicity' of how Africans—scholars and ordinary people alike—read Christian scripture. Ogbonnaya proves a trustworthy guide, subtly teasing out authentic developments in contextual, decolonial, liberative, and feminist approaches, while never shying away from naming missteps and dangers that have emerged in efforts to confront the continent's history of colonization, dispossession, and impoverishment."

  Jonathan Heaps, director of the Bernard J. Lonergan Institute, Seton Hall University

"*Under the Shade Tree* is a bold expression of biblical hermeneutics—a resistance against cultural and religious erasure in the art of interpreting Scripture. It invites us into the heart of the human library, not only as the locus but as the very reason for engaging Scripture. In the African context, this engagement has become an imperative, an obligation, and indeed, an emergency. *Under the Shade Tree* is not merely a book—it is a game-changer. It offers an immersive journey into a world where Scripture becomes alive in context. By the time you finish reading, you will not want to close the book—you will want to begin again. This work opens up fresh mindsets, reshaping how readers engage with the Bible across Africa and beyond."

Chammah J. Kaunda, author of *The Nation That Fears God Prospers: A Critique of Zambian Pentecostal Theopolitical Imaginations*

Reading the Bible in Africa

Under the Shade Tree

JOSEPH OGBONNAYA

FORTRESS PRESS
MINNEAPOLIS

UNDER THE SHADE TREE
Reading the Bible in Africa

Copyright © 2025 Fortress Press. All rights reserved. Except for brief quotations in critical articles or reviews, no part of this book may be reproduced in any manner without prior written permission from the publisher. Email copyright@fortresspress.com or write to Permissions, Fortress Press, PO Box 1209, Minneapolis, MN 55440-1209.

Library of Congress Control Number: 2025009683 (print)

Cover image: Tree in the desert, photo by Orest Sv/Pexels
Cover design: Brice Hemmer

Print ISBN: 979-8-8898-3434-2
eBook ISBN: 979-8-8898-3435-9

Contents

	Acknowledgments	vii
	Introduction	ix
1.	Early African Christian Biblical Hermeneutics	1
2.	The Bible and Missionary Activities in Sub-Saharan Africa	41
3.	Popular Reading of the Bible	65
4.	Academic Reading of the Bible in Africa	93
5.	Ecclesiological Foundations of Biblical Interpretation	133
6.	The Future of Bible Reading in Africa	173
	Conclusion	209
	Bibliography	215
	Index	243

Acknowledgments

Situations and dialogues have been combined to make this book possible. Gratitude is due to the Judaism, Christianity, and Antiquity area of theology department Marquette University colloquium that drew my interest to the reading of the Bible in Africa. Facilitating graduate seminar in Hermeneutic Theory provided me with theoretical framework to relate African reading with Western reading of the Bible. I am grateful to my students for the many ways they encouraged me as I researched in this book. I benefited from the research of the African biblical scholars without whom this book would not have had any meaningful direction.

Special thanks are due to Fortress Press editorial team for accepting my proposal for this book; the eagle eye of its copyeditor ensured nothing is taken for granted; and its editor, Ryan Hemmer, whose editorial skill brought this book to shape.

I am also grateful to my colleagues with whom I discussed this topic. Your feedback is well appreciated, and you will find some of your constructive criticisms reflected in the book. Thank you, Prof. Cyril Orji, for nudging me to complete the book.

Introduction

African theology is primarily contextual. It takes Africa and African situations to be the seedbed for speaking of God. Such theology cannot be done outside the socioeconomic, political, social, and religious realities of Africans. Outside of its ancient tradition in and around the Mediterranean coastlines on the continent's northern edge, African theology grew out of missionary activities. It formed around culture as a practice of making sense of Christianity and embedding Christ into cultures. "Thus, African theology has come to be characterized by the tendencies toward inculturation and liberation, key issues in contemporary theology of mission."[1] Jean-Marc Éla, the Cameroonian priest, sociologist, and liberation theologian, brought together these tendencies in African theology in his "shade-tree" theology. The shade tree invokes the African practice of gathering as a community to discuss issues (palaver) under a tree. Éla was concerned about the deprivation of his local Kirdi community among whom he ministered. Farmers were forced to cultivate cash crops such as cocoa, cotton, and cashew, and they were cheated out of the profits of those crops and the food they provided. They also suffered psychosocially, as their festivities and culture are interconnected with their subsistent farming. They thus suffered the trauma of meaninglessness and purposelessness. These were the issues Ela and members of his community discussed under the palaver tree.

According to Éla, shade-tree theology is a metaphor for "a theology that, far from the libraries and the offices, develops among brothers and sisters searching shoulder to shoulder with unlettered peasants for the sense of the word of God in situations in which this word touches them."[2] It is a grassroots

---

1. David T. Ngong, "The Theologian as Missionary: The Legacy of Jean-Marc Ela," *Journal of Theology for South Africa* 136 (2010): 8.
2. Jean-Marc Éla, *African Cry*, vi, cited in Jackson Nii Sabaah Adamah, "Food Insecurity, Eucharist, and Community: Reading Jean-Marc Éla's 'Shade-tree' Theology in Light of Balthasar's Ecclesiology," *Review and Expositor* 117, no. 4 (2020): 539.

INTRODUCTION

theology that arose out of Éla's in-depth study of the Bible and his daily discussions on variety of topics with the Kirdis. He confessed:

> My theology under the tree developed during my period in North-Cameroon. I learnt a lot of things there that I had not learned at school. All day I was among the people in the mountains. I only studied or wrote at night. The gospel contains an enormous potential. On the terraces of the mountain slopes, where they had their small fields, we discussed together matters like the water supply, the soil, the millet . . . Talking under the tree, that meant not only talking in the shade, because of the heat, but for me, and gradually also for us: the realization of the tree of the Cross, of the suffering Jesus assumes in his cry on the Cross, the suffering of all the African peoples, all the cries of distress of the world.[3]

The shade tree is a theological metaphor for the passion of Christ, whose paschal mystery is a prototype of the endurance of pain and suffering for the poor, the marginalized, the oppressed, and the excluded. Face-to-face with deprivations arising from colonial administration and draconian political structures out to frustrate and dispossess the poor, shade-tree theology offers resources for empathy as well as resistance, resources that restore the wounded and degraded dignity of the poor. Éla's interaction with the Kirdis will be an example of the rapport that ought to exist between the academic and the ordinary readers of the Bible in Africa. He asked: "Do not we, theologians, feel the need to go outside out of libraries or offices and to change over to a type of society where one sees the person of intellect together with farmers and planters, the person with a university training together with illiterates, the doctor together with people from the jungle, and where one finds the theologian and the priest in the villages where hunger, misery and despair determine the future and lead people to the path of resistance?"[4] Sociologically, shade-tree theology is a symbol of the egalitarian structure of Éla's communities, where each person is democratically included and has a say in discussion of issues (palaver) for the common good of the communities.[5] It is also a symbol of freedom and equality between and among members of communities. It bridges the gap between the rich and the poor, the elite and

---

3. Jan Heijke, "Thinking in the Scene of Disaster: Theology of Jean-Marc Ela from Cameroon," *Exchange* 29, no. 1 (2000): 64.
4. Heijke, "Thinking in the Scene of Disaster," 68.
5. Heijke, "Thinking in the Scene of Disaster," 65.

the commoners, the clergy and the laity, the expert and the ordinary people. It sets the template for an understanding of the church as the people of God. It's also an indictment of the gap often visible in churches, African churches included, between the hungry and the filled, the ordained and the laity, and other ways the church perpetuates the social stratification that distinguishes between people based on their wealth and status.

This book adopts Éla's shade-tree theology to express the contextuality of African biblical hermeneutics with a focus on Africa's sociopolitical, economic, and religious situations that inform its reading of the Bible.

CONTEXTUALITY OF BIBLICAL INTERPRETATION

People read texts with the aim of understanding them, making sense of them, finding their meaning. They want to know what the author is saying, the context of the author, the veracity of the truth claims of the text, and so forth, but they do so in the light of their own contexts as readers, contexts "derived from the world-view and the social-cultural context of a particular cultural community."[6] Particular conceptual frames can become paradigmatic, creating new ways of associating with texts. But no interpretation is universally applicable across diverse conceptual frames of reference. Humans think using the dynamic structure of human consciousness, experiencing, understanding, judging, and deciding, according to Bernard Lonergan,[7] but people's interactions with their environments—which include their history, culture, geography, ethics, values, and so on—are different from one another. And so, no biblical hermeneutic is universal, not even when a Christian church tradition legislates the method; its actual implementation must follow the patterns of the life of the people, their conceptual frames of reference. The historical-critical method and other literary forms of scriptural interpretation are themselves contextual, arising in Europe from the post-Enlightenment frame of reference. The historical-critical method, while appreciated, is also contextual. It will be much more accepted by the parts of the world that share

---

6. Justin S. Ukpong, "Reading the Bible in a Global Village: Issues and Challenges from African Readings," in *Reading the Bible in the Global Village: Cape Town*, ed. Justin S. Ukpong et al. (Society of Biblical Literature, 2002), 21.

7. Bernard J. F. Lonergan, *Insight: A Study of Human Understanding*, CWL 3, ed. Frederick E. Crowe and Robert M. Doran (University of Toronto Press, 1992).

its frame of reference and by the group of people trained in it as a method (i.e., biblical scholars), not by ordinary readers of the Bible. African biblical hermeneutics, for scholarly and ordinary readers, is no less contextual than European, Asian, North American, Australian, Latin American, or other biblical hermeneutics.

This work summarizes the elements of this contextuality in African hermeneutics, beginning with the fathers of the church from Africa, the missionary hermeneutics of the nineteenth century, ordinary African people reading, as well as the academic readings of the Bible, including the ecclesiological foundations of biblical hermeneutics. Finally, it will offer a critical appraisal of African biblical hermeneutics, concluding with strong support for and deepening of African biblical hermeneutics in its various forms: enculturated, liberative, and feminist.

Early African readers of the Bible from North African Christianity approached the Bible as the word of God and sought to understand it through the rule of faith. The early African church fathers read the Bible christologically, convinced that the Old Testament is fulfilled and has its fullest meaning in Christ. They applied the Bible to the varying challenges of their time, including persecutions, issues of apostasy and readmission into the faith, social and economic conditions, as well as struggles for independence from Roman domination. And so they engaged in contextual biblical interpretation, specifically, with the drama of salvation as key to interpretation. They held that Scripture must be interpreted in the light of the context of the readers, their cultures, and ways of life. At the same time, one must be conscious of the context of various scriptural passages and not quote practices that are no longer useful contemporaneously to justify an archaic practice for contemporary societies. For instance, in *On Christian Doctrine*, Augustine warned against castigating the cultural context of scriptural interpretation simply because it differs from one's cultural context (3.18.26).

Early fathers of the church from Africa distinguished scholarly reading from ordinary people's reading, the spiritual sense of interpretation from the plain sense of Scripture. They insisted on a deeper meaning of Scripture, distinguishing several distinct senses: allegorical, typological, moral, spiritual, and anagogical. Some rules of interpretation, like Tyconius's rules, link the Bible with the church, emphasizing the universality of the Bible for the unity of the church and the centrality of the church for scriptural interpretation. The spirit of God, which inspired the authors of the Bible, gives authority to Scripture as the word of God and serves to guide the reader to correct interpretation. The goal of all scriptural interpretation is the love of God and neighbor.

Christianity began to spread to sub-Saharan Africa again in the nineteenth century, thanks to the missionary activities of various European mission agencies. The context of their activities within the colonial period and the various ways the missionaries were assisted by colonial administrations of their home countries tied their missions inextricably with colonialism. Thus, they have been identified as agents of imperialism, as collaborators in the subjugation of the people, and as racists for not recognizing the humanity and the cultures of the African peoples whom they evangelized. They were seen as agents of modernization responsible for the cultural genocide of Africans and responsible today for the anthropological poverty of Africans suffering from a crisis of identity.

At the same time, European Christian missionaries' zeal for translation made the Bible available to the people. Granted, there are several mistakes in the translations (like the misinterpretation of ancestors as demons), but translations of the Bible into the vernacular enabled Africans to identify elements of their cultural values within the biblical narratives. Missionaries of the Protestant churches were keener on Bible translation and zealous for its dissemination across the continent; Catholic missionaries emphasized the catechisms in local languages. The languages of Africans were transcribed into workable orthography, thus contributing to the transition of African languages from orality to textualization. This equally promoted literacy and education, which became the pillar of the later nationalist struggles for political independence. Missionary hermeneutics sets the template for biblical interpretation. Unfortunately, it did not encourage Africans to appreciate their cultural values and hence their distinctness as a people. Its hermeneutics was aimed at turning them into what they were not, African Europeans capable of appreciating only Western values but denigrators of their own cultures. Hence the push for decolonization of the Bible to free the people from the ideological and Eurocentric readings of the missionaries.

Ordinary people untrained in the skills of biblical interpretation read the Bible in the plain sense as it appears in translated versions in any of the African colonial languages (English, French, Portuguese, Spanish) or in the local vernacular. Ordinary people's reading is functional. They apply the Bible to the various issues, challenges of existence, and riddles of life facing them. They regard the Bible as the word of God, as inspired by the Holy Spirit. Most hold onto verbal inspiration, according to which the Bible is dictated by God. Although not often clearly stated, ordinary people hold to the unity of Scripture. That is, the Old Testament is an intrinsic part of the Christian Bible even though most identify more with the New Testament. As the word of God, the Bible they hold is meant to guide moral decisions and, proleptically, to lead a believer to eternal life. They recognize that in some cases, biblical texts have deeper meaning beyond the plain texts they are reading. In other words, they recognize the spiritual senses of Scripture as well.

Ordinary people's reading is influenced by their contexts, including their varying cosmogonies, which heavily consist of belief in the spirit world, a world enchanted by spirits, including the good spirits of ancestors as well as evil spirits that inhibit people's progress and stand between them and their destiny. They believe that the miracles recorded in the Bible are still alive in the church, as God is faithful to his promises. Post-Enlightenment hermeneutics problematizes these miracles as an extraordinary rendition of natural occurrences. Ordinary readers of the Bible, however, are susceptible to literalism and bibliolatry, twin viewpoints that negatively affect African Christianity, leading to tendencies to magical views of Christianity as automatic tickets to health and wealth once one donates financially to the church, as preached by prosperity gospel preachers. It is imperative, therefore, to infuse critical analysis into ordinary readings.

African biblical scholars read the Bible as experts trained in the various methodologies of biblical interpretation and exegesis. Most are educated overseas and are familiar with the scientific post-Enlightenment historical-critical method and literary study of the Bible. Conscious of the inadequacy of the Eurocentric frame of reference to interpret the Bible for Africans, or to address African religious/spiritual issues, and convinced that one cannot read the Bible with another culture's frame of reference, they emphasize contextual readings of the Bible in light of the worldview of the Africans. Contextual biblical hermeneutics in Africa is enculturating and liberative, in line with the two major branches of African theology. Inculturation hermeneutics emphasizes readings from the backdrop of the meaning-making processes of Africans. Liberation perspectives read the Bible with the hermeneutics of suspicion, as texts that could become ideological and used to justify unjust political, social, or economic policies and other forms of imperialism, including religious imperialism of the missionaries who sought to impose European culture and civilization on Africa. The Bible, which had been used to justify segregations and unlawful acquisitions of African lands and resources also, ironically, becomes a tool for the liberation of Africans. Most liberation theological motifs read the Bible in the light of the Exodus liberation of the people of Israel from bondage in Egypt and the reconstruction of society undertaken during the Ezra-Nehemiah period. The Bible, once a tool of oppression, becomes an indispensable weapon of liberation from all forms of injustices.

Biblical scholars read "with" ordinary people to learn from them, especially the ordinary readers' hermeneutic based on the existential concerns of society. They also read to help them make sense of the various injustices arising from ideological uses of the Bible that justify such policies as the apartheid segregation endorsed by the Dutch Reformed Church and other situations of injustice and oppression. Academic readings of the Bible equally include feminist approaches that highlight the patriarchal nature of the Bible as well as the various ways interpretations of the Bible have marginalized women. Feminist approaches call for interpretations based on human dignity as intrinsic and embedded in all human beings.

More than any other scholar, Gerald O. West sees as central to his hermeneutics his alliance with ordinary readers. West suggests the way forward is in forming ordinary readers to a critical reading by introducing them to the historical-critical contexts of the texts so they can adequately read the texts in the light of their own contexts. Justin S. Ukpong concentrated on inculturation hermeneutics. Musa W. Dube's contextual interpretation is hinged on postcolonial hermeneutics of suspicion toward the Bible used as justification for ideologies of slavery, segregation, and oppression. Teresa Okure drums support for contextual hermeneutics, emphasizing the contextuality of all hermeneutics. Specifically, she advocates for feminist hermeneutics drawing attention to the various patriarchal readings of the Bible, even among African biblical scholars.

In line with the rule of faith and principles of interpretation of the early fathers of the church from Africa, biblical hermeneutics also has ecclesiological foundations. Most people's knowledge of the Bible is drawn from their various Christian traditions or perceptions of their various religions, in cases of non-Christians reading the Bible. The Second Vatican Council's Dogmatic Constitution on Divine Revelation (*Dei Verbum*) and the 1993 *Principles of Interpretation of the Bible in the Church* by the Pontifical Biblical Commission provide guidelines for biblical interpretation in the Catholic Church. Martin Luther's principles of salvation by faith alone, through grace alone, according to Scripture alone (*sola fides, sola gratia, sola scriptura*) are the ecclesial bases of scriptural interpretation in Protestant and Reformed churches. People read the Bible informed by these principles.

Both Catholic and (most) Protestant churches acknowledge the validity of the scientific method and train biblical exegetes to use hermeneutical approaches based on it. But they worry that the historical-critical method leaves the Bible as merely a piece of literature, that it ignores its spiritual, theological meaning as the word of God. For this reason, Christian biblical scholars insist on the Bible as the word of God, and any method of interpretation including the scientific method must recognize this. Reading the Bible must occur first in the light of its telos as the word of God, aimed at instilling the love of God and neighbor. The church is entrusted with the Bible as the deposit of faith, as the witness to revelation. The Bible, therefore, cannot be read comprehensively outside the church. This of course does not mean that ecclesiological foundations of biblical interpretation are monolithic. Various Christian traditions nuance ecclesiological principles of interpretation differently.

The future of African biblical hermeneutics lies in greater familiarity with the Bible as the word of God, the inculcation of critical analysis of the Bible to ordinary readers in Africa, and greater readiness of African biblical scholars to recognize and learn from ordinary people's faith-based hermeneutics. Instead of abandoning contextual biblical hermeneutics because of criticisms from their colleagues from the Global North, African biblical hermeneutics should penetrate to the grassroots to advance under-the-shade-tree discussions resolving global and local palaver through the Bible, discussions attuned to the sociopolitical, economic, and religious African conceptual frame of reference. This book is an attempt to promote such collaboration.

CHAPTER ONE

Early African Christian Biblical Hermeneutics

Early African readings of the Bible laid the foundation for subsequent developments in Christian biblical hermeneutics. By remembering this underappreciated aspect of intellectual history, we remind ourselves of an equally underappreciated aspect of religious history obscured by colonial fog: Christianity is not foreign to Africa. Africa shaped indispensable parts of the development of Christianity's doctrines, as well as its methods of biblical interpretation, theology, and spirituality. Through careful biblical exegesis and borne out of deep love of God and passion for the word of God, the early fathers of the church from Africa—Tertullian, Origen, Cyprian, Tyconius, Augustine of Hippo, and others—contributed to the universal church's biblical hermeneutics by distinguishing the plain sense from the spiritual senses of Scripture. They outlined the methods and laid down examples of theological interpretation by which the use of reason does not trump the rule of faith; the literal sense does not distract from Scripture as the word of God; inspiration does not necessitate inerrancy and infallibility; allegory and typology do not run wild; and the plain sense does not block one's recognition of deeper meanings.

The achievements of early African Christian hermeneutics formed part of patristic exegetical patrimony that extended to the Middle Ages, with its emphasis on the four senses of Scripture. Although Christianity faded in North Africa (the Maghreb), in antiquity the region was the epicenter of African Christianity, and its canons of biblical exegesis continue to form the basis of scriptural interpretation in Christianity: Orthodox, Roman Catholic, and Protestant. As Wendy Elgersma Helleman has argued, "African Christians can nonetheless take legitimate pride in the contribution made by their forebears for the development of Christianity in its earliest years. Even a cursory examination of outstanding leaders in those early centuries reveals the significant contribution of the North African Christian Church in the Roman Empire."[1] This chapter will survey the scope of the hermeneutical achievements of early Christian Africa through analyzing the teachings of several of its key thinkers and leaders. It also examines the legacy of these achievements in Coptic and Ethiopian Christianities.

TERTULLIAN OF CARTHAGE

There is not much material in the biography of Tertullian, who is regarded as one of the first great Latin theologians of the church. He was born in Carthage (present-day Tunisia) during the period of Roman colonial presence in Africa during the second century. While anthropological research favoring Roman occupiers presented North Africa as lacking civilization prior to the Romanization of North Africa, postcolonial studies have pointed to the constant revolt of Africans against Roman occupation.[2] This rubbishes the branding of North Africa as Roman North Africa, which was an attempt to exclude the region from the rest of Africa and attribute its achievements only to the civilizing influence of Roman occupation.[3] We should ask with David Wilhite, "Does Tertullian write with an African self-identity that exists alongside his other identities, such as that of a Christian?"[4] And if so, how do these identities interact in his theology? Tertullian wrote in Latin and "was responsible for much of the theological vocabulary of Western Christianity."[5] Little wonder, then, that he is regarded as the first Western theologian. However, "his African

---

1. Wendy Elgersma Helleman, "New Horizons in the Study of Early African Christianity," *Vox Patrum* 81 (2022): 129.
2. Cristina Andrei and Decebal Nedu, "The Campaign of Marcus Atilius Regulus in Africa. Military Operations by Sea and by Land (256–255 B.C.)," *Annals* (Constanța Maritime University) 11, no. 13 (2010): 206–9, recalls the various wars of resistance by the Carthaginians against Roman occupation.
3. David Wilhite, *Tertullian the African: An Anthropological Reading of Tertullian's Context and Identities* (Walter de Gruyter, 2007), 5.
4. Wilhite, *Tertullian the African*, 8.
5. Geoffrey D. Dunn, *Tertullian* (Routledge, 2004), 10.

context contributed something to his writings and therein can be explored in accordance with his vast array of non-African sources."[6] His theology is not identical with that of his European and Near Eastern counterparts. "He enables us to see something of African Christianity in its earliest years and, through a comparison of his thinking with other Africans, like Cyprian and Augustine, we can build up a detailed picture of Latin Christianity in one part of the Mediterranean."[7] The complexity of his North African community provided him with the mixture of indigenous African family traditions and Greco-Roman educational and cultural influences. David Wilhite captures the dialectics of Tertullian's identity and the wide appeal of his theology:

> Tertullian's influence over Western Theology does not negate his original context which had non-western aspects. Tertullian was from the Province of Africa and was therefore—at least by one taxonomy—an African. While the temptation to anachronistically compare Tertullian's "African Theology" with more recent sub-Saharan, post-colonial "African theology" could be viewed as precarious, such an approach could prove no more amiss than the traditional approach—conscious or otherwise—of reading Tertullian as a European. Instead, the juxtaposition of a competing branch of theology from the same continent as Tertullian provides a different framework that might better appreciate certain aspects of Tertullian's self-identity and theology.[8]

Our focus is Tertullian's scriptural exegesis. To this we now turn.

SCRIPTURAL EXEGESIS: BASIC ISSUES

Tertullian was engrossed with an apologetic defense of Christianity against heretics and detractors, so scriptural exegesis often served a defensive, polemical purpose. He was a controversialist who confronted doctrinal issues by arguing from biblical texts. He at times massaged the scriptural message to defend the Christian faith. "Exegesis for its own sake gave way to the need for 'more effective forms of apology and the refutation not so much of

---

6. Wilhite, *Tertullian the African*, 178.
7. Dunn, *Tertullian*, 11.
8. Dunn, *Tertullian*, 190.

interpretations regarded as faulty as of erratic doctrines in their entirety.'"[9] Instead of arguing with heretics over interpretation of Scripture, he focused on their right to use Scripture at all. Karlfried Froehlich sums up Tertullian's position: "Apostolic Scriptures belong to the apostolic church. The Gnostics with their claim to secret traditions have no right to use them, for only the public succession of teaching in the apostolically founded churches can be the measure of apostolicity and therefore of correct interpretation."[10] In other words, for Tertullian "Scripture is the property of the Church."[11] Those outside the house of faith "had no right to use them. They not only altered the text but also its meaning to suit themselves. A Christian should not enter into debate with a heretic about the meaning of Scripture because both sides would claim to be right and a third party would not be able to distinguish orthodox from heterodox interpretations."[12]

The major issue in biblical exegesis is the relationship between the Old Testament and the New Testament. In response to Marcion of Synope, who had taught that the God of the Old Testament was not the same as the God of the New Testament,[13] Tertullian argued for the unity and the continuity of Scripture, of the Old and the New Testaments, and expounded on "the historical nature of the Bible and its interpretation."[14] So, texts should not be quoted or used outside of their contexts in Scripture as heretics do—that is, quoting only those texts that support their arguments and ignoring the other parts of passages that do not support them. "For Christians, Tertullian maintains, the search has ended; the true faith has been found and must only be defended against its erosion by illicit curiosity."[15]

---

9. R. Kearsley, "Tertullian (fl. 200)," in *Historical Handbook of Major Biblical Interpreters*, ed. Donald K. McKim (InterVarsity Press, 1998), 62.

10. Karlfried Froehlich, *Biblical Interpretation in the Early Church* (Fortress Press, 1984), 14.

11. T. P. O'Malley, SJ, *Tertullian and the Bible: Language—Imagery—Exegesis* (Dekker & Van DeVegt, 1967), 119.

12. Dunn, *Tertullian*, 21.

13. Notger Slenczka of Humboldt University Berlin, in a 2013 essay titled "The Church and the Old Testament," argued, like Marcion, that the Old Testament is moribund for Christianity as its content does not address Christians but rather is "a document of a religious community with which the Church is no longer identical." Cf. Yaniv Feller, "The Specter of Marcion: Decanonizing the Old Testament in Twenty-First-Century Germany," *The Journal of Religion* 103, no. 4 (2023): 409–30.

14. Kearsley, "Tertullian (fl. 200)," 63.

15. Kearsley, "Tertullian (fl. 200)," 63.

GUIDING PRINCIPLES OF SCRIPTURAL INTERPRETATION

There is not merely one method of biblical exegesis for Tertullian.[16] However, his guiding principle for scriptural interpretation is the Christian rule of faith—the common doctrines of the church, "a kind of oral credal summary,"[17] or "the church's simple creed."[18] This rule, he believes, provides control over interpretation, serves as the confirming norm, and clears ambiguity. That belief is grounded in his earlier position that Scripture belongs to the church as a gift of the Holy Spirit, as part of the deposit of faith.[19] As he explains in *De praescriptione haereticorum*, what distinguishes proper from heretical use of Scripture is contextual, and the rule of faith is what determines the proper context. According to Dunn, "For Tertullian, one could judge the validity of a scriptural interpretation by its conformity with the *regula fidei*."[20] Tertullian also holds that Scripture could be self-explanatory when read in the light of other passages and the unity of Scripture.

While recognizing the value of allegory, he makes only limited use of it, when occasion arises to recognize and to show the inadequacy of the literal sense of Scripture.[21] An instance of his use of allegory is in his position on the unity of Scripture, when he argues that the Old Testament is preparatory to the New Testament, against Marcion's denial of the validity of the Old Testament for the Christian Scripture. And that the Old Testament should therefore be read in the light of the New Testament, with passages in the Old Testament prefiguring Christ. As Bernard S. Jackson remarks: "For Tertullian equally to have abandoned the 'Old Testament' entirely might have appeared to concede too much to his opponent (not to mention the value of the 'Old Testament' as indicating prophecies which would be fulfilled in the 'New'). Or, more fully: the revelation to the Jews spoke of a covenant to them which

---

16. J. H. Waszink, "Tertullian's Principles and Methods of Exegesis," in *Early Christian Literature and the Classical Intellectual Tradition: In Honorem Robert M. Grant*, ed. W. R. Schoedel and R. L. Wilken (Beauchesne, 1979), 17, cited in Geoffrey D. Dunn, "Tertullian's Scriptural Exegesis in *de praescriptione haereticorum*," *Journal of Early Christian Studies* 14, no. 2 (2006): 141.

17. Dunn, *Tertullian*, 21.

18. Froehlich, *Biblical Interpretation in the Early Church*, 15.

19. O'Malley, *Tertullian and the Bible*, 133.

20. Dunn, "Tertullian's Scriptural Exegesis," 141–55.

21. O'Malley, *Tertullian and the Bible*, 145–58, contains a history and the use of allegory up to Tertullian and a detailed study of Tertullian's cautious use of allegory, limited only to instances "where what we would call the literal meaning is not possible" (p. 148).

would be replaced by a 'new covenant' (Jer. 31:31), now revealed in the 'New Testament.'"[22] However, Tertullian's defense of allegory does not mean complete endorsement. He is cautious in its use, preferring much simpler reading. R. P. C. Hanson notes Tertullian's "insistence that a passage must be taken in its original sense, and interpreted according to the situation in which it was uttered."[23] As T. P. O'Malley aptly observes: "It is surely a paradox that Tertullian defends allegory, against Marcion, by showing the absurdity of a literal interpretation; and that it is precisely this literalism which makes him usually prefer the *simple* reading."[24] As an apologist (who argues to win a debate on any topic against real or imagined foes),[25] Tertullian "at times could argue for an allegorical or typological or spiritual interpretation of a scriptural passage . . . whereas at others he would support a more literal or obvious interpretation."[26] Following Dunn's advice, "perhaps we need to read Tertullian less like literary critics and more like judges and juries."[27] His use of rhetoric balances his positions on scriptural interpretation and on other topics of interest. He insists we not abandon common sense in biblical interpretation while also warning of the dangers of mere literalism. Thus he towed the middle ground between literalism and allegorism, which makes it difficult to accuse him of biblical literalism.[28] Hanson praises Tertullian's late work, *De Pudicitia*, where he balances the use of allegory with the literal interpretation as "one of the finest pieces of scriptural exposition in Christian

---

22. Bernard S. Jackon, "Why the Name New Testament," *Melilah: Journal of Jewish Studies* 9 (2012): 16–17.

23. R. P. C. Hanson, "Notes on Tertullian's Interpretation of Scripture," *The Journal of Theological Studies* 12, no. 2 (1961): 276.

24. O'Malley, *Tertullian and the Bible*, 128. By a simple reading of Scripture, Tertullian counters those who would like to see too much in a text by arguing that in specific passages, there is no deeper meaning.

25. Geoffrey D. Dunn observed that "there is a degree of polemic in everything Tertullian wrote—there was a point of controversy and Tertullian sought to persuade opponents to adopt his opinion. The polemic involved a theological difference of opinion and Tertullian utilized his rhetorical training to marshal his arguments to present his opinion in as persuasive a light as possible." Geoffrey D. Dunn, "Rhetoric and Tertullian's *De Virginibus Velandis*," *Vigiliae Christianae* 59, no. 1 (2005): 5.

26. Dunn, *Tertullian*, 22.

27. Dunn, *Tertullian*, 29.

28. Margaret M. Mitchell, "Christian Martyrdom and the "Dialect of the Holy Scriptures": The Literal, the Allegorical, the Martyrological," *Biblical Interpretation* 17 (2009): 177–72.

antiquity."[29] Hanson notes that "Tertullian displays a strong commonsense in exegesis which one wishes had been more contagious among ancient expositors than it was."[30]

Cyprian of Carthage

Cyprian was a prominent man in Carthage: a rhetorician, a lawyer, and a man of means and of senatorial rank.[31] His conversion to Christianity was celebrated, and not long after, he was ordained a bishop despite the opposition of some priests who protested, complaining that he had only been a Christian for a few years. With the persecution of Decius after an extended period of peace, he went into exile, from where he continued to oversee his diocese through letters. His return upon the death of Decius coincided with the crisis of deciding the future of lapsed Christians. He wrote his treatise *De lapsis* toward the solution to the problem.[32] After several years of relative peace, he was forced into another exile at the onset of a new persecution under Valerian in 257 CE. Upon his return to Carthage, he was beheaded on September 14, 258.[33] "From the period of 247 until his death in 258, Cyprian wrote only twelve treatises (*libelli*), for the sermons, parenetic exhortations, or testimonial collections of Scripture texts."[34] Our focus will be on his attitude toward Scripture: canon, inspiration, the unity of Scripture, and its exegesis.

---

29. R. P. C. Hanson, "Biblical Exegesis in the Early Church," in *The Cambridge History of the Bible*, vol. 1, *From the Beginnings to Jerome*, ed. P. R. Ackroyd and C. F. Evans (Cambridge University Press, 1970), 427.

30. Hanson, "Biblical Exegesis," 428.

31. J. Patout Burns, "Cyprian of Carthage," *Expository Times*, 120, no. 10 (2009): 469–77, is an excellent exposé of the life, times, writings, mission, and ministry of Cyprian of Carthage and his leadership role in African Christianity of the third century. However, it considers the role of Scripture as peripheral to Cyprian's work.

32. The chaotic nature of Cyprian of Carthage's African Christianity, occasioned by various persecutions and apostasies and the fractious nature of policies at readmission into Christian communion, has been articulated in Joseph A. Favazza, "Chaos Contained: The Construction of Religion in Cyprian of Carthage," *Questions liturgiques* 80, no. 2 (1999): 81–90.

33. I rely principally on Michael Andrew Fahey's *Cyprian and the Bible: A Study of Third-Century Exegesis* (J.C.B. Mohr [Paul Siebeck], 1971) for this brief study of Cyprian of Carthage.

34. Fahey, *Cyprian and the Bible*, 18.

ATTITUDE TOWARD THE BIBLE

Unlike Tertullian, his predecessor and mentor, Cyprian identified every scriptural text he uses as biblical and as the word of God. He occasionally uses the formula *scriptum est* or generically identifies scriptural texts as *scriptura* or *scripturae*, meaning "Christian revelation as contained in the Bible."[35] He also uses many words, expressions, and images for Scripture that we will not enumerate here.[36] Cyprian recognizes Scripture itself, its private reading, and its public use in liturgical worship. He aims primarily to stir God's people to faith with the Holy Scripture. Thus, he bases his teachings, writings, and homilies on Holy Scripture. And he relies on Scripture to guide his pastoral decision-making. According to Edwina Murphy, as a bishop Cyprian turned to the Scripture for answers to the various crises bedeviling his diocese: "persecution, schism, and plague."[37] His pastoral concerns and ministry were guided by Scripture, which he brings to bear on a variety of issues in his context: "the unity and uniqueness of the church and her sacraments, care for the poor and captive, the necessity of discipline and repentance, and the contrast between present privation and future reward."[38] With Cyprian, one can say there was an integration of theology and exegesis, which Rowan A. Greer observed was central to patristic exegesis: "For the church fathers the true meaning of Scripture was a theological one."[39] Frances Young agrees, arguing that reading the Bible "embraced the concerns we tend to separate out into scholarship, theology, praxis and spirituality. The purpose of biblical exegesis, implicit and explicit, was to form the practice and belief of Christian people, individually and collectively."[40] Thus, "Cyprian's numerous words for Scripture or Scriptural passages served not only as introductory formulas, separating the biblical text from his own words, but also described his understanding of the Bible as a collection of divine sayings and commands

---

35. Fahey, *Cyprian and the Bible*, 30.
36. See Fahey, *Cyprian and the Bible*, 29–40, for many of these expressions.
37. Edwina Murphy, "Divine Ordinances and Life-Giving Remedies: Galatians in the Writings of Cyprian of Carthage," *Journal of Theological Interpretation* 8, no.1 (2014): 81.
38. Murphy, "Divine Ordinances and Life-Giving Remedies," 81.
39. Rowan A. Greer, "The Christian Bible and Its Interpretation," in *Early Biblical Interpretation*, ed. James L. Kugel and Rowan A. Greer (Westminster, 1986), 177.
40. Frances M. Young, *Biblical Exegesis and the Formation of Christian Culture* (Cambridge University Press, 1997), 299, cited in Edwina Murphy, *The Bishop and the Apostle: Cyprian's Pastoral Exegesis of Paul* (De Gruyter, 2018), 1.

requiring obedience."[41] He wrote to acquaint his flock about the use of the Bible. For instance, Andy Alexis-Baker posits that his *Ad Quirinum Book Three*, besides laying out guidelines for a catechumenate program, "focus on *disciplina*, biblical book studies, and eschatological and baptismal concerns."[42] Similar emphasis on the use of Scripture is applicable to the two versions of Cyprian's *De Unitate* and his other writings.[43]

Cyprian upholds the belief in the human and the divine authorship of Scripture, the view that Scripture as the content of God's revelation is inspired by the spirit of God influencing the various human authors as they write the texts of Scripture.[44] "Cyprian expresses his belief in Scriptural inspiration more concretely by stating that a biblical author was '*constitutus*' by the Holy Spirit or that the Holy Spirit speaks through a human author."[45] Inspiration equally means that the Law and the Prophets speak in the name of Christ. While he does not engage in a theological elaboration of biblical inspiration, "he nonetheless asserts the belief without ambiguity and attributes the action to the Holy Spirit."[46]

UNITY OF SCRIPTURE

Cyprian affirmed the unity of the Old and the New Testaments of Scripture. He quoted from both testaments, arguing that God never fails to urge his people in both testaments of his covenant with them. Cyprian advised Christians of his community to read the entirety of Scripture to

---

41. Fahey, *Cyprian and the Bible*, 40.
42. Andy Alexis-Baker, "*Ad Quirinum* Book Three and Cyprian's Catechumenate," *Journal of Early Christian Studies* 17, no. 3 (2009): 357–80.
43. Stuart G. Hall, "The Versions of Cyprian, *De Unitate*, 4–5. Bévenot's Dating Revisited," *Journal of Theological Studies* 55, no. 1 (2004): 138–46. The other writings Hall mention in note 2 of his article include "Cyprian. *De lapsis and De Ecclesiae Catholicae Unitate*," text and trans. Maurice Bévenot, SJ (Oxford Early Christian Texts: Clarendon Press, 1971), x–xv; *Sancti Cypriani Opera*, I. *Ad Quirinum. Ad Fortunatum*, ed. R. Weber; *De lapsis* and *De ecclesiae catholicae unitate*, ed. Maurice Bévenot. Corpus Christianorum Series Latina, 3 (, 1972), 245–47.
44. Kyle R. Hughes, "The Spirit and the Scriptures: Revisiting Cyprian's Use of Prosopological Exegesis," *Journal of Early Christian History* 8, no. 2 (2018): 35–48, problematizes this use of the Holy Spirit in biblical inspiration.
45. Fahey, *Cyprian and the Bible*, 44.
46. Fahey, *Cyprian and the Bible*, 45.

gain strength and deeper understanding of the mysteries of Christianity. Despite giving similar weight to both the Old and the New Testaments, he recognizes that the Old Testament is fulfilled in the New, that the New Testament advances the Old Testament. In his commentary on the Lord's Prayer, he stated that the words of the Son of God are greater than those of the prophets who spoke about the Son. At the same time, his emphasis on the unity of Scripture allows him to quote the Old Testament to support the authority and meaning of the New Testament, thus reading the Old Testament symbolically as foretelling of Christ and Christian revelation. Christ unifies the Scripture, since in the incarnation, the Old Testament is fulfilled. "For Cyprian what gave unity to the OT and the NT was the presence of the Incarnate Word in the earlier testament."[47] Fahey interprets this as central to Cyprian's hermeneutics:

> Can we, at the risk of oversimplification, point to a characteristic Cyprianic method of interpretation? His most striking procedure, although not original with him, is an essentially Christological reading of the OT, a book which in his view was pregnant with allusions and prophecies about Christ. His Christologizing or Christianizing of the OT reflects a continuing preoccupation with the threat of Marcion, which perhaps was his principal legacy from Tertullian.[48]

As liturgist John D. Laurance notes, Cyprian teaches the Eucharist as the imitation of Christ through his Christological reading of the Old Testament. With the New Testament especially expounding Pauline writings, in Laurance's reframing, Cyprian affirms "that the unity of all creation in the Passover of Christ is the ultimate grounding for all Eucharistic theology."[49] In his Epistle 93, Cyprian draws upon Colossians 1:15–20 to formulate a sacramental theology that validates the imitation of Christ in the officiating minister of the Eucharist: "that priest truly functions in place of Christ who imitates that which Christ did, and consequently offers a true and complete sacrifice in the Church to God the Father."[50]

---

47. Fahey, *Cyprian and the Bible*, 48.
48. Fahey, *Cyprian and the Bible*, 624–25.
49. John D. Laurance, "The Eucharist as the Imitation of Christ," *Theological Studies* 47, no. 2 (1986): 294.
50. Ep. 63.14, cited in John D. Laurance, "The Eucharist as the Imitation of Christ," 295.

METHOD OF EXEGESIS

Methodologically, Cyprian's biblical exegesis employs typologies, by viewing some biblical figures like Noah, Melchizedek, Isaac, Joseph, and Joshua as "types" of Christ. Even though he does not employ allegory in the manner of the Alexandrian school, his typology is akin to allegory as there is not much technical difference between typology and allegory among the earlier church fathers. He emphasizes the contemporaneous nature of Scripture as not merely a record of past events but applicable to explicit situations of his third-century Carthaginian Church. "It (Scripture) has been written, it is read, it is heard, and it is proclaimed for our instruction by the mouth of the Church."[51] The relevance of Scripture for contemporary situations led Cyprian to appropriate Scripture to the varying contexts of the third-century Carthaginian Church. Whether it be on the pastoral office of bishops, the encouragement of Carthaginian Christians undergoing persecution, the crisis of the reabsorption of lapsed Christians, and even the devastating plague in Carthage in 252 CE, Cyprian thought that God addresses present situations through the words of Scripture. Nienke Vos notes that "the bishop uses Scripture in different ways. He links the day of persecution to the Day of Judgment, thereby evoking the dimension of eschatology and apocalyptic. Biblical words regarding persecutions can be directly applied to Cyprian's situation. The biblical context and the context of Cyprian's day become fused."[52]

Cyprian's hermeneutics is drawn from his view on the unity of Scripture. Scripture, he holds, must be interpreted in its totality. It is not enough to cite a scriptural passage without considering earlier and later passages. In other words, one should not take parts of Scripture and suppress parts of the passage that highlight the parts one is quoting or those that lay out the background of the passage one cites. That, he says, is corrupting the Scripture and citing it out of context, a habit characteristic of the heretic but not the faithful.[53]

---

51. Fahey, *Cyprian and the Bible*, 49.
52. Nienke Vos, "A Universe of Meaning: Cyprian's Use of Scripture in Letter 58," in *Cyprian of Carthage: Studies in His Life, Language, and Thought,* ed. Henk Bakker et al. (Peeters, 2010), 90. Further examples of Cyprian's use of Scripture for contemporary situations of the life of Carthaginians and in his ministry are contained in Fahey's *Cyprian and the Bible*, pp. 47–52.
53. Fahey, *Cyprian and the Bible*, 52–56, 495.

APPRAISAL

Cyprian was not a systematic theologian. He did not intend to or presume to have been engaged in systematized theological thinking. He was, as a bishop, confronted with complex issues, especially persecutions and the consequent apostasies as people struggled to survive and to practice their faith at the same time. He saw in the Bible answers to these myriads of challenges. He used the Bible to teach, nourish, encourage, and defend decisions bordering on faith and morals. He responded to the challenge of Marcionism by defending the unity of Scriptures, of the Old and the New Testaments. He, like his predecessor and mentor Tertullian, recognized the Old Testament as fulfilled in the New Testament. For this reason, passages of the Scriptures, especially the Old Testament, are to be read in the light of Christ and applied to the present, living context of Christian living.

Origen of Alexandria

Alexandria is often referred to as "thoroughly Greek since 331 BCE, when Alexander the Great founded it."[54] Yet, however successful the Ptolemies and their Roman successors were in colonizing Egypt, it remains that Egypt was and is African. Its predominant population and culture were African. Its soul was African. Even while integrating and appropriating Hellenistic and Roman learning, "the Coptic peasants [the majority of Alexandria's residents] . . . detested their Greco-Roman overlords, who left them little in return for the unequaled bounty their land produced."[55] This occasionally led to violent revolutions against the Roman occupying army and resulted in political instabilities, accompanied by hunger, diseases, plagues, atrocities, and massacres. This Alexandria was the home of one of the greatest, if also most controversial, thinkers in Christian antiquity: Origen. And while scholarship has largely ignored his African identity, it is simply not possible to adequately grasp his life and times without it.

Egyptian traditional religion was dominant despite the widespread recognition of the presence of the gods of the Hellenistic invaders. "The traditional

---

54. Joseph Wilson Trigg, *Origen: The Bible and Philosophy in the Third-Century Church* (John Knox Press, 1949/1983), 3.

55. Trigg, *Origen*, 5.

gods of Egypt, unlike those of Greece, still lived in Origen's time. Egyptians in the hinterland still read the hieroglyphics, practiced mummification, and worshipped animals as they had under the pharaohs. Greek-speaking Alexandrians despised the ways Egyptians worshipped, but they respected their gods as figures with real power."[56] Origen grew up and was educated in Alexandria and thus was influenced by the learning, culture, and religions of Egypt. He encountered there countless ideologies and theologies, including Gnostic doctrine, Marcion's denial of the God of the Old Testament, Platonic philosophy, and Greek hermeneutics, as well as Jewish theology and interpretation.[57] The most striking influences on Origen were Philo of Alexandria and Clement of Alexandria. Their approaches to allegory became central to Origen's biblical hermeneutics.[58]

Origen believed strongly in the Bible as a guide for life and observed its doctrines in full, including the rumored self-castration based upon Matthew 19:12 "in order to instruct his female students without fear of scandal."[59] Karlfried Froehlich described Origen as "one of the great minds and probably the most influential theologian of the early Christian era."[60] For Charles Kannengiesser, "Origen is still acclaimed as the founder of biblical criticism in the church, the most influential interpreter of Scripture, and the founder of systematic theology."[61] Jean Danièlou described Origen and Augustine of Hippo as "the two greatest geniuses of the early church."[62] Joseph Wilson Trigg compared him to St. Paul in assessing his contribution to the entire Christian tradition: "Paul was a leader and molder of traditions; Origen was a professional scholar. Paul could only hint at his thought in scattered letters; Origen could develop his at great length in volumes of treatises, commentaries, and published sermons. Paul was revered as an oracle of God; Origen was ultimately damned as a heretic."[63] Origen's greatness lies in his mastery

---

56. Trigg, *Origen*, 35.
57. Peter J. Youmans, "The Hermeneutical Method of Origen: The Influences upon Him and the View of Inspiration He Developed," *Journal of Dispensational Theology* 14 (2010): 9.
58. Ilaria L. E. Ramelli, "Philo as One of the Main Inspirers of Early Christian Hermeneutics and Apophatic Theology," *Adamantius* 24 (2018): 1.
59. Walter A. Elwell, ed., *Evangelical Dictionary of Theology* (Baker, 1984), 803.
60. Froehlich, *Biblical Interpretation in the Early Church*, 51.
61. Charles Kannengiesser, "Biblical Interpretation in the Early Church," in McKim, ed., *Historical Handbook of Major Biblical Interpreters*, 6.
62. Jean Danièlou, *Origen*, cited in Elizabeth Ann Dively Lauro, *The Soul and Spirit of Scripture Within Origen's Exegesis* (Brill, 2005), 1.
63. Trigg, *Origen*, 8.

of the Bible, most of which he committed to memory and used with ease in his christologically centered biblical hermeneutics. Jerome comments on the immensity of the volumes Origen wrote on scriptural interpretation: "Who of us can read everything he wrote? Who can fail to admire his enthusiasm for the Scriptures?"[64] Adolf von Harnack extolled him in glowing tributes regarding his love for the Scripture: "There has never been a theologian in the church who desired to be, and indeed was, so exclusively an interpreter of the Bible as Origen was."[65]

Origen based his allegorical interpretation of the Bible on the patristic premise that Christ fulfills the Hebrew Scriptures. The Laws, the Prophets, and the Writings, the fathers of the church believed, are fulfilled in Christ. In his *On First Principles*, Origen upholds biblical inspiration and presents methods of biblical interpretation. He makes use of prototypes, interpreting Moses, for example, as the prototype of Christ. The Pentateuch's accounts and stories refer to Christ. Even the psalms are directed to Christ. Origen states:

> In demonstrating the divinity of Jesus in this somewhat summary fashion by using prophetic pronouncements about him, we also offer proof that the Scriptures which prophesy about him are inspired and that those writings that announce his coming and his teaching speak with full power and authority; this is the reason they have won over the elect from among the nations. It must be admitted, however, that the divine quality of the prophetic statements and the spiritual character of the law of Moses came to light only with the coming of Jesus. Before Christ's advent it was hardly possible to present clear evidence that the old writings were inspired. But the coming of Jesus opened the eyes of readers who might have been skeptical about the divinity of the law and the prophets to the fact that these writings were indeed composed with the help of divine grace.[66]

Origen addressed different groups of people in his community: Judaizers, who insist on the Law without acknowledging allegory, and heretics like the Marcionites, who rejected the Hebrew Scriptures and their depiction

---

64. Jerome's Letter 84.8, cited in Peter W. Martens, *Origen and Scripture: The Contours of the Exegetical Life* (Oxford University Press, 2012), 3.
65. Jerome's Letter 84.8.
66. Origen, "On First Principles: Book Four," in Froehlich, *Biblical Interpretation in the Early Church*, 52–53.

of God. These groups, he writes, err because of their failure to recognize the Scripture "in its spiritual sense" and instead interpret them "according to the mere letter."[67] Consequently, Origen undertook to teach the correct method of interpretation of Scripture in accordance with the tradition—that is, "the rule of the celestial church of Christ resting on the succession of the apostles."[68]

METHOD OF BIBLICAL INTERPRETATION

Origen's method combines literal sense and allegorical sense of Scripture, acknowledging the role of plain sense in communicating the mystery of divine revelation to an extent but insisting that deeper meanings lay hidden in the narratives. Allegory implies that what one reads has a different sense than it appears in the text. It could be a proleptic telling of future events in veiled narration of present or past events. "Allegory by definition means saying something different from what one reads in the written source, allowing a legitimate appropriation of the cultural tradition . . . Generally labeled as the allegorical method of exegesis, biblical interpretation in Christian Alexandria went through many phases that militate against simplistic qualification."[69] Origen demonstrates some of those phases of allegorical interpretation in his methods of scriptural interpretation, which are evident in his distinction of literal and allegorical interpretation and his mention of mystic arrangements that God reveals as explanation for some texts with questionable morality. Using a story in *The Shepherd of Hermas*, he distinguished the bodily sense (literal) "exhorting those whose souls are children,"[70] the psychic sense (the lettered, the educated) addressed to "souls who have left the realm of bodily concerns and base thoughts,"[71] and finally, the pneumatic sense (the spiritual sense, the allegorical sense). As David S. Dockley observes, "Origen developed a threefold hermeneutical approach. He thought that Scripture had three different, yet complementary, meanings: (1) a literal or physical sense, (2) a moral or psychical sense, and (3) an allegorical or intellectual sense.

---

67. Origen, "On First Principles: Book Four," 56.
68. Origen, "On First Principles: Book Four," 56.
69. Kannengiesser, "Biblical Interpretation in the Early Church," 6.
70. Origen, "On First Principles: Book Four," 58.
71. Origen, "On First Principles: Book Four," 58.

The threefold sense was based upon his belief in a corresponding threefold division of humankind: (1) the physical, (2) the emotional or psychical, and (3) the spiritual or intellectual."[72]

For those at the bodily sense, at the literal level (that is, the people unable to handle the mystic arrangements of Scripture), the goal of the Spirit, Origen argues,

> was to hide his teachings... in texts which on the surface seemed to offer a plain narrative account of events such as the creation of the sensible world, the fashioning of man, and of the successive generations from the first parents to a multiplicity of human beings; the same holds true for other historical narratives which record the deeds of righteous people and of the mistakes they sometimes made because they were human beings... The intent was that the external cover of spiritual things, namely, the bodily element of the Scriptures, should not be rendered unprofitable for so many people; but rather, that it should be capable of improving the multitude according to their capacity.[73]

While distinguishing these senses of Scripture, Origen holds that one can get knowledge of Scripture through any of them but that the fullness of the sense of Scripture lies in the spiritual sense (i.e., the inner sense). This consists of recognizing the hidden meaning in the stories, the historical narratives, the prophetic messages, and the writings that point to Christ and the new covenant. "Spiritual exegesis, however, is reserved for the one who can identify the heavenly realities ... In one word ... 'the secret and hidden wisdom of God.'"[74] And it is realized "by carefully searching the plain texts and taking seriously the depth of their meaning"[75] under the guidance of the spirit of God.

Equally important to recognize is Origen's view of historical accounts in Scripture. Should they be read in the literal sense as a record of historical facts, or are they symbolic, an allegory of stories with different meaning altogether from the various narratives presented? What about some narrations that do not accord with the moral character of God and of some scandalous acts of important religious figures like Noah, David, Solomon, Abraham, or Jacob?

---

72. David S. Dockery, "The History of Pre-Critical Biblical Interpretation," *Faith and Mission* 10, no. 1 (1992): 14.
73. Origen, "On First Principles: Book Four," 62.
74. Origen, "On First Principles: Book Four," 59.
75. Origen, "On First Principles: Book Four," 61.

How are these to be read? Origen's position is consistent with his acceptance of allegorical interpretation and the different senses of Scripture. Some of the historical accounts are simply narratives aimed at conveying God's message in simplistic terms for people not yet ready to grasp the deeper meanings of the mysteries of God. In Origen's words, such a reading is "for the benefit of those who cannot carry the workload which the discovery of such matters requires."[76] In other words, some historical accounts are allegorical; some are embellished to convey the mystery of God; and others are plainly mythical and did not happen but are attempts at grappling with the mysteries of God that humans cannot explain in any other way. This is true of some historical narratives in both the Old Testament and the New Testament. Origen asserts:

> To be specific: What intelligent person can believe that there was a first day, then a second and third day, evening, and morning, without the sun, the moon, and the stars; and the first day—if this is the right term—even without a heaven [Gen 1:5–6]? Who is foolish enough to believe that, like a human farmer, God planted a garden to the east in Eden and created in it a visible, physical tree of life from which anyone tasting its fruit with bodily teeth would receive life; and that one would have a part in good and evil by eating the fruit picked from the appropriate tree [Gen 2:8–9]? When God is depicted walking in the garden in the evening and Adam hiding behind the tree, I think no one will doubt that these details point figuratively to some mysteries by means of a historical narrative which seem to have happened but did not happen in a bodily sense . . . What more can be said? Those who are not totally dull can collect innumerable examples of this kind, where something is presented as having happened but did not happen in terms of the literal and plain meaning of the text. Even the Gospels are full of passages of this kind, such as the devil leading Jesus up to a high mountain in order to show him from there all the kingdoms of the world and their glory [Matt 4:8] . . . The thorough investigator can find enough similar instances to convince himself that stories which happened according to the letter are interspersed with other events which did not actually occur. When we come to the legislation of Moses, if one attempts to observe it as it stands, many laws speak nonsense and others command the impossible.[77]

---

76. Origen, "On First Principles: Book Four," 61.
77. Origen, "On First Principles: Book Four," 63–64.

Even though it may give the impression of being ahistorical, Origen does not deny historical events in the Bible.[78] But he endeavors to highlight that they should not be read literally all the time. He writes,

> We mention all these examples in order to show that the purpose of the divine power offering us the holy Scriptures is not only that we understand what the plain text presents to us, for, taken literally, it is sometimes not only untrue but even unreasonable and impossible. We wanted to show also that some extraneous matter has been woven into the historical narrative of actual events and into the code of laws which are useful in their literal sense. No one, however, should suspect us of generalizing and saying that because a particular story did not happen, no story actually happened; or that, because a particular law is unreasonable or impossible in its plain reading, no law should be observed literally; or that the scriptural stories about the Savior are untrue in terms of the physical reality; or that none of the laws and commandments which he gave ought to be obeyed. On the contrary, it must be emphasized that the factual truth of the historical narrative is presented to us quite clearly in certain texts; for example, that Abraham was buried in the double cave at Hebron as were Isaac and Jacob and one wife of each [Gen 23:19; 25:9–10; 49: 29–32; 50:13] . . . In fact, instances which are true in terms of the historical narrative far outnumber the purely spiritual texts which have been woven in.[79]

APPRAISAL

R. P. C. Hanson's famed study of Origen's allegorical interpretation of Scripture, *Allegory and Event*, detailed the heightened interest and depth of the knowledge of the Bible in Origen's day and concluded that "Origen's life covered a period when the Bible was widely known and widely discussed in the Christian Church."[80] Hanson attributes to Origen the shift away from employment of proof-texts to carefully constructed methodical commentary.

---

78. See Peter W. Martens, "Origen Against History? Reconsidering the Critique of Allegory," *Modern Theology* 28, no. 4 (2012): 635–56, for a study of allegations of ahistoricity against Origen.

79. Origen, "On First Principles: Book Four," 66.

80. R. P. C. Hanson, *Allegory and Event: A Study of the Sources and Significance of Origen's Interpretation of Scripture* (SCM Press, 1959), 359–60.

"In this sense," Hanson argues, "we may say that Christian biblical exegesis begins with Origen."[81] Even though Hippolytus, Melito, Clement of Alexandria, and others had engaged the Scripture, "Origen brought the whole weight of contemporary scholarship—linguistic, critical, and philosophical—to bear upon the task of making the biblical commentary a permanent literary form for Christian writers, and he succeeded brilliantly. In fact, all writers of commentaries today owe a debt to Origen as in this sense the great Founding Father of their activity."[82] This statement should not give the impression that Hanson endorses Origen's allegorical scriptural interpretation. He thinks Origen reads meanings into texts. His glowing assessment of Origen is punctuated with mention of the major weakness of Origen's allegorizing, the lack of in-depth knowledge of the minds of the authors of Scripture:

> Competence, subtlety, ingenuity, symmetry—these are the leading qualities of Origen's interpretation of Scripture. He saw all the problems; he had thought them out. He knew his material thoroughly; he knew exactly how to handle it in the most effective way for his purposes. To a degree unparalleled before his time and not often equaled after it, he was a *sophisticated* expositor . . . all these convince us that Origen was a master of the art of exposition as only a few have been masters of it. Why can we not go further? Why can we not call Origen a great interpreter of the Bible, in the same sense that Augustine and Luther and Wescott and perhaps Barth can be called great interpreters? The answer in my opinion lies in the fact that in one important respect Origen's thought remained outside the Bible and never penetrated within it. Of the great interpreters . . . it is always evident that their minds were soaked in biblical thought; they give their reader the impression that they are speaking to him from inside the Bible; at least for the purposes of exposition, they have successfully put themselves into the minds of the biblical author whom they are interpreting. Origen never quite conveys this impression, and on countless occasions gives the opposite impression, that he is reading into the mind of the biblical author thoughts which are really his own. The critical subject upon which Origen never accepted the biblical viewpoint was the significance of history.[83]

---

81. Hanson, *Allegory and Event*, 360.
82. Hanson, *Allegory and Event*, 360.
83. Hanson, *Allegory and Event*, 362–63.

What must be affirmed of Origen's hermeneutics, which accounted for his contextualized exegesis, was his focus on the Christian drama of salvation and this as the driving force of biblical interpretation. According to Peter W. Martens, "For [Origen], as for other early Christian exegetes, the discipline of biblical scholarship embraced, yet also transcended, the application of prevailing philological principles to Scripture. Biblical interpretation was an extraordinarily rich practice, as much an intellectual as a spiritual exercise. It was, in short, a way of life."[84] Origen, as a philologist, embodies such exegetical life for whom scriptural interpretation is life. "He memorized the Scriptures, and he toiled day and night in the study of their meaning."[85]

Origen, however, was not clear on how to determine when a historical account is literal or when it is allegorical. He fails to give the criteria for "painstaking examination"[86] of scriptural texts; he leaves this to the reader's determination of "intelligible reality,"[87] which risks relativizing scriptural interpretation to the whims and caprices of the reader and the reader's cultural situation and literacy.[88]

Furthermore, while Origen understands the "literal" sense of Scripture to mean the straightforward, commonsense meaning of the words of Scripture, in contradistinction from figurative or metaphorical meaning, students of historical biblical method understand *literal* to mean the author's intention. But while it may be difficult to determine the literal sense of Scripture, Origen upholds the spiritual sense of the Scripture as a whole.

It is also not easy to determine what Origen means by the psychic sense of Scripture. While Trigg notes that some scholars take this to refer to the moral level of interpretation (a standard sense in the later, medieval approach), he suggests that "Origen considered the psychic level a non-mystic level of allegory."[89] Elizabeth Dively Lauro thinks Origen's three senses of Scripture correspond to the three human parts of the body (somatic), the soul (psyche),

---

84. Peter W. Martens, *Origen and Scripture: The Contours of the Exegetical Life* (Oxford University Press, 2012), 1.
85. Martens, *Origen and Scripture*, 2.
86. Origen, "On First Principles: Book Four," 67.
87. Origen, "On First Principles: Book Four," 67.
88. See Lauro, *The Soul and Spirit of Scripture Within Origen's Exegesis*, pp. 15–33, for a list of scholars like Eugène de Faye, who dismissed Origen's exegesis as "arbitrary" and thus not worthy of study and others like Henri de Lubac, who accept Origen's exegesis, recognizing its distinctive achievements like the inclusion of moral sense to Scripture.
89. Trigg, *Origen*, 126.

and the spirit (pneumatic), which interrelate to aid humans achieve perfect imitation of Christ. "For Origen, then, his exegetical method of three senses is drawn from Scripture's own structure in order to fulfill Scripture's purpose of preparing hearers for salvation."[90]

Despite its shortcomings, Origen's exegetical method was well received and attracted huge following as early fathers of the church adopted his allegorical method in scriptural interpretation.

Tyconius

Tyconius is described as "one of the most incisive thinkers of the African Church in the seventies and eighties of the fourth century. From his pen came the commentary on the Apocalypse that influenced exegetes for the next millennium. A second work, the *Book of Rules*, was the first treatise on biblical hermeneutics in the Latin West."[91] According to Pamela Bright, Tyconius's major question and concern was the relevance of prophetic books for the African church of his time. And with prophetic books, Tyconius does not limit himself to Israelite prophecy. In fact, "for Tyconius a 'prophetic' text is one that calls sinners to repentance by warning of the death and destruction that awaits those that are separated from the love of God."[92] In other words, for Tyconius, the purpose of the Scripture is to lead people back to the love of God and neighbor. Despite being a Donatist, he does not share the more strident Donatist ecclesiology that "championed the idea of a 'pure' church that was both 'without a spot or wrinkle' (Eph 5:27) and indivisible by nature, as the Song of Songs contended: 'a garden enclosed, a fountain sealed up'(Sg 4:12)."[93] Augustine notes that while Tyconius critiques Donatists, he remains part of them.[94] "He refused the notion of the apostasy of the non-Donatist Christian churches at the beginning of the Constantinian peace. Even more

---

90. Lauro, *The Soul and Spirit of Scripture Within Origen's Exegesis*, 4.
91. Pamela Bright, *The Book of Rules of Tyconius: Its Purpose and Inner Logic* (University of Notre Dame Press, 1988), 2.
92. Bright, *The Book of Rules of Tyconius*, 9.
93. Jean-Marc Vercruysse, "Tyconius Hermeneutics: The Way the Holy Spirit Expresses Itself Through Scripture," in *Patristic Theories of Biblical Interpretation*, ed. Tarmo Toom (Cambridge University Press, 2015), 20.
94. Saint Augustine, *On Christian Doctrine*, trans. D. W. Roberston (The Library of Liberal Arts, 1958), 3.30.42.

daringly for a Donatist, he refused to recognize the Donatist Church as the visible faithful remnant waiting the return of the Lord."[95]

Tyconius speaks of the spiritual sense of Scripture—that is, the spiritual interpretation of Scriptures by which the word of Scriptures is addressed to the church for its renewal and conversion through the grace of the Spirit. His position came about in response to the bitter argument and rivalry over scriptural interpretation and claims to the status of true church between the Donatists and the Catholics during the period of Constantinian peace. This peace followed a long period of persecution and subsequent apostasy of some Christians, including priests, bishops, and other leaders of the church. Donatists rejected the notion of bringing these apostates back into the fold, while the Catholics (especially Augustine) argued against this rejection. While Tyconius belonged to the Donatist party, he did not hold to its more extreme positions.

Tyconius's *Book of Rules* set out to uncover the key to the "mystic rules" of the Bible—that is, "a coherent pattern which would structure scripture itself,"[96] one that will help people in reading and interpreting the Bible. His theory of biblical hermeneutics relies on both the texts of the Old and the New Testaments, which he cites copiously, and treats christological, ecclesiological, and eschatological beliefs of the church with focus on the interrelationship of scriptural exegesis and the church. The seven rules according to Augustine, who is among our main sources of information on Tyconius, are (1) "Of the Lord and His Body"; (2) "Of the Bipartite Body"; (3) "Of Promise and the Law"; (4) "Of Species and Genus"; (5) "Of Time"; (6) "Of Recapitulation"; and (7) "Of the Devil and His Body."[97]

The first rule enjoins readers of the Bible to relate to Christ and his body, the church. It urges the church to persevere, to not give up hope, and to be strengthened by the passion of the Christ. "Tyconius envisions the biblical text as means to help the church shaped by her suffering toward Christlikeness."[98]

---

95. Bright, *The Book of Rules of Tyconius*, 11.
96. Charles Kannengiesser, "A Conflict of Christian Hermeneutics in Roman Africa: Tyconius and Augustine," in *Protocol of the Colloquy of the Center for Hermeneutical Studies in Hellenistic and Modern Culture*, ed. Charles Kannengiesser and Pamela Bright (Center for Hermeneutical Studies in Hellenistic and Modern Culture, 1989), 6.
97. Saint Augustine, *On Christian Doctrine*, 104; see Pamela Bright, *The Book of Rules*, 43–48.
98. Matthew R. Lynskey, *Tyconius' Book of Rules: An Ancient Invitation to Ecclesial Hermeneutics* (Brill, 2021), 122.

Rule two on the bipartite nature of the church addresses the reality of evil in the church by using the image of Esau and Jacob. It equally extends to the conflict between good and evil morally and metaphysically drawn from the evil of the persecution of North African Christians and the conflict of good and evil in our moral choices. "This bipartite ecclesiology was an anvil on which Tyconius forged his hermeneutic theory. The dual nature of the church was the means by which the church could understand its sullied present and labor continuously toward a *purified future*."[99]

The third rule is a reminder of the role of the Holy Spirit, of divine authority, both in the inspiration and in the interpretation of Scripture. It urges reading the Scripture as the work of the spirit of God with a willingness to surrender to the Spirit both to interpret the text correctly and to be renewed by the biblical text. "Tyconius stresses, with a strong systematic rigor, the fact that only such a 'mystic rule' overcomes the apparent contradiction between the distinct levels of salvation, the one of 'promise' and the other of 'law.'"[100]

Rule four uses genus and species, not in the secular usage of human speech but in reference to the ahistorical and historical elements in biblical prophecy. The reader is to discern when reference is being made to the historically possible and to the ahistorical in text. "A 'genus' text is that class of prophecy in which the extremity of its language and imagery militate against its literal application. In other words, readers should refrain from struggling to justify the historical truth of the text, and focus their attention immediately on the universal church to which the prophecy is directed, that is, it is directed at the church."[101] Tyconius's message here emphasizes the universality of the biblical message, with the aim of unifying the divided Christian communities of North Africa. "As a hermeneutics of unity, Tyconius offered his set of mystical rules as a means to repair the internal quarrelling that divided the contemporary church of his day."[102]

Rule five, "Of Time," presents the eschatological hermeneutic of Tyconius's ecclesiology and situates that eschatology for the present church in his typological reading of history. According to Pamela Bright, "Rule VI, 'on Recapitulation,' is concerned with that area of eschatological expectation so

---

99. Lynskey, *Tyconius' Book of Rules*, 126.
100. Kannengiesser, "A Conflict of Christian Hermeneutics in Roman Africa," 9.
101. Bright, *The Book of Rules of Tyconius*, 72.
102. Lynskey, *Tyconius' Book of Rules*, 273.

important to the early Church, the discernment of the 'signs of the times.' While not denying that the end is approaching, Tyconius insists that the interpreter is to recognize the signs of the separation of the two parts of the one Body, the Church, already manifest in the deeds of love or of hate within the membership of the Church."[103]

Rule seven's mention of the devil and his body is an allegorical reference to the antichrist, not to Satan as the evil spirit but to members of the community of the faithful who had fallen from their faith and are thus within the church. This supports rule two on the bipartite nature of the church as a community made up of good and bad, of saints and sinners, of the faithful and the possible apostates. They represent the "mystery of iniquity" mentioned already in the prophetic texts.[104]

Through these rules, one reading the Bible is imbued with the keys to navigate the secrets of the "immense forest" of prophecies and obscurities of the Scripture about the reality of good and evil and remains steadfast to the faith through commitment to Christ. That has always been the goal of hermeneutics, from the ancient to the modern world: to remove obscurities, the veil covering the inner meaning of Scripture from the plain literal sense the Bible presents.[105] The task of hermeneutics was unmasking these obscurities to reveal the treasures of the texts. Augustine speaks of Tyconius's rules as being "of no little assistance in penetrating what is covert in the Holy Scriptures."[106] According to Augustine,

> I thought it necessary before all the other matters which occurred to me to write a book of Rules, and to fabricate, as it were, keys and windows for the secrets of the Law. For there are certain mystic rules which reveal what is hidden in the whole Law and make visible the treasures of truth which are invisible to some. If the sense of these rules is accepted without envy as we have explained it, whatever is closed will be opened, and whatever is obscure will be illuminated, so that he who walks through the immense forest of prophecy led by these rules as if by pathways of light will be defended from error.[107]

---

103. Bright, *The Book of Rules of Tyconius*, 82.
104. Bright, *The Book of Rules of Tyconius*, 85.
105. See Origen, "On First Principles," IV 2.8, cited in Bright, *The Book of Rules of Tyconius*, 59.
106. Saint Augustine, *On Christian Doctrine*, 104.
107. Saint Augustine, *On Christian Doctrine*, 105.

Karlfried Froehlich suggests that Augustine shared Tyconius's general understanding of hermeneutics and that Augustine's theology, including his "eschatology, ecclesiology, soteriology, and hermeneutics were more deeply influenced by Tyconius than one might notice at first glance."[108] Thus, "Augustine's hermeneutics was a commentary on this Tyconian theme: the goal of all biblical interpretation must be the double love of God and neighbor, the ordering of the Christian life toward our heavenly home."[109] In accordance with the understanding of hermeneutics during his time, for Tyconius, " the immediate task of Christian hermeneutics is to address the 'obscurities' of the biblical text."[110] According to Froehlich, "Patristic hermeneutics . . . concerns itself with the developing principles and rules for a proper understanding of the Bible in the early Christian church . . . It was in the hermeneutical circle of biblical text, tradition, and interpretation that Christian theology as a whole took shape."[111]

TYCONIUS'S NORTH AFRICAN CHRISTIANITY

Froehlich describes Tyconius's *Book of Rules* as "the first hermeneutical treatise written in the Latin West."[112] In it the general interpretation of Scripture in North African Christian communities is manifest—the unity of Scripture, of the Old and the New Testaments, and the applicability of Scripture to the contemporary situation, as well as the ecclesial goal of biblical hermeneutics, "the centrality of the church in the exegesis of Scripture."[113] Tyconius's mental world, as a late-fourth-century North African Donatist, shaped not only his hermeneutics in general but also his writing.

Maureen A. Tilley's book, *The Bible in Christian North Africa: The Donatist World*,[114] gives a bird's-eye view of the North African Christian scriptural belief that influenced Tyconius's *Book of Rules*. First, North African Christians related to the Scripture's world and constructed and legitimated their own

---

108. Froehlich, *Biblical Interpretation in the Early Church*, 26.
109. Froehlich, *Biblical Interpretation in the Early Church*, 28.
110. Bright, *The Book of Rules of Tyconius*, 60.
111. Froehlich, *Biblical Interpretation in the Early Church*, 1.
112. Froehlich, *Biblical Interpretation in the Early Church*, 25.
113. Lynskey, *Tyconius' Book of Rules*, xi.
114. Maureen A. Tilley, *The Bible in Christian North Africa: The Donatist World* (Fortress, 1997).

world and approved or disapproved of others in the light of the Bible. Second, during periods of intense state persecution, the Exodus liberative motif, the Israelite journey in the desert, exile in Babylon, and bondage under foreign rule shaped their thought pattern. They were the new Israelites and were bound to triumph just as the Israelites of old were liberated from bondage and slavery. Third, they saw their bishops as Moses types and thus viewed those outside their fold as the Israelites who decided to go back to Egypt instead of suffering during the journey to the promised land. Fourth, "when, during the latter half of the third century, Donatism experienced serious internal schism at the very time it was becoming the majority church in North Africa, Donatist writers utilized Scripture to develop new ecclesiologies that accounted for the presence of evil even within a pure church."[115] The collapse of the once strong collegiality of North African Christianity coupled with a lack of indigeneity by the Latin Christianity weakened this Christianity, leaving it vulnerable to Islamic Arabic invaders in the mid-seventh century. Tilley sums up the situation:

> Between the fifth and seventh centuries the distinctively collegial and episcopal structure of North Africa was weakened by persecution during the Vandal occupation and then was attacked by two converging factors: from the East, by changes in relationships between the African bishops and civil power of the Byzantine Empire; and, from the West, by attempts of the bishops of Rome to take on a larger role in North Africa. Between the two piercing prongs of the pincers, the leadership structure of the North African Church was severely weakened well in advance of Islam. With the collapse of the episcopacy the stage was set for the eclipse of Christianity.[116]

Matthew R. Lynskey's scholarly work on Tyconius sheds more light on the background of North African Christianity nurtured in the seeds of persecution and martyrdom, which seasoned North Africans and toughened their practice of Christianity, with demands for authentic witness characterized by fidelity to the Scripture. While persecution was off and on, it later intensified under Diocletian. Lynskey describes the situation well:

---

115. William Tabbernee, review of *The Bible in Christian North Africa: The Donatist World*," by Maureen A. Tilley, *Church History* 67, no. 4 (2009): 749.

116. Maureen A. Tilley, "The Collapse of a Collegial Church: North African Christianity on the Eve of Islam," *Theological Studies* 62 (2001): 4.

This background of violent persecution and heated controversy compelled the church to define its essential matters of orthodoxy and the doctrinal beliefs for which Christians would be willing to die . . . It hastened the church to prepare its members for imminent danger, cultivating an ethos of urgency and devotion throughout its ranks. As the church grew increasingly defined by this martyrological badge, many of its other aspects became shaped *en route* . . . The harsh and caustic surround of this persecuted people was met with an equally robust and rigorous legacy of ecclesiastical and theological servants, who put to writing to aid the members of the assaulted church in finding their identity as a marginal pilgrim people. To Tyconius belongs this heritage.[117]

Lynskey describes the Donatist North African Christianity as characterized by "*rigorism, purism, sectarianism, apocalypticism, and biblicism.*"[118] Their rigorism made them loyal to the end and explained their commitment even in the face of suffering, death, and martyrdom. It also formed the backdrop to Tyconius's ecclesiocentric hermeneutics "that highlighted the affinity of Christ (the head) and the church (the body) through shared suffering"[119] Purism explains their extreme dedication to holiness and sanctity up to the point of demanding it as a criterion for validity of the sacraments performed by priests. Perhaps this explains Tyconius's inclusion of the concept of bipartism in his rule, the view that the church is composed of pure and impure members and that both coexist side by side and the impure cannot contaminate the pure ones. Lynskey explains:

> Readers see how Tyconius' ecclesial hermeneutics shows the relationship between holiness and Bible reading. Specifically, his view of the church as a sacred communion of the Holy Spirit underscores his hermeneutic concerns of purity, holiness and character formation. Not only is holiness important for the right interpretation of the Bible, but it is also one of the dynamic effects of Spirit-led interpretation of the Bible itself. But as with rigorism, Tyconius maintained a hermeneutical concern for purity that should coincide with, and not do damage to, the unified church.[120]

---

117. Lynskey, *Tyconius' Book of Rules*, 36–37.
118. Lynskey, *Tyconius' Book of Rules*, 39 (italicized in the original).
119. Lynskey, *Tyconius' Book of Rules*, 42.
120. Lynskey, *Tyconius' Book of Rules*, 44.

The duo of rigorism and purism led to sectarianism and the distinction of Donatist Christian communities from other Christians, states, and surrounding cultures that they considered to be unholy and sought to separate themselves from. Yet again, Tyconius distinguished himself from such sectarian sentiment in his quest for integrated society and church. "Tyconius, in his hermeneutical endeavors, wrote within a setting and history that experienced sectarian animosity and proliferated separatism. He not only experienced this rift and 'fell between two stools' in the Catholic-Donatist divide but he also wrote to oppose these sectarian sentiments."[121]

Tyconius sought to unify Catholics and Donatists through Bible reading. He aimed at giving hope to the beleaguered Christian communities by giving them identity not only through the apocalyptic bent of Scripture but also through its practical, present tense value. Tyconius and North African Christians took the Bible seriously as a guide for life. He shared this diligent and assiduous biblicism with his contemporaries. For him, "the Bible was written *about* the church and *to* the church in a way that it is rightly understood *by* the church."[122]

Augustine of Hippo

Of all the early theologians of North African Christianity, none exert so profound an influence on what we now call "the West" than Augustine of Hippo. His conversion from Manicheism to Christianity, so vividly documented in his autobiographical *Confessions*, ushered in not just a radical change in the life of one man but a radical change in the development of an entire religion. On nearly every topic—grace and freedom, Trinity, Christology, political theology, the liberal arts, marriage, discipleship—Augustine had something to say. And nearly everything he said influenced what was said after him. His approach to biblical interpretation is no exception.

On Christian Doctrine, which Augustine started in 396 or 397 CE and stopped working on three years later before 400, was finished before his death in 430. This book lays the groundwork for scriptural interpretation and church doctrine in the double love of God and neighbor. Charity, Augustine says,

---

121. Lynskey, *Tyconius' Book of Rules*, 49.
122. Lynskey, *Tyconius' Book of Rules*, 53.

is the central message of the Scriptures; charity is the basic attitude toward the Scriptures, and the reader must interpret in line with this intention of the author.[123] He asserts:

> Whoever, therefore, thinks that he understands the divine Scriptures or any part of them so that it does not build the double love of God and of our neighbor does not understand it at all. Whoever finds a lesson there useful to the building of charity, even though he has not said what the author may have shown to be intended in that place, has not been deceived, nor is he lying in any way.[124]

Augustine divides *De Doctrina* (*On Christian Doctrine*) into two methodical phases based on his view of scriptural interpretation. "There are two things necessary to the treatment of the Scriptures: a way of discovering those things which are to be understood, and a way of teaching what we have learned."[125] Books 1–3 treat the way of discovery, while Book 4 addresses the way of teaching. This means that, for Augustine, scriptural interpretation involves understanding the text of Scripture and disseminating, teaching, or sharing the text, communicating what is understood with others. Books 1–3 aim at setting out the rule of faith (*regula fidei*) and the rule of love (*regula dilectionis*) as central to scriptural interpretation. "The *regula fidei* comprises those things of faith and hope, the *objects* to which one relates in love."[126]

In Book 1 (2.2–4.4), Augustine distinguishes between signs and things as a springboard to his distinction between things we enjoy and things we use. The purpose of these distinctions is to emphasize enjoying God because we love God and using things for the purpose of loving God. Scripture points to the things to be enjoyed: "The things which are to be enjoyed are the Father, the Son and the Holy Spirit, a single Trinity, a certain supreme thing common to all who enjoy it, if indeed, it is a thing and not rather the cause of all things, or both a thing and a cause."[127] Scripture's purpose is to enable us cultivate the love of God, the enjoyment of the Trinity:

---

123. Saint Augustine, *On Christian Doctrine*, 1.36.42.
124. Saint Augustine, *On Christian Doctrine*, 1.36.
125. Saint Augustine, *On Christian Doctrine*, 1.1.
126. James A. Andrews, *Hermeneutics and the Church* (University of Notre Dame Press, 2012), 3.
127. Saint Augustine, *On Christian Doctrine*, 1.5.5.

The sum of all we have said since we began to speak of things thus comes to this: it is to be understood that the plenitude and the end of the Law and of all the sacred Scriptures is the love of a Being which is to be enjoyed and of a being that can share that enjoyment with us, since there is no need for a precept that anyone should love himself. That we might know this and have the means to implement it, the whole temporal dispensation was made by divine Providence for our salvation.[128]

Augustine begins Book 2 by discussing signs that he distinguishes as either natural or conventional. Natural signs lead the mind from sign to signified according to the sign's nature, like smoke moving the mind to imagine fire. Conventional signs are intentional and are aimed at expressing something one has sensed or understood. Written words have become the dominant way of signifying whatever people want to communicate. While other forms of communication fizzle away, written words remain.[129] The human words of Scripture, then, are examples of those written words, the signs through which God communicates. Thus, Augustine affirms scriptural inspiration: the divine and the human authorship of Scripture. "We propose to consider and to discuss this class of signs in so far as men are concerned with it, for even signs given by God and contained in the Holy Scriptures are of this type also, since they were presented to us by the men who wrote them."[130] Scripture aims at presenting the will of God through the words of the human authors of Scripture.[131] Scriptural interpretation aims at discerning this purpose of Scripture, which is discovering God's will. Augustine warns against casual reading precipitating obscurities, ambiguities, or erroneous interpretations.

In 2.16.23, he presents similitude as figurative language used to express a deeper meaning. It serves as a metaphor, like an allegory that interprets symbols beyond the immediate expressive symbols to a deeper, often spiritual sense. An allegorical reading of the Bible interprets events of the past as having been fulfilled in the present without correlating events to justify such interpretation.[132] Allegorizing is central to the Christian reading of the

---

128. Saint Augustine, *On Christian Doctrine*, 1.35.
129. Saint Augustine, *On Christian Doctrine*, 2.3.4.
130. Saint Augustine, *On Christian Doctrine*, 2.2.3.
131. Saint Augustine, *On Christian Doctrine*, 2.5.6.
132. It is slightly different from the Jewish typological interpretations of the Hebrew Scripture where events of the present are interpreted as the fulfillment of events or personalities found in the Jewish Scripture.

Tanak—that is, the reading of the Hebrew Scripture in the light of Christ. Ignorance of the meaning of these symbols, like the snake in the story of creation in the book of Genesis, is responsible for the impediments in interpretation, Augustine claims.

The prerequisites for scriptural interpretation are attitudes of love of God and neighbor for the sake of God's love (2.7.9–11); reading the whole Scripture (2.8.12); learning biblical languages like Hebrew and Greek (2.11.16); correct translation (2.12–15); avoiding the deceit of sophistry, which is never after truth but after the use of words to outsmart others; and being guided by the principle of valid inference, which states that if the consequent is false the antecedent must also be false (2.32.50). He asserts: "In the Sign of the Cross the whole action of the Christian is described: to perform good deeds in Christ, to cling to Him with perseverance, to hope for celestial things, to refrain from profaning the sacraments" (2.41.62). He clarifies further in this summary of Christian doctrine of the Scriptures:

> A man fearing God diligently seeks His will in the Holy Scriptures. And lest he should love controversy, he is made gentle in piety. He is prepared with a knowledge of languages lest he be impeded by unknown words and locutions. He is also prepared with an acquaintance with certain necessary things lest he be unaware of their force and nature when they are used for purposes of similitudes. He is assisted by the accuracy of texts which expert diligence in emendation has procured. (3.1.1)

Book 3 is an instruction on the interpretation of Scriptures when words are used either literally or metaphorically. When words are used literally, they are to be interpreted according to the context established by the previous and following passages. When these fail, Augustine allows for "whatever blameless interpretation the reader wishes may be used" (3.3.6). Besides ambiguous constructions in texts, there are ambiguities in figurative words. We must be careful, Augustine admonishes, lest we take figurative expressions literally. It consists of "taking signs for things so that one is not able to raise the eye of the mind above things that are corporal and created to drink in eternal light" (3.5.9).

Just as we must not confuse figurative expressions with the literal, we must also not confuse literal expressions with the figurative. Augustine lists ways of determining and avoiding this confusion: whatever in the Scripture does not literally pertain to virtuous behavior or to the truth of faith is figurative. And virtuous behavior he described as love of God and neighbor; the truth of faith is knowledge of these loves. He specifies: "Those things which seem almost shameful to the inexperienced, whether simply spoken or actually performed either by the person of God or by men whose sanctity is commended to us, are all figurative, and their secrets are to be removed as kernels from the husk as nourishment for charity" (3.12.18). Actions we might consider shameful in the Scripture, like a man marrying many wives, are to be interpreted not literally but figuratively as people of the time tell the heavenly kingdom imaginatively after the earthly kingdom (3.12.20). He also insists we recognize the place of contextuality in biblical interpretation: "When those inexperienced in the customs of others read about these deeds, they think them to be shameful, unless they are restrained by authority. Nor can they observe that their entire way of living with respect to marriage, banquets, clothing, or other necessities and customs of human life might seem shameful among other peoples and at other times" (3.14.22).

In Book 4, Augustine reminds the reader he is not going to be using rhetoric in the second part of *On Christian Doctrine* dedicated to the way of teaching. In other words, it is not going to be based on eloquence even though eloquence will help in teaching, in clarifying what is being taught. But eloquence can equally be used to teach evil and to manipulate people to accept what is false. The teacher or expositor of sacred Scriptures should dedicate themselves to teaching "the good and extirpate the evil" (4.4.6). One who has read widely and understood the sacred Scriptures speaks wisely. In other words, the word of Scripture is to be preferred to eloquence of the speaker or of the teacher. Yet the eloquence of the wise person equally makes the words of Scripture evident. He cites Paul's 2 Corinthians 2:16–30 as an example.

Teachers or expositors of the divine Scripture, while eloquent, must not abandon wisdom. In teaching they should not necessarily imitate the eloquence so exemplified in the text but should teach with clarity: "In their utterances they should first of all seek to speak so that they may be understood, speaking in so far as they are able with such clarity that either he who does not understand is slow or that the difficulty and subtlety lie not in the manner of speaking but in the things which we wish to explain and show, so that this is the reason why we are understood less, or more slowly" (4.8.22). When what is being taught is grasped there is no need dwelling on it lest it bores people or become tedious. Also, when the purpose is to elicit action, what is being taught is not grasped unless it is put into action. Instruction should come before persuasion. To get people to listen no matter how important our message, we must speak in a manner that is pleasing (4.14.30).

APPRAISING *ON CHRISTIAN DOCTRINE*

Augustine's classic hermeneutical text has been praised both inside and outside theological contexts. John D. Schaeffer notes that the text is "a landmark text in the history of rhetoric that set the agenda for Christian education until the end of the seventeen[th] century."[133] Kathy Eden praises the book "as an outstanding contribution to this human science."[134] James Andrews describes *On Christian Doctrine* as an "expanded hermeneutics"—that is, "a hermeneutics that includes rhetoric."[135] Carol Harrison observes that the text is Augustine's attempt "to communicate and teach the truth of the Christian gospel from the pulpit."[136] Eugene Kevane agrees and affirms that "Augustine's *De doctrina Christiana* contains the guidelines for organizing the teaching, and the rules or precepts for carrying it out in actual classroom practice."[137] Augustine makes Scripture the guideline for all teaching and learning, the foundation of Christian culture.

Yet, for as much praise as Augustine has received and however universal his place in the Western literary canon remains, we must not forget or ignore his African origin and his contribution as an "outsider" to Western history and theology. As aptly articulated by Miles Hollingworth, "Late antiquity describes the transitional period between the late Roman Empire and the Middle Ages: it is a European phenomenon. But before Augustine come the African theologians Tertullian, Cyprian and Lactantius—and Augustine himself is famous proof of the African preoccupation to have a Christianity of the heart as much as of the mind."[138] According to James J. O'Donnell, there

---

133. John D. Schaeffer, "The Dialectic of Orality and Literacy: The Case of Book 4 of Augustine's *De Doctrina Christiana*," *PMLA* 111, no. 5 (1996): 1133.

134. Kathy Eden, "The Rhetorical Tradition and Augustinian Hermeneutics in *De Doctrina Christiana*," *Rhetorica: A Journal of the History of Rhetoric* 8, no. 1 (1990): 45.

135. James Andrews, "Why Theological Hermeneutics Needs Rhetoric: Augustine's *De doctrina Christiana*," *International Journal of Systematic Theology* 12, no. 2 (2010): 184.

136. Andrews, "Why Theological Hermeneutics Needs Rhetoric," 122.

137. Eugene Kevane, "Augustine's *De Doctrina Christiana* in World-Historical Perspective," *Augustiniana* 41, nos. 1–4 (1991): 1016.

138. Miles Hollingworth, *St. Augustine of Hippo: An Intellectual Biography* (Oxford University Press, 2013), 2.

remains in Augustine's context the continued influence of African character and lifestyle, the aboriginal Berber language, and clothing as well as religion, the old local pagan cults. Christianity is not a foreign religion in Africa. African theologians were at the forefront of world Christian hermeneutics.

THE COLLAPSE OF NORTH AFRICAN CHRISTIANITY

As Philip Jenkins recounts in his widely read book *The Lost History of Christianity*, Christianity in North Africa collapsed in the seventh century following Islamic invasion and expansion.[139] In the words of Kenneth Scott Latourette,

> In Western Asia and North Africa were the remnants of the churches which had existed before the conquests by the Arabs and by religion, Islam, of which the Arabs were the bearers. . . . through the centuries, under the encircling pressure of Islam, the churches had been slowly dwindling and by 1800 had completely disappeared in North Africa west of Egypt. Occasionally they were subjected to persecution and always they suffered from restrictions on the public exercise of their faith and from social discrimination against their members. Their members could defect to Islam, but no converts could be made from that religion: the penalty for apostasy from dominant faith was death—or at least social ostracism.[140]

One of those churches that is still surviving, albeit under extreme pressure, is the Coptic Orthodox Church of Egypt. Another ancient church with a little different history that has endured to this day is the Church of Ethiopia, "an ancient body which conserved its faith in the highlands of that country as yet unengulfed by Islam."[141]

THE COPTIC CHURCH

The infancy narrative in Matthew's Gospel mentions Egypt as a place of refuge for the Holy Family from the persecution of Herod, who sought to kill the

---

139. Philip Jenkins, *The Lost History of Christianity* (Oxford University Press, 2009).
140. Kenneth Scott Latourette, *Christianity in A Revolutionary Age: A History of Christianity in the Nineteenth and Twentieth Centuries*, vol. V, *The Twentieth Century Outside Europe* (Michigan: Zondervan Publishing House, 1969), 279.
141. Latourette, *Christianity in A Revolutionary Age*, 280.

infant Jesus (Matt 1–2). Egypt thus holds a place of prominence in Christian memory. According to Azmi Bishara, "Copts" is the alteration of the Greek name for Egypt and the Nile Valley "Egyptos." It denotes the indigenous people of the land prior to the Arab settlement of Egypt. This explains why Arabs called "the indigenous people of Egypt 'the Copts,' and called Egypt 'the Land of the Copt.'"[142] During the Islamic period, the term *Copts* came to be used to designate "Christian" Egyptians, especially after the conversion of the region's majority to Islam.

"'Coptic' was the pre-Islamic language of Egypt which flourished from the fourth through the tenth centuries C.E. and is still in liturgical use . . . and served as a vehicle for the translation of the New Testament. The Coptic Old Testament is based on the Greek Septuagint rather than on Hebrew texts.[143] Complete versions of the New Testament appear both in Sahidic (the Southern dialect) and Bohairic (the Northern dialect)."[144] Established according to tradition by St. Mark in Alexandria in 62 CE,[145] Coptic Christianity flourished for centuries and was home to famous schools, including the Alexandrian Catechetical School, traditionally connected with apostles. It served as the center for the integration of Christian faith with Hellenistic culture. The foremost leaders of this school were biblical scholars: Pantaenus (a Stoic philosopher), Clement, and Origen.[146] On account of the influence of the Alexandrian school extending upward to Rome, John Baur claimed that "Christian theology in the proper sense of the word first started in Alexandria."[147]

Following the Arabian conquest of Egypt, Christians were initially tolerated. Some converted to Islam for economic reasons, while Greeks in the area largely fled to other places, but the Copts remained. During Mamluk's dynasty (1257–1517), many Coptic churches and monasteries were burnt down. The proclamation of Arabic as the official language after the conquest meant that Coptic language survived only in the Coptic Church for over four

---

142. Azmi Bishara, "Can We Speak of a 'Coptic Question' in Egypt?," *Arab Center for Research & Policy Studies* (2011): 7.

143. This is not surprising given that some three hundred years before Christ, Egypt had been conquered by Alexander the Great, who imposed Greek as the language of literacy. Hence the intense influence of Greek language and civilization on major Egyptian cities. Even the names "Egyptos" and "Copts" were Greek.

144. Wendell G. Johnson, "'Out of Egypt Have I Called My Son': A Bibliographic Essay on Egyptian Christianity from its Origins to the Arab Conquest," *Journal of Religious & Theological Information* 18, no. 2–3 (2019): 46.

145. John Baur, *2000 Years of Christianity in Africa* (Daughters of St. Paul, 1994), 21.

146. Johnson, "'Out of Egypt Have I Called My Son,'" 47.

147. Baur, *2000 Years of Christianity in Africa*, 22.

centuries. "This century-long oppression slowly reduced Egyptian Christianity to a minority. The isolation from the rest of the Christian world caused a certain spiritual stagnation, but also brought about the very important identification of the Christian faith with the national heritage, that helped the Copts to preserve both their national character and Christianity up to the present time."[148]

THE ETHIOPIAN ORTHODOX TEWAHEDO CHURCH

Ethiopian Christianity dates to the times of the apostles, with specific mention of the conversion of the Ethiopian eunuch already reading the Bible without understanding and seeking Philip's assistance (Acts 8:27). And even in the Old Testament prophets, Ethiopia is mentioned. The Septuagint version of Isaiah 18:1 and 20:3 referred to Ethiopia as the biblical land of Kush. Psalm 68:31 envisions that "Ethiopia will stretch out its hands to the Lord." Ethiopian Christianity traces its roots in the Bible to the Solomonic dynasty in the famed relationship between King Solomon and the "queen of the South" (1 Kgs 10:1–13), the queen of Sheba. Thus, Baur writes: "Even today below the altar of every church in Ethiopia there is an ark, called tabot—and all the descendants of Menelik are proud of the title 'Lion of Judah.'"[149]

According to tradition, Ethiopia was evangelized by Matthew the evangelist; he suffered martyrdom there as well. Emperor Ezana declared Christianity the official religion of the empire in 328 CE. St. Frumentius was appointed its first bishop by St. Athanasius of Alexandria. Thus, the Ethiopian Church "fell under the apostolic headship of the Coptic Church for sixteen hundred years, until it became an autonomous Patriarchate in the mid-twentieth century. The bond with the Coptic Church significantly influenced the subsequent translation of Scripture from Syrio-Arabic texts."[150] The Bible of the Ethiopian Church was comprised of the Old and the New Testaments, with the inclusion of many more books than the

---

148. Baur, *2000 Years of Christianity in Africa*, 26.
149. Baur, *2000 Years of Christianity in Africa*, 34.
150. Bruk A. Asale, "The Ethiopian Orthodox Tewahedo Church Canon of the Scriptures: 'Neither Open nor Closed,'" *The Bible Translator* 67, no. 2 (2016): 207.

regular canon of other Christian denominations. Traditionally, the Ethiopian Orthodox Tewahedo Church (EOTC) Scriptures is made up of eighty-one books[151] comprising the Old and New Testaments translated into Ge'ez and other deuterocanonical/pseudoepigraphal books, including Jubilees, 1 Enoch, and the Ethiopic Didascalia. The history of this Scripture passed through the five different periods of the church: "(1) the earliest period before and at the birth of Christianity, when the religion of Israel and Christianity were introduced; (2) the fourth century C.E., when Christianity had become the state religion; (3) the fifth to sixth centuries, typically believed to be the time of the arrival of 'the Nine Saints,' [missionaries from Syria in the fifth and sixth centuries], when the faith spread widely and the church was structurally consolidated; (4) the fourteenth to fifteenth centuries, when the church underwent a major reform [the Ge'ez version of the Scriptures revised based on the Arabic version]; and (5) the twentieth century with the formal autonomy of the church and a translation shift from Ge'ez to Amharic."[152] Major factors internally and externally influenced the formation of the Scripture through the history of the EOTC and, in the process, the canon was not fixed but left open.

The favored interpretive tradition emphasizes the unity of the plain sense and the inner sense of Scripture. As Yimenu Adimass Belay notes, "The use of Scripture in the religious and cultural context is deeply rooted in the use of *sëm ena wërq* (wax and gold) hermeneutics of *Qiné* that address the plain meaning and the hidden meaning of the biblical text. Unlike a Platonic philosophical outlook, marked by duality between knowledge and practice, the Ethiopian Church tradition of *sëm ena wërq* considers *Tëwahedo* (unity) in interpretive and philosophical creativity."[153] This contextual reading of Scripture that incorporates the horizon of the reader in applying a scriptural text in different contexts is the *andəmta* interpretive tradition, which also informs teaching and commentary on the Bible. According to Ralph Lee, "The andəmta corpus of Amharic commentary on Ge'ez biblical

---

151. Asale, "The Ethiopian Orthodox Tewahedo Church Canon of the Scriptures," 209. This should not be taken to mean that there is a fixed canon of Scripture as found in Western Christianity, Roman Catholic and Protestant.
152. Asale, "The Ethiopian Orthodox Tewahedo Church Canon of the Scriptures," 204–5.
153. Yimenu Adimass Belay, "Scripture and Context in Conversation: The Ethiopian Andəmta Interpretative Tradition," *Conspectus* 34 (2022): 44.

and patristic texts derives its name from the repeated use of 'andəm,' meaning 'and (there is) one (who says),' to introduce different interpretations."[154]

Scholars are divided as to the constituents of the interpretive tradition, whether it is original to Ethiopia and designed for their context by integration of elements within and external to Ethiopian context or a continuation of the Antiochene literary tradition and/or Alexandrian allegorical tradition. The predominant view, though, is that the EOTC "developed its own unique tradition by weaving together elements from different sources of both internal and external traditions through dynamic interaction with other traditions. These include Ethiopian primal, Hebraic, Jewish, apostolic, Syriac and Egyptian Coptic."[155]

While remaining faithful to the Amharic translation of the Ethiopic Ge'ez text, the *andəmta* interpretive tradition refers to other texts and illustrates them with stories. This contextual biblical interpretation is often referred to as "four-eyed." According to Belay, "The characterization of the traditional practitioners as 'foureyed' suggests the idea of discovering different horizons of understanding, entertaining multiple viewpoints, and comparing, critiquing and coordinating them. The Ethiopic interpretive tradition gives an interpretation and application to the text, supporting each possibility to address the intellectual and spiritual needs of people in different contexts."[156] The Ethiopians' affinity with Israel's history, their national belief of being the replacement of Israel, and their faith in being the chosen people of God all cement the unique interpretation of Scripture to their contexts.[157] "The Ethiopian *andəmta* interpretive tradition in the OT and NT claims that

---

154. Ralph Lee, "Symbolic Interpretations in Ethiopic and Ephremic literature" (PhD diss., University of London, 2011), cited in Belay, "Scripture and Context in Conversation," 45.

155. Keon-Sang An, "Ethiopian Contextualization: The Tradition of the Ethiopian Orthodox Tewahido Church," *Mission Studies* 33, no. 2, (2016): 147.

156. Belay, "Scripture and Context in Conversation," 46.

157. Belay's examples succinctly explain the basis of this "four-eyed" interpretive tradition: "The interpretation of different biblical texts both in the OT and NT are highly connected with the Ethiopian identity. For instance, King Melchizedek of Salam in Gen 14:18 is considered an Ethiopian king (57). Even though Melchizedek is identified with Christ in Heb 7, Ethiopian tradition asserts that he ruled Ethiopia based on the belief that Ethiopia is the land of origins (EOTC 2015, 64142; Hancock 1992, 48–53). In addition to the above, the Ethiopian *andəmta* commentary on the gospel of Matthew interprets the wise men of Matt 2:1 as Ethiopians, claiming they understood the birth of the Messiah as God leads them towards the newly-born king of the Jews." Belay, "Scripture and Context in Conversation," 46.

Ethiopians have worshipped God from the creation, continuing through the giving of the law to Moses, and to the reception of the gospel in the NT as referenced in Acts 8."[158]

CONCLUSION

Christianity is not foreign to Africa. Africa formed part of the tradition that shaped the formulation of doctrine, biblical interpretation, theology, and Christian spirituality. Through careful biblical exegesis arising from in-depth analysis of Scripture borne out of deep love of God and passion for the word of God, the early fathers of the church from Africa contributed to the universal church's biblical hermeneutics by distinguishing the plain sense from the deeper spiritual senses of Scripture. The use of reason does not trump the rule of faith; the literal sense does not distract from Scripture as the word of God; inspiration did not necessitate inerrancy and infallibility. Allegory and typological sense do not run wild; the plain sense does not becloud one's vision to recognize the obvious deeper meanings of Scripture. The authority of the Bible, while incontestable, does not negate the tradition of the Church that formed the content of Scripture. Scriptural interpretation was not individualistic but communal, arising from the faith of the Christian communities. It was also not an independent interpretation limited to the local community of believers but was universally applicable to the church as the body of Christ. Even though influenced by their contexts, the interpretations were models of biblical interpretation for the church universal. The achievements of the early African Christian hermeneutics that formed part of patristic exegesis extended to the Middle Ages with its emphasis of the four senses of Scripture. Although Christianity may have been decimated in North Africa, the epicenter of early African Christianity, its biblical exegesis continues to form the basis of scriptural interpretation in Christianity: Orthodox, Roman Catholic, and Protestant.

---

158. Belay, "Scripture and Context in Conversation," 46.

CHAPTER TWO

The Bible and Missionary Activities in Sub-Saharan Africa

INTRODUCTION

Apart from the Coptic and Ethiopian remnants, Christianity in North Africa collapsed in the seventh century. It was only in the fifteenth century that new attempts were made to spread Christianity to South, West, and East Africa, championed by the Portuguese missionaries who accompanied Portuguese expeditions. In some places, like the kingdoms of Kongo, Angola, Warri, and Zimbabwe, the attempts lasted for two hundred or three hundred years. But this era of African Christianity was doomed by the transatlantic slave trade.[1] Conversion to Christianity could not save Africans from being victims of the slave trade.[2] Even Christian missionaries participated in the enslavement of Africans who embraced Christianity.[3] This second encounter of Africans with Christianity was a result of the dual interest of the Portuguese. They came to Africa with a primary focus on commerce. Missions were secondary and, ultimately, a means of securing commerce.[4]

---

1. Emilia Viotti da Costa, "The Portuguese-African Slave Trade: A Lesson in Colonialism," *Latin American Perspectives* 12, no. 1 (1985): 41–61; Joaquim Romero Magalhães, "Africans, Indians, and Slavery in Portugal," *Portuguese Studies* 13 (1997): 143–51.

2. Katie Geneva Cannon, "Christian Imperialism and the Transatlantic Slave Trade," *Journal of Feminist Studies in Religion* 24, no. 1 (2008): 127–34.

3. Justine Walden, "Capuchins, Missionaries, and Slave Trading in Precolonial Kongo-Angola, West Central Africa (17th Century)," *Journal of Early Modern History* 26, nos. 1–2 (2022): 38–58.

4. J. O. Ijoma, "Portuguese Activities in West Africa Before 1600: The Consequences," *Transafrican Journal of History* 11 (1982): 136–46; Allen Isaacman and Jennifer Davis,

Mission activity consolidated the control of land and resources in accordance with the Padroado treaty that empowered the Portuguese and gave them rights over any land on which they set foot.[5] In the name of evangelization, the papal bulls *Dum Diversus* (1452 CE),[6] *Romanus Pontifex* (1455 CE) and *Inter Caetera* (1456 CE) gave the Portuguese rulers spiritual, political, and commercial authority of the lands they "discovered."[7] The affected areas included

---

"United States Policy Toward Mozambique Since 1945: 'The Defense of Colonialism and Regional Stability,'" *Africa Today* 25, no. 1 (1978): 29–55; Thomas Henriksen, "Portugal in Africa: A Noneconomic Interpretation," *African Studies Review* 16, no. 3 (1973): 405–16.

5. Eugenia W. Herbert, "Portuguese Adaptation to Trade Patterns Guinea to Angola (1443–1640)," *African Studies Review* 17, no. 2 (1974): 411–23.

6. This papal bull authorizes the Portuguese crown to subjugate, enslave, and own the land and the peoples they conquer, provided they win the souls for the Catholic Church. It states in part: "We grant to you full and free power, through the Apostolic authority by this edict, to invade, conquer, fight, subjugate the Saracens and pagans, and other infidels and other enemies of Christ, and wherever established their Kingdoms, Duchies, Royal Palaces, Principalities and other dominions, lands, places, estates, camps and any other possessions, mobile and immobile goods found in all these places and held in whatever name, and held and possessed by the same Saracens, Pagans, infidels, and the enemies of Christ, also realms, duchies, royal palaces, principalities and other dominions, lands, places, estates, camps, possessions of the king or prince or of the kings or princes, and to lead their persons in perpetual servitude, and to apply and appropriate realms, duchies, royal palaces, principalities and other dominions, possessions and goods of this kind to you and your use and your successors the Kings of Portugal." 1452—Dum Diversas—Issued by Pope Nicolas V to Alfanso V of Portugal," The Complete Doctrine of Discovery, accessed January 20, 2024, https://www.doctrineofdiscovery.net/1452-dum-diversas-issued-by-pope-nicolas-v-to-alfanso-v-of-portugal.html.

7. Scholars referred to these papal bulls as reasons for the forced annexation of American Indian lands, as well as other non-Christian peoples, nations, and so forth. "In the years 1452, 1454, and 1493, Popes Nicholas V and Alexander VI issued papal bulls that together form the original text of what has been called 'the Doctrine of Discovery.' The age of expansion and exploration by the Christian nations of Europe was just beginning." Anthony F. C. Wallace and Timothy B. Powell, "How to Buy a Continent: The Protocol of Indian Treaties as Developed by Benjamin Franklin and Other Members of the American Philosophical Society," *Proceedings of the American Philosophical Society* 159, no. 3 (2015): 262–63.

Also, cf. Philiphe Bỉnh and Prince Dom João, "Invoking the Padroado," in *Vietnamese Moses: Philiphe Binh and the Geographies of Early Modern Catholicism*, ed. George E. Dutton (University of California Press, 2017), 119–58; Pius Malekandathil, "Cross, Sword and Conflicts: A Study of the Political Meanings of the Struggle Between the Padroado Real and the Propaganda Fide," *Studies in History* 27, no. 2, (2011): 251–67; Wilfred Prakash D'Souza Prabhu, "'Padroado Versus Propaganda Fide': The Jurisdictional Conflict Between Portugal and Rome: State—Church Relations in Sixteenth-Seventeenth—Eighteenth Century Indo-Portuguese History, Its Repercussion on Konkani Roman Catholics of Coastal Karnataka," *Proceedings of the Indian History Congress*, 66 (2005–2006): 974–98;

Asia, Africa, and Brazil. This royal patronage (Portuguese: Padroado), a monumental fusion of the state and the church that Portugal would later interpret as giving the country a divine mission and use as an excuse for colonialism until 1974, entrusted the king with the powers of appointing bishops, parish priests, and chaplains for the mission.[8] It also meant that only missionaries from Portugal protected by the Padroado treaty could operate in the lands entrusted to the Portuguese crown. Pope Nicholas V's bull *Romanus Pontifex* of January 8, 1455, declares: "All lands and seas that have been discovered or will be discovered belong forever to the king of Portugal." The implications of this right were several. It meant that no European (presumably) could enter the African territories without the prior consent of the king; it also meant that the king would have a monopoly over commerce, with the whip of excommunication for all who trespassed. In addition, it included the right to construct churches, to maintain them, and to provide them with priests, besides the exclusive rights to navigation, commerce, and trade.[9] In a sense, then, the evangelization of sub-Saharan Africa was initiated by the expeditions of the Portuguese merchants.

However, the success or the failure of these missions would depend on African agency, on the role of African agents. For instance, by 1915, "351 Protestant mission societies had about 24,000 foreign missionaries working mostly in Asia and Africa. The 109,000-strong native or indigenous workers who toiled alongside them outnumbered these missionaries."[10] As Professor Lamin Sanneh argued, "The historical roots of the preponderance of African agents over the Western missionary are firm and clear. It is by that factor, more than any other, that we have to explain and assess the apparent failure of missions between about 1480 and 1785."[11] The role of African agents in the missionary activities in Africa is gaining traction. Elochukwu Uzukwu's recent study on the role of the laity in the ancient Kongo Church shows that

---

Joseph A. Griffin, "The Sacred Congregation De Propaganda Fide Its Foundation and Historical Antecedents," *Records of the American Catholic Historical Society of Philadelphia* 41, no. 4 (1930): 289–327.

8. Hugo Gonçalves Dores, "The Road to an Agreement on Missions: The Quarrel Between Portugal and the Holy See Regarding the Missionary Policy for the Portuguese Empire in Africa (c.1880–1910)," *Journal of Religion in Africa* 51, nos. 1/2 (2021): 86–110.

9. Prabhu, "Padroado Versus Propaganda Fide,' 975.

10. Lalsangkima Pachuau, *World Christianity: A Historical and Theological Introduction* (Abingdon Press, 2018), 35.

11. Lamin Sanneh, *West African Christianity: The Religious Impact* (George Allen & Unwin, 1983), xii.

missionaries only built on the lay-led church "suffused with an enduring, creative, and complex theological culture."[12] This must be borne in mind in the discussion of the work of Western missionaries. As Richard Gray notes,

> Already we were beginning to recognize that right from the start of the modern history of Christian missions in West Africa, from the earliest days in the settlements at Freetown, the role of African ministers and evangelists and of African Christian traders, teachers and craftsmen had been of crucial importance in the development of the mission-connected churches in West Africa. And already one wondered whether a similar reorientation, away from an emphasis on the policies and activities of the European missionaries, would not likewise transform our understanding of church history in East and Central Africa.[13]

The African Christianity we are familiar with today was kick-started with nineteenth-century missionary activities.[14] This included the colonial and postcolonial periods and the stages of indigenization and inculturation. So much has been written about this period by historians.[15] We will not repeat that work here. But suffice it to say that African Christianity will be studied within the context of world Christianity, with an emphasis on the autochthonocity of Christianity within the cultural framework of Africans. This chapter hopes to contribute to a contextual approach to the Bible within a particular context of world Christianity. It takes for granted the imperative of context or situation as a prerequisite in reading a text, specifically the Bible.

The Bible became much more prominent and disseminated during the colonial period as propagated by the missionaries. While it is not necessary to recount the history of the Bible during this period, especially the initial

---

12. Elochukwu Uzukwu CSSp, *Memorializing the Unsung: Slaves of the Church and the Making of Kongo Catholicism* (Penn State University Press, 2024), Kindle.

13. Richard Gray, "Christianity and Religious Change in Africa," *African Affairs* 77, no. 306 (1978): 89.

14. R. Elliot Kendall, "The Missionary Factor in Africa," in *Christianity in Independent Africa*, ed. Edward Fashole-Luke, et al. (Indiana University Press, 1978), 16–25; Chukwudi A. Njoku, "The Missionary Factor in African Christianity," in *African Christianity: An African Story*, ed. Ogbu U. Kalu (Africa World Press, 2007), 191–223.

15. Cf. Lamin Sanneh, *Translating the Message: The Missionary Impact on Culture*, 2nd ed. (Orbis Books, 2009); Baur, *2000 Years of Christianity in Africa* (; Fashole-Luke et al., *Christianity in Independent Africa*; Kalu, *African Christianity: An African Story*; Kwame Bediako, *Christianity in Africa: The Renewal of Non-Western Religion* (Orbis Books, 1997).

hesitance to translation, reading the Bible by the few literate common people was not encouraged, especially in the Roman Catholic Church, owing to its fears of possible misinterpretation by people unable to grasp its varying complexities and possible confusion of its various meanings: figural, typological, allegorical, and anagogical.[16] It is worthy of note that mass circulation and campaigns urging people to read the Bible in the vernacular originated with the Protestants. In British West Africa, this was led by the Foreign Bible Society, which imbibed the Reformation principle of *sola scriptura*, by which knowledge of God is limited to textualization of the Scripture.

COLONIALIST AND MISSIONARY HERMENEUTICS

Missionary hermeneutics takes the texture of colonialism even though it is distinct from the colonial governments.[17] Missionary activities, despite being distinct from and on several occasions opposed to various forms of misrule of colonialism, were structured on the colonial principle of the one universal history, the Western history, upon which every other history and culture must abide.[18] According to Eric Anum, this universalization of Western history is equally the foundation of Western missionary activities: "*Kulturprotestantismus* served as the basis for the formulation of colonial ideology and European value-setting for biblical interpretation in the non-Western world, including Africa in the nineteenth and twentieth centuries."[19] This generated what Bernard Lonergan would describe as the classicist mentality, according to which European culture, thought patterns, history, values, and so forth are synonymous with the human culture.[20] Little wonder that it was difficult for the European missionaries to support indigenizing of the clergy or the

---

16. Louis B. Pascoe, "The Council of Trent and Bible Study: Humanism and Scripture," *The Catholic Historical Review* 52, no. 1 (1966): 18–38, has a history of the deliberations of the study of the Bible in the Council of Trent.
17. Brian Stanley, *The Bible and the Flag* (Apollos, 1990), treats the various claims of Christian missionaries as agents of colonialism.
18. Cf. J. Comaroff and Jean Comaroff, *Ethnography and the Historical Imagination* (Westerview, 1992).
19. Eric Anum, "The Usage of the Bible in African Missionary History: The Legacy of New Testament Usage in Africa," *Ghana Journal of Religion and Theology* 1 (2006): 72.
20. Bernard Lonergan, "The Transition from a Classicist World-View to Historical-Mindedness," in *A Second Collection*, ed. William F. J. Ryan and Bernard J. Tyrrell (Westminster Press, 1975), 3.

struggle for political independence from colonialism, even though they were in support of biblical translation.

The missionary hermeneutic flowing from the colonial hermeneutic changed Christianity with a civilizing role to rescue the barbarian, primitive, and disorderly people without culture. The Bible, then, is associated with the orderliness, cleanliness, and improved well-being under the salvific power of the gospel. Christian evangelization, then, meant the inculcation of European lifestyle and values into the colonized peoples and the extrapolation of Christianity and the Bible as the only vehicle for redemption and liberation from the powers of darkness that had held the people in bondage. The imperialists subjugating the people were now wearing the garb of redeemers and liberators. Practically, as R. S. Sugirtharajah argues, the consequence is the alteration of cultural values, the injection of foreign values, the outright condemnation of the patterns of life and thought of Africans, and the burning of their cultural and religious artifacts, regarded as idols, as proof of conversion to Christianity and their substitution with the Bible.

> Instead of discerning the revelation of God afresh for the time, colonial hermeneutic was unthinkingly content with concepts and formulations suitable for the people of the Mediterranean world nearly two thousand years earlier, and re-applied them to Asian, African and Latin American contexts without recognizing the cultural and theological differences between the two.[21]

African elites suggest that the Christian missionaries using the Bible hoodwinked the people into submitting their land in exchange for prayers. In the famous statement of Jomo Kenyatta in his anthropological work, *Facing Mount Kenya*, "When the Missionaries arrived, the Africans had the land, and the missionaries had the Bible. They taught us how to pray with our eyes closed. When we opened them, they had the land, and we had the Bible."[22]

The Bible was used to cushion the effects of the difficult conditions facing the people, especially ones engendered by colonial cruelty and exploitation. *Fuga mundi* (flight from the world) spirituality with emphasis on the joys of

---

21. Rasiah S. Sugirtharajah, *The Bible and the Third World* (Cambridge University Press, 2011), 52.
22. Jomo Kenyatta, *Facing Mount Kenya: The Tribal Life of the Gikuyu* (Secker and Warburg, 1953). Cf. Barbara Celarent, "*Facing Mount Kenya* by Jomo Kenyatta," *American Journal of Sociology* 116, no. 2 (2010): 722–28.

the beatific vision were introduced as more important for the people. African novelists like Ngugi Wa Thiong'o,[23] Chinua Achebe,[24] and Wole Soyinka[25] have critiqued the activities of the Christian missionaries in this regard. However, Africans were not merely hapless and passive agents, toyed with and buffeted mindlessly by the colonial and missionary hermeneutics. As will be discussed later, they responded in many ways to the introduction of the Bible. Yet the positive impact of European civilization on Africa should not be glossed over, especially in terms of education, infrastructure, development of languages, and so forth, as Chukwudi A. Njoku has pointedly observed.[26]

MAKING THE BIBLE AVAILABLE: TRANSLATIONS INTO VERNACULAR

The first step in the dissemination of the Bible was its translation into the vernacular of the various sub-Saharan African languages, which during the missionary era, were oral. It ought to be emphasized that the first Bible translation in the church was in Africa, with the translation of the Hebrew Bible into Greek, called the Septuagint.[27] Translation brings out the meaning of texts in different languages to a new one. As has been rightly observed, "An intelligible Bible in the vernacular is and always has been one of the most important factors influencing church growth in Africa."[28]

The orthography of these languages had first to be standardized, often by isolating one of the languages or by selecting one dialect in a language to be used in the translation. Initially, the process was haphazard and incredibly diverse, with each language producing its own orthography depending on the idiosyncrasies of the inventor. "The same sound is represented in various ways, and it may happen that two separate sounds are represented by the

---

23. Ngugi Wa Thiong'o, *Weep Not, Child* (Heinemann Educational Publishers, 1964).
24. Chinua Achebe, *Things Fall Apart* (Penguin Books, 1994).
25. Wole Soyinka, *Chronicles from the Land of the Happiest People on Earth* (Pantheon Books, 2020). See also *The Trials of Brother Jero* and *Jero's Metamorphosis*, both first produced in Ibadan in 1960, then published in 1964; *The Lion and the Jewel*, first produced in Ibadan in 1959, then published in 1963; and *Madmen and Specialists*.
26. Njoku, "The Missionary Factor in African Christianity," 213.
27. Julius Gathogo and John Kennedy Kinyua, "Afro-Biblical Hermeneutics in Africa Today," *Churchman* 124 no. 3 (2010): 254–55.
28. Ernst R. Wendland, "The Challenge of Bible Translation in Africa Today," *Wisconsin Lutheran Quarterly*, 80, no. 4 (1983): 284.

same letter. More frequently it happens that essential features of a language are not indicated in any way, and it has never been quite clear whether a given orthography has been designed for the benefit of the Native, with a view to teaching him to read and write his language, or for the benefit of the European desirous of studying the language."[29] Efforts at standardization came when the missionary societies of England, North America, and the European Continent entrusted the production of such orthography, not only for Africa but also for all languages of the world, to an Egyptologist of great repute, C. R. Lepsius. Lepsius's book *Standard Alphabet* "first appeared in 1855, followed by a second edition in 1863, and was much used in missionary circles, particularly in Africa."[30] Imperfect as it was, it was successful in grasping the sounds of various languages and articulating them into written symbols. Yet the missionaries encountered difficulties with the orthography of African languages.

As the first memorandum issued by the International Institute of African Languages and Cultures observed, the problems of African orthography are threefold: (1) phonetic, (2) psychological and pedagogical, and (3) typographic. There must be phonetic—that is, the accurate "resolution of a spoken language into its constituent sounds"[31] before any meaningful orthography can occur or else the language is distorted and different meanings are misrepresented. Some favor the purely phonetic principle, according to which words are written as they are pronounced, while others favor "the etymological principle, by which words are written so that their derivation may be recognized."[32] Psychological and pedagogical problems arise when one thinks about how to represent thirty consonant sounds using the letters of a language that only has twenty-one. Do you have to add new letters for African languages? Do you add diacritical marks? In these problems, the missionaries were faced with enormous challenges that resulted in some errors in translations. Using Ghana as an example, Emmanuel Kojo Ennin Antwi pointed to some of these mistranslations: "In an attempt to produce translated versions of the Bible for the natives, they ended up producing translations, some of which

---

29. A. Lloyd James, "The Practical Orthography of African Languages," *Africa: Journal of the International African Institute* 1, no. 1 (1928): 125.

30. Carl Meinhof and Daniel Jones, "Principles of Practical Orthography for African Languages," *Africa: Journal of the International African Institute* 1, no. 2 (1928): 228.

31. A. Lloyd James, "Phonetics and African Languages," *Africa: Journal of the International African Institute* 1, no. 3 (1928): 358.

32. Meinhof and Jones, "Principles of Practical Orthography," 229.

did not reflect the thoughts of the indigenous people. This has called for an enterprise whereby these texts need to be retranslated and interpreted to reflect the thoughts of the indigenous people."[33]

Thus, orthography of African languages was a long time in the making. For instance, when the Church Missionary Society convened to finalize the Romanized Yoruba language in 1875, the orthography they chose had taken thirty-five years of hard work by Bishop Samuel Ajayi Crowther, Christian clergy, and specialist linguists.[34] The work of translation had to deal with conflicting orthographies and political agendas of local communities looking toward translation as a tool for peddling their ideologies. This was true of the Luyia of western Kenya. According to Julie MacArthur, "Controversies over orthography, pronunciation, and translation revealed the competing interests of missionaries and African linguists."[35] Writing about the Shona peoples of Zimbabwe, Lovemore Togarasei notes the absence of a written version of the language and the differences in the dialect of the language: "What this then means, is that when the missionaries translated the books of the Bible, they used the dialect of the region in which they were operating. Not only were the missionaries to translate the Bible, but they also had to devise an orthography of the language, since the Shona themselves were then a non-literate society."[36]

Without diminishing the importance of oral cultures, the transcription of African languages made possible the textualization and the written word and the transition to literacy through various forms of education. Difficult as this was, and despite lapses in various African countries and language areas, Bible translations in the various languages in Africa made the Bible available to the people in their native tongues. This was a daunting task considering the multiplicity of languages, estimated to be about two

---

33. Emmanuel Kojo Ennin Antwi, "Assessing the Mode of Biblical Interpretation in the Light of African Biblical Hermeneutics: The Case of the Mother-Tongue Biblical Interpretation in Ghana," *Religions* 15, no. 203 (2024): 1.

34. Isaac Adejoju Ogunbiyi, "The Search for a Yoruba Orthography Since the 1840s: Obstacles to the Choice of the Arabic Script," *Sudanic Africa* 14 (2003): 77–102. See also Stephen Ney, "Samuel Ajayi Crowther and the Age of Literature," *Research in African Literatures* 46, no. 1 (2015): 37–52.

35. Julie MacArthur, "The Making and Unmaking of African Languages: Oral Communities and Competitive Linguistic Work in Western Kenya," *The Journal of African History* 53, no. 2 (2012): 152.

36. Lovemore Togarasei, "The Shona Bible and the Politics of Bible Translation," *Studies in World Christianity* 15, no. 1 (2009): 53.

thousand in Africa. According to Ernst R. Wendland, Africa "is one of the most linguistically complex regions of the world and many of the threads still remain to be unraveled, but recent investigations put the figure at somewhere between 1,600 and 2,000 distinct languages (each different from the other at least as much as Spanish from Portuguese or French from Italian) . . . The effect of such language diversity upon the translation of Scripture is almost intimidating."[37]

Apart from the difficulties posed by the multiplicity of languages in Africa, Bible translation in and of itself is not easy. According to Lynell Zogbo, a United Bible Societies (UBS) translation consultant based in Abidjan, Côte d'Ivoire, "Bible translators worldwide face a number of challenges as they attempt to render the Scriptures in a way that is faithful to the original, natural, and understandable in the target language. This job is never an easy one, no matter where it is carried out. Translators and exegetes working on the African continent face a unique set of challenges, even if they benefit as well from some important advantages."[38] Specifically, "the missionary linguists who shouldered the burden of translation grappled with numerous technical issues of alphabet, script, text, tone, orthography, grammar, semantics, usage, culture, and currency, matters of great importance to specialists, it has to be stressed."[39] At times, they try to solve this problem by creating one single language out of the numerous ones in existence.[40] The success or failure of such practice we will see shortly.

While recognizing the role played by African linguists, European and North American missionary societies participated in this translation. Deeply involved in the process and worthy of note are "the Anglican Society for the Propagation of the Gospel in Foreign Parts (1701), the Church Missionary Society (1790), the British and Foreign Bible Society (1804) and the Roman Catholic Association for the Propagation of the Faith (1822)."[41] To this must be included the UBS, "which dates its official origin to 9 May 1946, in England, [and] is the major Bible translation agency in both Africa and throughout her

---

37. Wendland, "The Challenge of Bible Translation in Africa Today," 285.
38. Lynell Zogbo, "Issues in Bible Translation in Africa," *Review and Expositor* 108 (2011): 280.
39. Lamin Sanneh, *Whose Religion Is Christianity? The Gospel Beyond the West* (William B. Eerdmans, 2003), 106.
40. Cf. MacArthur, "The Making and Unmaking of African Languages, 151–72.
41. Gosnell Yorke, "Bible Translation in Anglophone Africa and Her Diaspora: A Postcolonialist Agenda," *Black Theology* 2, no. 2 (2004): 154.

Diaspora."[42] UBS works in tandem with Wycliffe Bible Translators in Central Africa (Malawi and Zambia). According to church historian Brian Stanley, "The role of the Bible societies in effecting the transformation of Christianity into a global religion is still undervalued."[43] However, the attempted creation of a common language as standard for the translation of the Bible has not always fared well. Nigeria's case serves as an example.

The success of Samuel Ajayi Crowther's Bible translation into Yoruba helped to establish the use of Roman script for the writing of Yoruba instead of the Arabic *anjemi* script used by the Yoruba Muslims. This led to the attempt at replication among the Igbos of Southeast Nigeria, resulting in the much-criticized Union Igbo Bible.[44] Completed between 1906 and 1912 in Egbu, near Owerri, and the handiwork of Archbishop Thomas Dennis and T. D. Anyaegbunam of the Church Missionary Society, the Union Igbo was in circulation by 1913. Aimed at the unification of the Igbo language and supported by the British and Foreign Bible Society, the translation ended up being a mix of Igbo that no one speaks. The production of the Union Igbo may be informed by the age-long European interest in language as key to human identity and categorization of people.[45] The Union Igbo came about because of the European missionaries' conviction of the existence of an Igbo lingua franca.[46] The Union Igbo may have been rejected because of its attempt at unification of the Igbo language, which had remarkably diverse dialects. According to Lamin Sanneh, the translation failed because it was an attempt to impose uniformity against translations of the Bible in local dialects.[47] The Catholic Church in the region could not settle on the translation of the Bible

---

42. Yorke, "Bible Translation in Anglophone Africa," 155.

43. Brian Stanley, *Christianity in the Twentieth Century: A World History* (Princeton University Press, 2018), 59.

44. Ben Fulford's "An Igbo Esperanto: A History of the Union Igbo Bible 1900–1950," *Journal of Religion in Africa* 32, no. 4 (2002): 457–501, chronicles such criticisms from scholars like the great novelist Prof. Chinua Achebe, eminent Igbo linguist Nolue Emenanjo, and Igbo historian Adiele Afigbo, who blamed the loss of Igbo identity and culture to the activities of the Christian missionaries.

45. Frederick Lugard, the one-time governor-general of Nigeria, wrote that "the language of the Native was his soul, and the appeal to him must be through his soul." Cf. F. D. Lugard, "The International Institute of African Languages and Cultures," *Africa: Journal of the International African Institute* 1, no. 1 (1928): 12.

46. Demitiri van der Bersselaar, "Creating 'Union Igbo': Missionary and the Igbo Language," *Africa: Journal of the International African Institute* 67, no. 2 (1977): 273–95.

47. Sanneh, *Translating the Message*, 185. Van der Bersselaar, "Creating 'Union Igbo,'" presents much more comprehensive reasons for the failure of the Union Igbo Bible.

(despite its criticisms of the Union Igbo)[48] until many years after the Second Vatican Council when, in the year 2000, it produced the Igbo Catholic Bible (ICB).[49]

One wonders to what extent the missionary's conception of the worldview of the African peoples they were evangelizing affected the translations of the Bible. What political-social anthropological views were carried into the translations? In the work of translation, how did the religious and spiritual belief systems of Africans determine the choice of words used? What biblical hermeneutical assumptions serve as a backdrop for the Bible translations? As Lovemore Togarasei observed, "Translation does not take place in a vacuum. Each translator is guided by a certain ideology or ideologies."[50]

Since Christianity had already splintered into various denominations before coming to sub-Saharan Africa, Bible translation was done along denominational lines. The views of Scripture of these Christian churches impacted their attitude to the Bible and their translations as well. The diverse notions of inspiration between the Protestants, the Catholics, the Orthodox, and the Pentecostals play out in Bible translation. The Protestant-sponsored Bible translations would of course exclude the deuterocanonical books and stick to the King James Version of the Bible. The Catholic and the Orthodox translations would include these extra books. Bible translations of difficult passages, words, or phrases or of "crucial theological concepts such as 'grace' and 'justification' along with key terms like 'prophet' and 'angel,'"[51] often follow denominational paths. As articulated by a Lutheran translator in Central Africa: "Above all, we try to make sure that no rendering of a passage where there is a difference of opinion excludes the confessional Lutheran position on the matter."[52]

The rejection of the Union Igbo Bible by the Catholic Church is partly because of the differences between the Catholic and the Anglican views of the

---

48. Nicolas Omenka, "The Role of the Catholic Mission in the Development of the Vernacular Literature in Eastern Nigeria," *Journal of Religion in Africa* 16, no. 2 (1986): 121–37.

49. Uchenna Oyali, "Bible Translation and Language Elaboration: The Igbo Experience" (PhD diss., Universität Bayreuth, 2018), https://epub.uni-bayreuth.de/4298/1/Bible%20Translation%20and%2 0Language%20Elaboration%20%E2%80%93%20The%20Igbo%20Experience.pdf.

50. Togarasei, "The Shona Bible and the Politics of Bible Translation," 51.

51. Zogbo, "Issues in Bible Translation in Africa," 281.

52. Wendland, "The Challenge of Bible Translation in Africa Today," 291.

Bible, particularly the former's preference for catechisms over Bible translations at the time. According to Brian Stanley, "The Catholic Church before Vatican II placed a low priority on the production of vernacular scriptures: in East Africa at the end of the 1950s there were only three Catholic translations of the New Testament compared with fifty by Protestants, plus thirteen Protestant translations of the entire Bible."[53] Also, there was the issue of the quality of the translation, which was poorly done. This is true not only of the Union Igbo Bible but of most Bible translations in sub-Saharan Africa. Wendland is right:

> A number of these translations are over half a century old and transmit an archaic form of the language which is not familiar to contemporary speakers. Most of them are also literal renderings which reflect the grammatical structures of Hebrew and Greek (or English and French) rather than the natural flow of the African language into which the translation was done. And finally, many of these original versions were done by those who were not mother-tongue speakers, missionaries in particular, with the result that the message often gets obscured, or even obliterated, by unnatural and incorrect usages.[54]

The translated Bibles were produced and distributed to the people through various agencies focused on the distribution of the Bible. Worthy of note is the British and Foreign Bible Society (BFBS), devoted to publishing the Bible and making it available across the world.[55] Next is the international and interdenominational organization Scripture Union, formed in England sometime between 1867 and 1879. By 1890, SU (as it's fondly called) was engaged in evangelism in West Africa, encouraging people to read the Bible and to live by it. According to Andrew Olu Igenoza, SU thrived by stamping evangelism with "indigenous authenticity through the process of contextualization."[56]

---

53. Stanley, *Christianity in the Twentieth Century*, 59; also 77.
54. Wendland, "The Challenge of Bible Translation in Africa Today," 285–86. Most Christian denominations are also revising the translations done by Western missionaries.
55. A concise elaboration of the work of the Bible Society can be found in Sugirtharajah, *The Bible and the Third World*. Also, Ype Schaaf, *On Their Way Rejoicing: The History and the Role of the Bible in Africa* (Paternoster Press, 1994), chronicles the activities of BFBS in publication and distribution of the Bible.
56. Andrew Olu Igenoza, "Contextual Balancing of Scripture with Scripture: Scripture Union in Nigeria and Ghana," in Gerald O. West and Musa W. Dube, eds., *The Bible in Africa: Transactions, Trajectories and Trends* (Brill, 2001), 294.

BIBLE, EDUCATION, AND POLITICS

The act of translation could be as political as it was religious. Using the translation of the Gîkuyù New Testament as a case study, Johnson Kīriakū Kīnyua shows, first, "that Bible translation in colonial Africa, though in most cases defended as a neutral, legitimate, and benevolent act of redemption, actually disguises the colonial power situation. Secondly, even though Bible translators aimed at dominating and restructuring the colonized's view of reality, the translation process was not in itself immune to the restructuring power of decolonization."[57] In a sense, one can say that the various ways the Christian missionaries used to evangelize and spread Western Christianity, including its civilizations, were a mix of blessing and curse. The negative impact on African cultures must not be glossed over. At the same time, the fact of African agency means that despite Western influence, Africans remained conscious of their unique culture and endured the initial crisis of identity that the demeaning of African culture caused. The practices and institutions created for the creation and promulgation of the Bible in Africa exemplify this ambiguity.

The effort to make the people read the Bible was first done through developing an orthography that transcribed their oral languages into alphabets that could be written down. Second, this effort necessitated schools to promote literacy.[58] The African feminist biblical scholar Musa W. Dube affirmed that in sub-Saharan Africa, "schools were introduced to educate and bring up Bible readers—literacy itself was introduced to promote bible translation, interpretation, conversion and training of preachers."[59] But once literacy takes hold, teachers no longer control what their students do with it. So, while initial waves of literacy spread through missionary initiative during the colonial period, the subsequent nationalist movements that eventually gave rise to the political independence of African countries are themselves the fruit of the introduction of the Bible and Christian evangelization through the schools.

---

57. Johnson Kīriakū Kīnyua, "A Postcolonial Analysis of Bible Translation and Its Effectiveness in Shaping and Enhancing the Discourse of Colonialism and the Discourse of Resistance: The Gîkûyû New Testament—A Case Study," *Black Theology* 11, no. 1 (2013): 53.

58. Criticisms of the deficiency of the missionary schools and their education systems aimed at training workers for the missions and junior staff for the colonies abound. Cf. Gray, "Christianity and Religious Change in Africa," 89–100.

59. Musa W. Dube, "The Scramble for Africa as the Biblical Scramble for Africa: Postcolonial Perspectives," in *Postcolonial Perspectives in African Biblical Interpretations*, ed. Musa W. Dube (Society of Biblical Literature, 2012), 4.

Dube expresses this well: "The writing is on the wall. In sub-Saharan Africa, biblical interpretation, its institutions, and readers will always be related to modern colonial history, for the Scramble for Africa was the Scramble for Africa through the Bible. As we shall observe, the scramble to get Africa back from the colonial clutches was and still is waged through the Bible (yet the Bible is not the only viable weapon). That the Scramble for Africa was a scramble through the Bible is therefore an interpretation crux."[60] Dube's position here indicates that Africans were not only introduced to the Bible, but they also appropriated the Bible as subjects and made use of it as an object to achieve political independence. This agrees with Gerald O. West's view that the Bible not only played a significant role in the formation of African Christianity, but Africa has also equally played a role "in the interpretation, and construction, of the Bible. Africa is no longer acted upon, but is itself an actor. The Bible is no longer the agent, but is the object of the actions of (African) others."[61]

Nationalist movements that arose from the political will of Africans for African rule and independence from colonialism got from the Bible the notion of the inherent dignity of humankind as created in the image and likeness of God. Nnamdi Azikiwe, the first governor-general of independent Nigeria, alludes to the biblical image of human creatureliness in God's image as the principle of equality and freedom, the repugnance of racism and discrimination. He asserts:

> The challenge of Nigeria as a free State in twentieth century Africa is the need to revive the stature of man in Africa and restore the dignity of man in the world. Nigerians believe passionately in the fundamental human rights. We regard all races of the human family as equal. Under no circumstance shall we accept the idea that the black race is inferior to any other race. No matter where this spurious doctrine may prevail, it may be in Lodwar or Sharpville or Decatur, we shall never admit that we are an inferior race, because if we accept the Christian or Muslim doctrine that God is perfect and that man was made in the image of God, then it would be sacrilegious, if not heretical, to believe that we are an inferior race.[62]

---

60. Dube, "The Scramble for Africa," 4.
61. Gerald O. West, "On the Eve of an African Biblical Studies: Trajectories and Trends," *Journal of Theology for Southern Africa* 99 (1997): 99.
62. Nnamdi Azikiwe, "Respect for Human Dignity," *Negro History Bulletin* 24, no. 6 (1961): 126.

The nationalists saw the contradictions in the practices of colonialism, which diminish their dignity. They saw the hypocrisy of some Western missionaries for not regarding Africans as equal human beings, contrary to the teachings of the Bible. As aptly articulated by Ndabaningi Sithole:

> One of the unique teachings of the Bible, especially in the New Testament, is the worth and dignity of the individual in the sight of God, and there is a relation between this teaching and the present African nationalism. According to African tradition, at least in some parts if not in the whole of Africa, the individual counted in so far as he was part and parcel of the group, outside of which he lost his real worth ... Individual initiative was crippled. But now ... we find individuals venturing beyond the confines of the group ... The same Bible is helping the African individual to reassert himself above colonial powers! It is inconceivable to a logical mind that the Bible could deliver the African from traditional domination without at the same time redeeming him from colonial domination. If the Bible teaches that the individual is unique, of infinite worth before God, colonialism in many respects, says just the opposite; so that, in actual practice, Biblical teachings are at variance with colonialism, and it becomes only a matter of time before one ousts the other.[63]

And so, in some sense, one can say that the Bible became a subversive force both against the submissive education of the missionary schools and colonialism by opening the eyes of Africans to see themselves as eagles, and to fly to freedom.[64]

James S. Coleman points out the critical role education played in the quest for nationalist movements for political independence when he observed that "Western education has created the new African elite."[65] William E. Phipps expatiates, linking nationalist movements to the languages taught in schools and the standardization of the vernacular translations of the Bible, arguing

---

63. Ndabaningi Sithole, *African Nationalism* (Oxford University Press, 1959), 53, cited in William E. Phipps, "Christianity and Nationalism in Tropical Africa," *Civilisations* 22, no. 1 (1972): 96.

64. George W. Reid, "Missionaries and West African Nationalism," *Phylon* 39, no. 3 (1978): 225–33.

65. James Coleman, *The Politics of the Developing Areas*, 278, cited in Phipps, "Christianity and Nationalism in Tropical Africa," 93.

that "vernacular translations accelerated the pace of African nationalism."[66] What this means is that African agency, through vernacular translations and the accompanying education, exposure to overseas travel, and assistance of international institutions, engendered the struggle for political independence by the African elites through the nationalist movements. According to Ndabaningi Sithole: "Christianity has played an important role in the development of Africa. Even its worst enemies admit this. It was Christianity that introduced literacy on a continent-wide basis. Functionally too the continent of Africa owes Christianity an irrecoverable debt. Such distinguished African political leaders as Dr. Kwame Nkrumah, Dr. Julius Nyerere, Dr. Hastings Banda Messr. Obote, Kaunda, Nkomo and many others were helped to a great extent in their education by Christian missions."[67]

THE BIBLE AND RELIGIOUS CHANGE

In *Disciples of All Nations: Pillars of World Christianity*,[68] Lamin Sanneh referred to "pillars" for world Christianity. In "charismatic and primal pillars," he "highlighted the contributions of indigenous Africans and African Americans in the nineteenth and twentieth centuries, which set in motion the movement toward African Christianity."[69] Sanneh made mention of William Wade Harris ministries, which arose based on a divine calling Harris felt after reading the Bible.[70] The Harris ministries, which will be discussed briefly in the next chapter, is an example of numerous African responses to the Bible in the formation of what came to be called "African Indigenous Churches," "African Initiated Churches," or "Independent African Churches" (AICs). The AICs emerged at times in response to perceived exclusion due to the racist, demeaning attitudes of Western missionaries in the mainline churches; denial of leadership positions in these churches; lack of tolerance of charismatic gifts; and/or outright expulsion from the mainline churches. A lot

---

66. Cited in Phipps, "Christianity and Nationalism in Tropical Africa," 94.
67. Ndabaningi Sithole, "African Nationalism and Christianity," *Transition* no. 10 (1963): 37.
68. Lamin Sanneh, *Disciples of All Nations: Pillars of World Christianity* (Oxford University Press, 2008).
69. Pachuau, *World Christianity*, 12.
70. John Zarwan, "William Wade Harris: The Genesis of an African Religious Movement," *Missiology* 3, no. 4 (1975): 431–50.

has been written about AICs because of their uniqueness and rootedness in African cosmology, spirituality, and culture.[71] The vastness of their influence lies in their formulation of Christianity, which claims that relying on the Bible overcomes the dualism of Western Christianity and philosophy. Their appeal to many Africans and fascination to Westerners lie beyond their purported exoticness to the deep-seated human desire toward integral spirituality that recognizes the connection between the secular and the spiritual worlds. Our interest in the AICs lies in their significant contributions to inculturation, leading subsequently to inculturation hermeneutics.

David Barrett attributes the emergence of the AICs to the publication of the Bible in the local languages of African peoples. According to him, among other factors, "the danger period when movements begin to secede is on average sixty years after the arrival in the tribe of the first mission body, Protestant or Catholic; or sixty years after the first publication of the New Testament; or a hundred years after the arrival of colonial rule." Independence, Barrett continues, becomes "increasingly more probable as more of the scriptures become available in a tribe's language."[72] Barrett is right. One of the famous AICs in Kenya, the Akurinu, emerged in 1927 under leaders Joseph Ng'ang'a and John Mung'ara. The fame of Akurinu attracted the attention of Jomo Kenyetta, who described them in his anthropological tome, *Facing Mount Kenya*, thus: "The members of this religious sect strongly believe that they

---

71. For the various ways AICs have been studied by various scholars, see Sibusiso Masondo, "The History of African Indigenous Churches in Scholarship," *Journal for the Study of Religion* 18, no. 2 (2005): 89–103; AIC on inculturation, see Terence Ranger, "African Initiated Churches," *Transformation* 24, no. 2 (2007): 65–71; as a positive response to the gospel, see C. M. Pauw, "African Independent Churches as a 'People's Response' to the Christian Message," *Journal for the Study of Religion* 8, no. 1 (1995): 3–25; as an anthropology of Christianity in Africa, see Birgit Meyer, "Christianity in Africa: From African Independent to Pentecostal-Charismatic Churches," *Annual Review of Anthropology* 33 (2004): 447–74; as a new religious movement, see José Antunes da Silva, "African Independent Churches Origin and Development," *Anthropos* Bd. 88, H. 4./6. (1993): 393–402; Itumeleng Mosala, "Race, Class, and Gender as Hermeneutical Factors in the African Independent Churches' Appropriation of the Bible," *Semeia* 73 (1996): 43–57. Book length study: Nathaniel I. Ndiokwere, *Prophecy and Revolution: The Role of Prophets in the Independent African Churches and in Biblical Tradition* (SPCK, 1981); Bengt G. M. Sundkler, *Bantu Prophet in South Africa*, (Lutterworth Press, 1948); Bengt Sundkler, *The Christian Ministry in Africa* (SCM Press, 1960); David B. Barrett, *Schism and Renewal in Africa* (Oxford University Press, 1968).

72. Barrett, *Schism and Renewal in Africa* (Oxford University Press, 1968), 6, cited in John S. Mbiti, "The Role of the Jewish Bible in African Independent Churches," *International Review of Mission* 93, no. 369 (2004), 221.

are the chosen people of God to give and interpret his message to the people. They proclaim that they belong to the lost tribes of Israel."[73]

The Old Testament has a strong appeal to the AICs. This may be because of the similarity between the African worldview and those of the cultures recorded in the Old Testament. AICs came to this knowledge because of the translation and publication of the Bible in various African languages. While they recognize the whole Bible, including the New Testament, they could relate their history, customs, and cultures to the Old Testament. They felt the exhilarating freedom and personhood that had been denied them through colonialism and the put-downs by Western missionaries, including the vicious attacks on their local cultures. As has been expressed by Bishop John Henry Okumu, "The missionaries who brought Christianity, rid Africa of all its traditional values and religious concepts in order to have a clean plate on which to put the new faith."[74] But with the Bible, Africans saw an exact replica of their worldview expressed in the word of God. According to John S. Mbiti, one of the foremost African theologians and philosophers,

> among other injustices that it did, colonial occupation eclipsed African peoplehood. Colonial presence, domination, ignorance and arrogance, plus a certain amount of (sometimes, cheap) missionary teaching, projected an attitude towards Africans as though "they were no-people." In contrast, we opened the scriptures in our own languages and saw the Jewish people in the Bible as a mirror in which we viewed ourselves. This insight was something contrary to the image that colonial and missionary presence projected about us. For us, the Bible had a greater authority than that of colonial rulers, anthropologists and missionary preachers. We could find anthropological refuge and protection within the pages of the Bible, and nowhere else. Furthermore, it was and is the word of God, the very God that we knew and trusted through traditional religion long before missionaries arrived. Africans already knew something about the same God and offered worship to the same. The Bible accepted and described that same God, which was something that

---

73. Kenyatta, *Facing Mount Kenya*, 275, cited in Nahashon W. Ndung'u, "The Role of the Bible in the Rise of African Instituted Churches: The Case of the Akurinu Churches in Kenya," in West and Dube, *The Bible in Africa*, 237.

74. Bishop John Henry Okumu, *Church and Politics in East Africa* (Uzima Press, 1974), 8, cited in Israel K. Katoke, "Christianity and Culture: An African Experience," *Transformation* 1, no. 4 (1984): 7.

foreign presence had denied us. In the pages of the Bible, the people identified themselves together with God the creator of all things.[75]

In other words, with the Bible, "the missionaries, served by local interpreters and catechists [no] longer have the final word."[76] Through reading the Bible, Africans began appropriating Christianity in the light of their traditional religious cultures by incorporation of elements of African traditional religions into Christianity.

Thus, Lamin Sanneh extols the "vernacularization" of Christianity through the translation of the Bible, which "ushered in a fundamental religious revolution, with new religious structures coming into being to preside over the changes."[77] This provided an independent standard of reference that African Christians were quick to seize on.[78] Through the Bible, they who had been identified as having no history now have one, an identity as "the people of the Bible." "They retrieve their historical and anthropological identity that foreign presence had eclipsed, denied or falsified."[79] As a product of a process of acculturation, the African origins of AICs is undoubtable. While Christianity is never truly a "Western" religion because Africa has always been involved with Christianity, as we discussed in chapter 1, the AICs "serve as a correction to the earlier identification of Christianity with Western civilization."[80] AICs are truly the people's response to the Christian message in the light of their cultures. As C. M. Pauw writes, "AICs are to be seen as reflecting a positive response to a widespread religious need among African peoples, a response which is given within the framework of the Christian Bible and which is fulfilling a need not being satisfied elsewhere."[81]

Another important religious change is the emergence of a truly world Christianity owing to the massive conversion of Africans to Christianity. For instance, "in 1900 there were 9 million Christians on the entire continent of Africa. A little more than 100 years later, the number of Christians

---

75. Mbiti, "The Role of the Jewish Bible in African Independent Churches," 221.
76. Nathaniel I. Ndiokwere, *Prophecy and Revolution* (SPCK, 1981), 22–23.
77. Sanneh, *Translating the Message*, 159, cited in Solomon K. Avotri, "The Vernacularization of Scripture and African Beliefs: The Story of the Gerasene Demoniac Among the Ewe of West Africa," in West and Dube, *The Bible in Africa*, 313.
78. Barrett, *Schism and Renewal in Africa*, 127, cited in Ndiokwere, *Prophecy and Revolution*, 23.
79. Mbiti, "The Role of the Jewish Bible in African Independent Churches," 222.
80. Pauw, "African Independent Churches," 14.
81. Pauw, "African Independent Churches," 14.

in Africa numbered more than 667 million!"[82] Lamin Sanneh attributes the rise of world Christianity to the role of the Bible in Christian life and practice. Just as the translation of the Bible into the various European languages and in English led to the expansion of Christianity, and its cultural appropriation by the West, so it was for Africa: The Bible in the vernacular or mother tongue, through the translation of the Bible into the local languages of various parts of Africa, gave rise to the emergence of indigenous Christianity.

Translation has presented Christianity in a new and different light. Christianity is not a closed-circuit religion but one that is dynamic, open to localization and anchored in indigenization and encouraging creativity, cross-cultural, global, and adaptable local cultures. Christian theology is transformed by translation; it is no longer classicist but attuned to the empirical notion of culture, to use Bernard Lonergan's terminology.[83] Sanneh argues:

> Translation is evidence that Christianity's neurological center is in flux, that its vocabulary is growing and changing, that historical experience has had cumulative force, that the allotment of "neurons" is continuing because "neurogenesis" is a living process rather than a relic of evolution, that foreign idioms have lodged in the system like oxygen in the bloodstream, and that "localizationism" in the frontal lobe of northern Christianity has shifted to the central cortex of Southern Christianity where new, expanded tasks have stimulated tolerance and diversity in the religion. Translation has shifted the "genetic determinism" of the established canon by encrypting the religion with the most diverse cultural chromosomes of other societies. The growing statistics of the resurgence shows the scale of what is afoot. And in this new milieu old school theology has appeared as a relic, which may explain its reported decline in its once hallowed cultural strongholds.[84]

---

82. F. Lionel Young III, *World Christianity and the Unfinished Task: A Very Short Introduction* Cascade Books, 2021), 22. Young's statistic is from Tom M. Johnson and Gina Zurlow, eds., *World Christian Encyclopedia* (Edinburgh University Press, 2020), 4.
83. Lonergan, "The Transition from a Classicist Worldview to Historical Mindedness," 3–10.
84. Lamin Sanneh, "Post-Western Wine, Post-Christian Wineskins? The Bible and the Third Wave Awakening," in *Understanding World Christianity: The Vision and Work of Andrew F. Walls*, ed. William R. Burrows et al. (Orbis Books, 2011), 104.

Sanneh's "third wave awakening" resembles but goes beyond Walbert Buhlmann's *The Coming of Third Church*[85] and Philip Jenkin's *The Next Christendom*[86] by focusing on the resurgence of Christianity, not on the Western model of global Christianity but on the autochthonocity of world Christianity.[87] The Gospels and the New Testament are translated versions of the message of Jesus. This makes Christianity a translated religion. "Translation is the church's birthmark as well as its missionary benchmark: the church would be unrecognizable or unsustainable without it."[88] Andrew Walls affirms Sanneh's view on translatability of Christianity: "Christian faith must go on being translated, must continuously enter into vernacular culture and interact with it, or it withers and fades."[89] Thus, today, the center of gravity of Christianity has shifted from the Global North to the Global South.

CONCLUSION

The chapter argued that the translation of the Bible into the various African languages led to the autochthonocity of Christianity in the cultures of sub-Saharan African peoples. This accounts for the massive conversion to Christianity, to the surprise of those who taught that Christianity would collapse after colonialism and attainment of political independence. Reading the Bible in their various cultures equally gave rise to the emergence of indigenous expressions of AICs, which led the way in the inculturation of Christianity in sub-Saharan African.

The reintroduction of Christianity by the missionaries to Africa, beginning with the efforts of the Portuguese missionaries in the fifteenth century and proceeding to the translation efforts of the nineteenth century, was bound up with European colonialism. For this reason, colonial mentality filtered into the work of European missionaries, as their attitude to culture coincided with the idea of the European culture and framework as human culture. But

---

85. Walbert Buhlmann, *The Coming of the Third Church: An Analysis of the Present and Future of the Church* (Orbis Books, 1977).

86. Philip Jenkins, *The Next Christendom*, 3rd ed. (Oxford University Press, 2011).

87. Lamin Sanneh and Michael J. McClymond, introduction to *World Christianity*, ed. Lamin Sanneh and Michael J. McClymond (Wiley & Sons, 2016), 1–18.

88. Sanneh, *Whose Religion Is Christianity?*, 97.

89. Andrew F. Walls, *The Cross-Cultural Process in Christian History: Studies in the Transmission and Appropriation of Faith* (Orbis Books, 2002), 29.

the translation of the Bible into the vernacular initiated the process for the emergence of a Christianity formed from the cultural expressions of Africans. Thus, today we can boast of an enculturated African Christianity. Literacy accompanying the translation through the schools and education led to the nationalist movements through which African peoples of the sub-Sahara gained political independence from their various colonial overlords. The Bible empowered the people to identify themselves as part of the people of God. It forms the basis of the demand for equality and justice from others and from themselves for one another. The Bible equally engendered the AICs as truly African churches at the grassroots of people's belief, experiences, desires, and deep spiritual yearnings.

CHAPTER THREE

Popular Reading of the Bible

To call an approach "common" or "popular" is not a pejorative statement. It does not imply defect. It specifies only a manner or pattern of knowledge. It situates and describes the achievements of common sense while also being honest about the limitations and pitfalls that often accompany those achievements. The Canadian philosopher Bernard Lonergan offers an analysis of common sense, the questions it asks and answers, the forms of community it fosters, and its contrast to other forms of knowledge and inquiry in his landmark work, *Insight*. Whether in matters of science and theory or in realms of practicality and prudence, "in every case, the man or woman of intelligence is marked by a greater readiness in catching on, in getting the point, in seeing the issue, in grasping implications, in acquiring knowhow."[1] Lonergan is "endeavoring to conceive the intellectual component of common sense."[2]

He seeks to articulate the form of understanding or insight proper to commonsense knowledge and the function of intelligence that operates within common sense's domain of competence. "It is an accumulation of insights," he writes, "in which each successive act complements the accuracy and covers over the deficiency of those that went before."[3] Insights are not just individualistic; they are also communal. They are influenced by one's situation and duration, by space and time, by one's context. One learns from one's context and contributes to the development of the community. Common sense, therefore, refers to the community's accumulated wisdom in which people

---

1. Bernard Lonergan, *Insight: A Study of Human Understanding*, CWL 3, 197.
2. Lonergan, *Insight*, 203.
3. Lonergan, *Insight*, 197.

are acculturated and enculturated and to which people equally contribute to and advance. But common sense has limits. Its domain of competence has clear boarders. The common fund of understanding it makes possible "may suffer from blind spots, oversights, errors, bias."[4] These liabilities, though, do not obviate the need for common sense. They merely indicate the potential pitfalls that accompany its progress and must be reversed for that progress to continue. Common sense is concerned with the concrete and the practical, with finding solutions to everyday problems, issues, and riddles of life. So, too, is much of the Bible.

This chapter will show that a popular or commonsense reading of the Bible is not an unintelligent, unquestioning, or nonliterate reading. Commonsense reading of the Bible relates the Bible to us; seeks for lessons, especially moral lessons from the Bible; and applies the Bible to various contemporaneous issues—spiritual, political, social, educational, psychological, metaphysical. Commonsense reading is contextual, concerned primarily with linking the biblical texts "with the realities of African contexts."[5] Justin S. Ukpong has studied popular, ordinary, or commonsense reading of the Bible and associates it with "the poor, the marginalized, non-biblical experts."[6] He writes,

> As a general category the term "ordinary people" refers to a social class, the common people in contradistinction to the elite. In most of Africa they live by the world-view provided by their traditional cultures, they are poor and marginalized, they suffer economic, social and political disadvantage, and are found in both rural and urban areas. They are not trained in the theological sciences, and are generally illiterate, semi-literate or functionally illiterate. However, they have a high sense of self-worth and would not be compromised because of their low social status. Scars of struggle for survival mark their lives. Even though in most cases they live below the subsistence level, they never give up on living (one rarely finds cases of suicide among them). They are "incurably" religious. All these in different ways constitute their conditioning of reading.[7]

---

4. Bernard F. Lonergan, *Method in Theology*, CWL 14, ed. Robert M. Doran and John D. Dadosky (University of Toronto Press, 2017), 44.
5. Justin S. Ukpong, "Reading the Bible in a Global Village," 10.
6. Ukpong, "Reading the Bible in a Global Village," 11.
7. Ukpong, "Reading the Bible in a Global Village," 23.

Ukpong's pilot study on popular readings of the Bible in Africa and the West, the Bible in Africa project, was carried out in Port Harcourt, Nigeria, and Glasgow, Scotland. The aims of the study include an examination of the oral and literary approaches to the Bible in Africa and Europe, how the classical biblical interpretation reflects the perspectives of the West, and ways it is being used by African biblical scholars to develop specific ways of reading the Bible for African contexts. It's also aimed at exploring the connection between academic study of the Bible and popular reading in Europe and Africa and on how sociopolitical contexts and issues influence the reading of the Bible. Ukpong's study highlights popular reading in Africa. This includes determining the attitude of ordinary Nigerians to the Bible, how they interpret and apply the Bible to their daily lives, the cultural influences on their interpretations, the passages they find difficult, and how they resolve the conflict in applying the Bible to their daily lives.[8] Ukpong's study was interdenominational. Christians from four Christian traditions participated: "Roman Catholic, Protestant, (Presbyterian), African Instituted Churches, and Evangelical churches."[9]

Responses from the participants unveil the popular conception of the Bible among Nigerians. First, because the Bible is inspired, it is authoritative and has the final say in all aspects of life. It is the word of God, given by God through the Holy Spirit, which humanity should revere and to which it should submit. Second, by virtue of its divine origin, the Bible has power over principalities and powers—that is, over all evil forces, especially witches and wizards, that inflict suffering, pain, and all kinds of misfortune against the people. Third, the Bible is a book of devotion, meant for prayer, interaction, and communion with God. It is the guide to actions, "a rule of life and a norm for morality."[10] Fourth, the Bible is used not only to overcome forces of darkness but also to promote prosperity and material welfare. "The bible is used in seeking deliverance from material afflictions like poverty, childlessness, etc. which they believe is caused by evil spirits . . . Passages of the bible are also read for consolation and enlightenment."[11] Finally, the Bible is read literally: "The historical veracity of its content is not questioned as such questioning

---

8. Justin S. Ukpong, "Popular Readings of the Bible in Africa and Implications for Academic Readings," in West and Dube, *The Bible in Africa*, 583.
9. Ukpong, "Popular Readings of the Bible," 587.
10. Ukpong, "Popular Readings of the Bible," 588.
11. Ukpong, "Popular Readings of the Bible," 588.

would detract from this reverence . . . They are interested neither in the literary analysis of biblical texts nor in the history behind the text. They are interested in the historical message in the text and how that message might be useful to their lives. The bible is thus treated not as any other literature but as literature of a special category."[12] Johnson Kīriakū Kīnyua observes that "the kind of common sense hermeneutics that the ordinary African 'non-scholars' developed were simple, literalistic, and highly selective."[13]

Some argue that this African perception of the Bible is an extension of its notion of authority. Others insist that the African worldview is characterized by belief in the dual but integrated worlds of matter and spirit, of the cosmos and the spirit world, and that African Christians apply that worldview to the Bible. According to Ukpong, the responses could be "a true representation of what the people think the bible stands for and communicates . . . a reflection of the needs of the people, that is, what the people look for in the bible and expect to get from it . . . a reflection of what they have been told by their churches to be the central message of the bible."[14] What is obvious, though, is that ordinary people read the Bible in existential terms in the light of their various life situations and varieties of contexts. Despite the resonances between the Old Testament and African culture, most of the respondents are drawn more to the New Testament, mainly because of the miracles of Jesus in the Gospels and the power of God in Jesus. This attraction is not surprising as the people read the Bible in the first place for spiritual support and for material prosperity. Ukpong asserts:

> The Bible is believed to provide a spiritual resource for combatting spiritual forces. Since these forces are spiritual, only spiritual resources can overcome them. It is on this ground that the mainline churches, which do not use the bible in this way, lose their members to the "Spiritual churches" which do use the bible for this purpose. The search for such support makes Christians move from one church to another in search for the one that best provides the needed support, for not all the "Spiritual churches" are equally endowed with the "power." . . . No distinction was therefore made between the use of the bible for spiritual

---

12. Ukpong, "Popular Readings of the Bible," 588.
13. Johnson Kīriakū Kīnyua, *Introducing Ordinary African Readers' Hermeneutics: A Case Study of the Agīkūyū Encounter with the Bible* (Peter Lang, 2011), 167.
14. Ukpong, "Popular Readings of the Bible," 589.

needs and for material needs. Prosperity, happiness, good health, etc. are regarded as a sign of divine blessing, while a life of deprivation on earth is a negation of the expected happiness of the afterlife. There is therefore no purely spiritualized interpretation of the bible.[15]

The Bible is indispensable in African Christianity and theology.[16] Embedded in Ukpong's assessment are the impacts of spiritism and prosperity theology in African Christianity. Both forces shape the face of African Christianity to the world, giving rise to the perception of African Christianity as spiritually charismatic and theologically conservative (about the use and authority of the Bible), and explain the wave of prosperity gospel in Africa. Since these are engendered by the popular reading of the Bible, let us look at believing the Bible in Africa.

BELIEVING THE BIBLE IN THE GLOBAL SOUTH

Philip Jenkin's book *The New Faces of Christianity* gives the impression that ultraconservative biblical literalism is peculiar to African and Asian Christianities, while North American and European churches are much more accommodating and open to liberalizing trends, owing to theological sophistication and critical interpretation of the biblical texts. But such neat geographical sorting is not supported by fact. Both conservative and liberalizing approaches are found in churches of both the Global South and the Global North. And so "the conservative traditions prevailing in the global South"[17] are equally found in the Global North. "A decisive move toward literal and even fundamentalist readings of the Bible"[18] are headquartered in the church universally, "to the horror" of both American and European churches, as well as Asian and African churches.

Liberals are found in all churches as well. The issues of sexual morality, LGBTQ relations, and their climax in the ordination of Gene Robinson as a

---

15. Ukpong, "Popular Readings of the Bible," 590.

16. Edward W. Fashole-Luke, "The Quest for African Christian Theologies," in *Mission Trends No 3: Third World Theologies*, ed. G. H. Anderson and T. F. Stransky (William B. Eerdmans, 1976), 141.

17. Philip Jenkins, *The New Faces of Christianity: Believing the Bible in the Global South* (Oxford University Press, 2006), 1.

18. Jenkins, *The New Faces of Christianity*, 2.

bishop remain controversial in the worldwide Anglican Church, and indeed in Christianity and in world religions, societies, and nations. Opposition to Robinson's ordination came not only from the Global South but from the Global North as well. It "appalled many church leaders in the global South,"[19] as well as in the Global North. To illustrate this with another, more recent example, the declaration by the Dicastery for the Doctrine of the Faith, *Fiducia Supplicans*, On the Pastoral Meaning of Blessings (2023), endorsed by Pope Francis, was vehemently opposed by conservative Catholics across the globe. Despite the rejection of the declaration as contrary to their cultures, none of the African or Asian bishops conferences attacked the pope as Joseph Strickland (the deposed US bishop of Tyler, Texas) did when he charged Francis with "undermining the Deposit of Faith."[20] Cardinal Gerhard Müller, a German (European) and former prefect of the same dicastery that issued the declaration, "dismissed the possibility that two persons of the same sex who love each other with fidelity could be blessed by God." "When we take the Word of God seriously, this is not possible," he said. "To bless homosexual couples is blasphemy."[21] He later doubled down, ridiculing the declaration and the efforts to clarify and explain it as "bowing down to this absolutely wrong LGBT and woke ideology."[22] Simply put, characterizing Christians of the Global South as uniquely socially or religiously conservative ignores a vast range of opinion both in the Global South and the Global North.

Jenkins's book illustrates what popular, commonsense, ordinary reading of the Bible looks like: "a much greater respect for the authority of scripture, especially in matters of morality; a willingness to accept the Bible as an inspired text and a tendency to literalism; a special interest in supernatural elements of scripture, such as miracles, visions, and healings; a belief in the continuing power of prophecy; and a veneration for the Old Testament,

---

19. Jenkins, *The New Faces of Christianity*, 3.
20. Colleen Dulle, "When Bishops Attack: How Pope Francis Handles His Critics," *America*, May 25, 2023, https://www.americamagazine.org/faith/2023/05/25/bishop-strickland-pope-francis-criticism-245363.
21. Gerard O'Connell, "Cardinal Müller Calls Blessing of Homosexual Couples 'Blasphemy,'" *America*, March 24, 2023, https://www.americamagazine.org/faith/2023/03/24/cardinal-muller-homosexuality-244963.
22. Edward Pentin, "Cardinal Müller: Efforts to Explain 'Fiducia Supplicans' Add to Confusion Over Document," *National Catholic Register*, February 12, 2024, https://www.ncregister.com/interview/cardinal-mueller-efforts-to-explain-fiducia-supplicans-add-to-confusion-over-document.

which is considered as authoritative as the New."[23] Literalistic interpretations of Scripture are the result not only of inadequate social, political, and economic realities but also from an abiding belief in the divine authority of Scripture. Understood in this way, "the Bible speaks to everyday, real-world issues of poverty and debt, famine and urban crisis, racial and gender oppression, state brutality and persecution."[24] Belief in the authority of Scripture in ordinary people's reading of the Bible equally responds to the secular humanism engendered by modernity and the need for discipline to counter licentiousness, which could result from consumerist culture and unfettered capitalism, where everything becomes an object for profit and consumption. In other words, irrespective of one's context, whether rich or poor, developed or developing, religious or secular, free or oppressive, some people will read the Bible in a literalist manner, while others (depending on training and exposure) will read it critically.

Ordinary people read the Bible in and through their contexts and situations and look to it as a guide and power to overcome life's challenges. This is true of popular reading of the Bible in Sao Paolo, Brazil,[25] just as it is true of reading the Bible in revolutionary and imperial times.[26] Commonsense Bible study approaches are also well documented in the United States in the 1860s, especially among evangelicals, and are known to have been fueled by "the democratic revivalism of the Second Great Awakening as well as the American and British revivals of the late1850s."[27] Jenkins recognizes this as well:

> I am not, of course, proposing a simple kind of geographical determinism shaping religious belief. We can hardly speak of how "Africans" approach a given topic, any more than how Europeans do ... Attitudes toward biblical interpretation and authority follow no neat North-South pattern, still less a rigid chasm between liberal North and conservative South. We find "Southern" expressions in the North, in the form of

---

23. Jenkins, *The New Faces of Christianity*, 7.
24. Jenkins, *The New Faces of Christianity*, 5.
25. Pothin Wete, "The Popular Reading of the Bible," *The Pacific Journal of Theology* 6 (1991): 107–10.
26. Dario Barolín, "Popular Reading of the Bible in Revolutionary and Imperial Times," *Exchange* 44, no. 1 (2015): 27–44.
27. Daved Anthony Schmidt, "Scripture Beyond Common Sense: Sentimental Bible Study and the Evangelical Practice of 'the Bible Reading,'" *Journal of Religious History* 41, no. 1 (2017): 61.

charismatic, fundamentalist, and deeply traditionalist belief; and those currents exist, however unhappily, in most liberal-dominated churches. If global South express their faith that God will intervene to reward or punish contemporary states and societies, so do such high-profile American Christians as Pat Roberston and Jerry Falwell. Nor is it difficult to find North Americans who accept pristine New Testament views of exorcism and spiritual healing. For Pentecostal believers in North America and Europe, spiritual warfare is a strictly current reality, while the modern Vatican accepts a clear, if limited, role for exorcists—to the embarrassment of most Northern Catholic faithful, and many clergy.[28]

Ordinary people's reading of the Bible often characterized a literalism that can lead to a version of bibliolatry, where the Bible itself is the foundation of faith and trust in Christianity as a religion. Christianity is based on the Bible because according to the ordinary people's reading, the Bible as inspired is inerrant, does not contain error, and is thus an infallible guide to life.

While such attitude to the Bible is termed fundamentalistic, it hardly applies to the ordinary reader in Africa. Debates around creationism and education that are so common in North America do not arise in Africa. Believing the story of creation in Genesis does not prevent an African from believing the stories of origins in their various cultural traditions. Theories of evolution are regarded as scientific and are for education, learning, and the classroom and do not negate the story of creation in the Bible. In a similar vein, Jenkins notes, "liberal" and "conservative" do not apply in the same way for ordinary African readers of the Bible. "Many churches take very seriously the supernatural worldview that pervades the Christian scriptures, with the recurrent themes of demons, possession, exorcism, and spiritual healing. Yet readings that appear intellectually reactionary do not prevent the same believers from engaging in social activism."[29]

THE FOUR SENSES OF SCRIPTURE

Ordinary readings of the Bible in Africa are focused on the existential issues that confront people and on how to prepare themselves for eternal salvation.

---

28. Jenkins, *The New Faces of Christianity*, 6.
29. Jenkins, *The New Faces of Christianity*, 12–13.

Ordinary, popular readers, like their patristic and medieval forebears, evince an integral unity of "faith, ethics, praxis and eschatology."[30] That is, ordinary people's reading of the Bible in Africa can be understood in terms of the four senses of Scripture, the "spiritual exegesis":[31] the literal (historical sense), allegorical (doctrinal sense), tropological (moral sense), and anagogical (eschatological, futuristic sense).

The literal, or historical, sense describes the context or the events that were going on when the text was written. The allegorical sense understandably flows from the historical sense since texts have meaning beyond themselves. Hence, allegorical sense, often used by the fathers of the church (as discussed in Chapter 1), specifies the deeper meaning of the events of the Old Testament in the New Testament, in the light of Christ. As a guide to life, the Bible offers ways of living as a Christian; hence, biblical texts give moral, or tropological, sense. As the word of God, as divine revelation, the Bible offers insight into divine mysteries and hence has spiritual anagogical sense. "The text had a literal sense, but it also involved allegory which taught doctrine, it offered moral directions, and pointed to the future, either to the heavenly kingdom at the end of time, or at least to the ongoing life of the Church."[32] In medieval exegesis, the four senses of Scripture are contained in the quatrain written by Augustine of Dacia: "The letter teaches events, allegory what you should believe, morality teaches what you should do, anagogy what mark you should be aiming for."[33] Thomas Aquinas clarified that "as a result those things [in the NT] which are said of Christ himself by the letter are able to be explained both allegorically by referring to his mystical body, and morally by referring to our acts which should be conformed to his, and anagogically in as much as in Christ himself the road to glory is shown to us."[34]

---

30. Hans de Wit, "Exegesis and Contextuality: Happy Marriage, Divorce or Living (Apart) Together?," in *African and European Readers of the Bible in Dialogue: In Quest of a Shared Meaning*, ed. Hans (J. H.) de Wit and Gerald West (Brill, 2008), 8.

31. Susan K. Wood, *Spiritual Exegesis and the Church in the Theology of Henri De Lubac* (William B. Eerdmans, 1998).

32. John Hilary Martin, OP, "The Four Senses of Scripture: Lessons from the Thirteenth Century," *Pacifica* 2 (1989): 88.

33. Henri de Lubac, SJ, *Medieval Exegesis*, vol. 1, *The Four Senses of Scripture* (William B. Eerdmans, 1998), 1.

34. Thomas Aquinas, *Quaestiones quodlibetales*, 7, q. 6, a. 2, ad 5, cited in Matthew Thomas Gerlach, *Lex Orandi, Lex Legendi: A Correlation of the Roman Canon and the Fourfold Sense of Scripture* (PhD diss., Marquette University, 2011), 134, https://epublications.marquette.edu/dissertations_mu/122.

For ordinary Africans who read and/or listen to the Bible in the churches, in group Bible study, as individuals, or in the open spaces, markets, fields, homes, and other places, the Bible is read as the word of God, as inspiration to deepen one's faith since the Bible is the witness to God's revelation and God is the author of the Bible. The Old Testament is read in the light of the New Testament—that is, in the light of the person of Christ, as reiterated in Christian tradition that "the spiritual sense of the Old Testament is the New Testament."[35]

Even though the Old Testament resonates with the patterns of life of Africans, and references are made to the Old Testament religious practices, stories, and events, great emphasis is placed on the person of Jesus in the New Testament, which is considered the fulfillment of the Old Testament. This in no way implies that African ordinary readers compartmentalize the Bible. To the contrary, both testaments are valued as the word of God. The Bible is filled with stories and statements about faith, grace, salvation, and redemption. For ordinary readers of the Bible, the literal sense is literalistic, and historical, in the sense of the continuity in meaning of the texts of Scripture. It is not historical in the medieval sense of the context or the events during which the various books of the Bible were written because the Biblical texts are believed to record reality.

Bob Wielenga, a South African Reformed theologian, captures the attitude of the common unlettered who hear the Bible: "In an oral culture written texts were read out loud to an audience which could not read. The letters of Paul were read to the churches, and were experienced as addressed by him to them personally. In the oral cultures of Africa one experiences, behind the written Bible, the original Speaker, who gives authority to it as holy Writ."[36] They listen and in faith apply the text to their lives. Human life is lived by faith: "For we live by faith not by sight" (2 Cor 5:7).

The story of the child suffering from epilepsy that the apostles couldn't cure and Jesus's response to the doubting father ("Everything is possible for anyone who has faith" [Mark 9:24]) fill the ordinary reader with faith in the Bible as the word of God with authority to fulfill what it says. In fact, the following signs associated with believers ring a constant bell to ordinary readers of the Bible in Africa: "In my name they will cast out devils; they

---

35. De Lubac, SJ, *Medieval Exegesis*, xiv.
36. Bob Wielenga, "Bible Reading in Africa: The Shaping of a Reformed Perspective," *In die Skriflig* 44, nos. 3–4 (2010): 704.

will have the gift of tongues; they will pick up snakes in their hands, and be unharmed should they drink deadly poison; they will lay their hands on the sick, who will recover" (Mark 16: 17–18). Ordinary readers of the Bible in Africa, according to John S. Mbiti, conceive Christ as *Christus Victor* (miracle worker and risen Lord). Christ "is the conqueror of those evil powers (spirits, magic, disease, death) feared by the African, and is guarantor of immortality."[37] Of course, such literalist understanding of the Bible is problematic, as we will explore shortly.

Even though they may not advert to it explicitly, ordinary African readers of the Bible regard the Bible as a unit, as Scripture. The grassroots Christology of African Christianity regards Jesus Christ as the answer to human quest. Ordinary Africans read the Bible bearing Christ in mind. Christ as the savior is the cornerstone of Christian life. Even the story of creation leads to the coming of the messiah. The Laws and the Prophets, the Psalms and the Writings, the stories of Job and even Moses are prefiguring of Christ. The Old Testament is in the Bible because it segues into the story of Jesus Christ, the savior, in the New Testament. Afterall, Jesus confirms to the disciples on the way to Emmaus that the Scriptures contain things concerning him (Luke 24:27; cf. Philip and the Ethiopian reader of Isaiah in Acts 8:29–35). We recall in this context the statement of Jerome, the fifth-century biblical interpreter that "ignorance of Scripture is ignorance of Christ."[38] The preponderance of opinion on the perception of the ordinary readers of the Bible in Africa is their regard of the continuity of the Old Testament in the New Testament and of "the Israelite story as demonstrating God's involvement in history, so that the old Israel, the new Israel, and the *goyim* (nations) are in effect within the same situation: that of God's rule over the world."[39]

Going by R. P. C. Hanson's definition of allegory as "the interpretation of an object or person or a number of objects or persons as in reality meaning some object or person of a later time, with no attempt made to trace a

---

37. Charles Nyamiti, "African Christologies Today," in *Jesus in African Christianity: Experimentation and Diversity in African Christology*, ed. J. N. K. Mugambi and Laurenti Magesa (Acton Publishers, 2003), 18.

38. Cf. Pope Benedict XV, *Spiritus Paraclitus*, 1920, https://www.vatican.va/content/benedict-xv/en/encyclicals/documents/hf_ben-xv_enc_15091920_spiritus-paraclitus.html.

39. Kwesi A. Dickson, "Continuity and Discontinuity Between the Old Testament and African Life and Thought," in *African Theology En Route*, ed. Kofi Appiah-Kubi and Sergio Torres (Orbis Books, 1979), 99.

relationship of 'similar situation' between them,"[40] one has no hesitation to affirm that ordinary African Bible readers allegorize the Old Testament in the New Testament. This allegorical reading appears to be the intent of the story of the disciples on the road to Emmaus who encountered Jesus without recognizing him. Jesus began to explain to them how all the Scriptures speak of him. Even though allegorizing the Old Testament in the light of Christ is a subject of controversy,[41] for ordinary readers in Africa, the Bible is the revelation of God's mystery in Christ. They will agree with R. W. L. Moberly on the allegorical sense of Scripture because the truth of Scripture is hidden in Christ:

> Presumably part of the logic of Jesus' expounding the Scriptures to his puzzled disciples is that these Scriptures provide a context and a content for making sense of Jesus, when all that the disciples know about him already somehow has not "clicked"; Israel's Scriptures help one make sense of Jesus . . . So presumably a further part of the logic of Jesus' exposition is that the disciples need to be able to read these Scriptures in a new way, in the light of all that had happened surrounding Jesus, so that they can see in these Scriptures what they had not seen before; Jesus helps one make sense of Israel's Scriptures.[42]

For ordinary African readers, the Bible as the word of God is the authoritative guide for life as a Christian. Hence, the Bible is read for its moral lessons, to decipher from the word of God values for action in everyday existential struggles. Even when Christian virtues conflict with African cultural values, like on issues of polygamy, sacrifice to idols, observing Sabbath rest, and so on, ordinary readers of the Bible in Africa persevere in opting for Christian morality contained in the Bible. Because the authority of the Bible is not doubted, and because of the deep-seated acceptance of biblical inerrancy, the Bible is preferred as a guide for ethical conduct.

---

40. Hanson, *Allegory and Event*, 7.

41. Martin Luther had only negative words for allegorizing the Scriptures: "Allegory is a sort of beautiful harlot, who proves herself specially seductive to idle men"; "To allegorize is to juggle with Scripture"; "Allegorizing may degenerate into a mere monkey game (Affenspiel)"; "Allegories are awkward, absurd, in vented, obsolete, loose rags." cited in Paul K. Jewett, "Concerning the Allegorical Interpretation of Scripture," *The Westminster Theological Journal* 17, no. 1 (1954): 1.

42. R. W. L. Moberly, "Christ in All the Scriptures? The Challenge of Reading the Old Testament as Christian Scripture," *Journal of Theological Interpretation* 1, no. 1 (2007): 80.

I am not of course presuming that ordinary readers of the Bible are always faithful to biblical ethical values, but often the guilt and consciousness of sin indicates remorse and preference for biblical ethical codes over other options. Such use of the Bible arises because the ordinary reader's attitude to the Bible is literal and historical in the sense of continuity and stability of the Bible as the word of God. Hence, the meaning of biblical texts remains the same irrespective of differences in epochs of composition, the intention of the author, and the gap in the value system of biblical times from those of our contemporary societies. Morality is an integral part of African traditional religion, and hence is God-centered, even when it appears to emphasize human values of life and community,[43] as reflected in Laurenti Magesa's *What is Not Sacred?*[44]

Societal taboos that protect communal infrastructure, like lakes that provide drinking water, or prevent sexual relationships detrimental to the health of the community, like incest or bestiality, are not merely negative legislations but are positive injunctions for mutual coexistence, progress, and advancement of a healthy community. As Bénézet Bujo affirms: "The main criterion for evaluating and establishing ethical norms is the life of the individual and of the entire community; the aim is not the realization of isolated individuals—perhaps even against the community, as is possible on the natural-law model—but rather a mutual relationship of all persons, which alone can make the human person truly human."[45] Ordinary person reading of the Bible draws from biblical texts ethical codes that enable them to transcend the individual consanguineal African ethics and incorporate the African values like hospitality and love, a much more universal ethics of love of humanity, including love of one's enemies. This expands the principles of life and community central to African ethics.[46] A recovery of the African concept of *ubuntu*, "the heart of African ethics,"[47] in its various forms, of universal brotherliness, of love of each other as fellow human beings, based

---

43. Laurenti Magesa, *Anatomy of Inculturation: Transforming the Church in Africa* (Paulines Publications Africa, 2005), 77.
44. Laurenti Magesa, *What Is Not Sacred? African Spirituality* (Orbis Books, 2014).
45. Bénézet Bujo, *Foundations of an African Ethic: Beyond the Universal Claims of Western Morality*, trans. Brian McNeil (Crossroad Publishing Company, 2001), 161–62.
46. Agbonkhianmeghe E. Orobator, "Ethics Brewed in an African Pot," *Journal of the Society of Christian Ethics* 31, no. 1 (2011): 3–16.
47. Ramathate Dolamo, "Botho/Ubuntu: The Heart of African Ethics," *Scriptura* 112 (2013): 1–10.

on the indispensability of the community, deepens interrelationships and communal peace in Africa.[48]

In his groundbreaking work on the New Testament eschatology, John S. Mbiti notes the eschatological bent of Christianity and aligns it with the eschatological background of African traditional religion. He asserts:

> The Christian faith is intensely eschatological, and wherever the Church expands it brings and displays its eschatological presence, manifested in activities and experiences like the kerygma, repentance, conversion, salvation, sacraments, mission and Christian hope . . . Akamba religious ideas and practices, like those of many other African societies, are directed primarily to "eschatological" aspects of life, concerning death, the departed, the spirits, and the hereafter . . . Akamba Christians show great interest in eschatological themes like the parousia, death and destiny of Christians, heaven and the hereafter. This means that, *inter alia*, Christianity is embraced and pictured primarily as an eschatological Faith.[49]

Though African concepts of time and history might be cyclical rather than linear, life at some point terminates in the remoteness of the indefinite past. "There is, therefore, both an 'endless' and an 'endlessness' about them: they have a finality and a repeatability, a constant and a rhythm. There is no room in this scheme of thought for teleology and fulfilment."[50] But there is room for eschatology, albeit materially, as manifest in the belief in reincarnation when diseased ancestors from a disincarnate realm, a sort of limbo, "are eager to return to a new terrestrial life."[51] Christian eschatological concepts that emphasize futurism, using materialistic symbols to describe realities of the afterlife with reward for a good life and punishment for the evildoers is nonexistent in African concepts of death and dying or life after death. The New Testament concepts used to describe the afterlife, like Gehena, fire, treasure, city, country, eating and drinking, tears and pain, heaven, and

---

48. Kwame Gyekye, "African Ethics," in *Stanford Encyclopedia of Philosophy*, ed. E. N. Zalta (Stanford University Press, 2011), accessed March 12, 2024, https://plato.stanford.edu/archives/fall2011/entries/african-ethics/.

49. John S. Mbiti, *New Testament Eschatology in an African Background: A Study of the Encounter Between New Testament Theology and African Traditional Concepts* (Oxford University Press, 1971), 2–3.

50. Mbiti, *New Testament Eschatology in an African Background*, 31.

51. Ian Stevenson, "The Belief in Reincarnation Among the Igbo of Nigeria," *Journal of Asian and African Studies* 20, no. 1 (1985):13.

hell, are strange ideas to Africans.[52] They have been bought wholeheartedly by the ordinary African readers of the Bible as an eternal place of peace or punishment, "a glorious future, a utopia to which they may escape at death or at the Parousia."[53] According to Mbiti,

> Many of the biblical concepts we have examined are alien to Akamba ideas, as far as their theological content is concerned. The same seems true about these ideas in other African societies. In attempting to reach some understanding of the ideas in this materialistic language, Akamba people have created a similarly materialistic future located away from the earth: in heaven (for Christians) or in Gehena (for non-believers). The same world is also imagined to be a contrast, for better or worse, to this earth. People have little or no notion of how to relate this life to the life in that other world, except insofar as they can psychologically escape to that dreamland. This whole conceptual area is new to Akamba and other African peoples, in that traditionally they never thought of or expected a future world situated somewhere in the heavens. Both in terms of Time and geography, African peoples are undergoing a radical change in their conception as far as their understanding of the hereafter is concerned.[54]

Mbiti is a respected voice and authority in African thought. He may be right in his expression of the Akamba people, and it may well be true of most African peoples. However, there are some exceptions whose end-myth symbolisms depict apocalypticism like the Judeo-Christian apocalypticism, of an end of the cosmos and the reconciliation of all things in the supreme being.

Aylward Shorter points to the Sonjo of Tanganyika as a people whose futuristic eschatology trumps Mbiti's thoughts of teleology being strange to Africans. Shorter argues that "African end-myths are nevertheless often a form of parousia. There is a prediction that a divinity, a deified hero or eminent ancestor or, indeed, several such figures, will return to play a role similar to the one for which they are remembered. Such beliefs have appeared at various times in connection with the concept of the Bachwezi hero-rulers known to several of the East African lake kingdoms."[55] The African concept

---

52. Mbiti, *New Testament Eschatology in an African Background*, 64–89.
53. Mbiti, *New Testament Eschatology in an African Background*, 64.
54. Mbiti, *New Testament Eschatology in an African Background*, 90.
55. Aylward Shorter, "Eschatology in the Ethnic Religions of Africa," *Studia Missionalia* 32 (1983): 5.

of the ancestors and their roles in their families and in their communities—because of the different state of their lives after death, as protector and shield, as intercessors, and as a spirit presence—predispose Africans for Christian eschatological concepts.

Ordinary readers transpose the concept of the living dead in the reverence of the ancestors onto the person of Jesus, who by virtue of his resurrection, now becomes the great ancestor, a prototype of the everlasting life, of the ever-living present embedded in traditional African eschatology. Kwame Bediako expresses this transposition well:

> ... the insights about Jesus Christ in the epistle to the Hebrews are perhaps the most crucial of all ... Our Savior is our Elder Brother who has shared in our African experience in every respect, except our sin and alienation from God, an alienation with which our myths of origins make us only too familiar ... From the standpoint of Akan traditional beliefs, Jesus has gone to the realm of the ancestor spirits and the "gods." We already know that power and resources for living come from there, but the terrors and misfortunes which could threaten and destroy life come from there also. But if Jesus has gone to the realm of the "'spirits and the gods, so to speak, he has gone there as Lord over them in the same way that he is Lord over us. He is Lord over the living and the dead, and over the 'living-dead,' as ancestors are also called. He is supreme over all gods and authorities in the realm of spirit, summing up in himself all their powers and cancelling any terrorizing influence they might be assumed to have upon us.[56]

Ordinary readers of the Bible in Africa have no difficulty with the anagogic sense of Scripture. Jesus brings eternal life to believers through his word. He promises everlasting life with God. He rewards the righteous and punishes the unjust. Whether eschatological concepts were introduced into Africa by Christianity or whether Africans transposed the eschatological concepts from their traditional religious cultures, what is evident is that the ordinary readers of the Bible believe and hope for everlasting life in the afterlife, in a place of peace and joy. Dreams of such eternal rest and peace gleaned from the Bible

---

56. Kwame Bediako, *Jesus and the Gospel in Africa: History and Experience* (Orbis Books, 2004), 26–27.

on last things and Jesus's teachings about the end-time, though figurative, are read literally by ordinary readers of the Bible in Africa. There is thus the sense of the end and the consummation of all things. The colonial missionary Christianity equally emphasized this otherworldliness as an important end goal of Christians. In some ways, it has given rise to *fuga mundi* (flight from the world) spirituality in various parts of Africa.

Doubt and disparagement of popular reading of the Bible only came about toward the end of the Renaissance in Europe because of abuses in the popular reading of the Bible. "Against the background of war, tribal disputes and bloodshed, people such as Spinoza and Descartes search for a universal criterion. They arrive at reason, or better expressed as: the intellectual obligation to formulate knowledge clearly and distinctly. It is good to realize that turning to reason as the universal criterion for dealing with the Scripture was a turn that was intended to serve the text as Gospel."[57] This statement indicates a boundary marker, a universal fixing of the Bible and its limitation to the dictates of the mind. It is a domestication of the Bible and, by extension, a domestication of Christianity, its ultimate privatization, and its final subjugation to the authority of the state. It marked the beginning of the creation of civil religion, which is not Christianity. Such doubts have not happened in Africa, because its societies were not shaped by the Enlightenment. For this reason, it is wrong to expect African Christianity, and reading of the Bible by ordinary people, to mimic the European contextual realities. And so, ordinary, popular reading of the Bible as the word of God that teaches the way of salvation is still in vogue in Africa. This of course does not mean it does not have its limitations and dangers, which is why ordinary people or popular reading of the Bible needs academic and critical historical study. The danger signals of manipulation, deceit, and abuse are becoming obvious. As Lamin Sanneh observes, "False prophets have appeared, schisms have spread, the simple and ignorant have been taken advantage of, ethnic hostility has flared into grim killings, and ethical standards have slipped with political corruption."[58]

Ordinary people reading of the Bible in Africa is the result of the translation of the Bible into African languages. This gave rise to what Sanneh calls "the *indigenous discovery of Christianity* rather than the *Christian discovery*

---

57. De Wit, "Exegesis and Contextuality," 9.
58. Sanneh, *Whose Religion Is Christianity?*, 32 (italicized in the original).

of indigenous societies."[59] The difference between both, though simple, is stark. When Christian discovery of indigenous societies is emphasized, it means that the missionaries' enterprise are intent on establishing a Eurocentric brand of Christianity and subjugating African cultures. The indigenous discovery of Christianity, on the other hand, is about the people encountering Christianity in the light of their cultures and in their native tongues , retaining their indigenous names for God and remaining Africans, while being transformed by the gospel, which they appropriate and make their own in the light of their ways of living and thinking, their needs, and their experiences.[60]

The immediate outcome of this was the adoption of indigenous names for God in biblical interpretation. Since the names of God are foundational to the structure of African societies bringing together the various aspects of societal life, they set the tone for the natural indigeneity of African Christianity, giving Christianity in Africa its distinctive indigenous touch, enabling it to grow and expand more despite the end of colonialism and later the expulsion of the missionaries. Reading the names of God they were familiar with through their traditional religions assured African Christians of the relevance of their cultural values, patterns of thought, and traditional institutions to Christianity. It made their comprehension of Christian doctrines easier because Christianity resonates with the patterns of their lives.

What is needed, then, is the rooting out of those aspects of their cultures that have been found to be bad in the light of Christianity and the expansion into broader global society beyond the limited confines of closed societies promoted by African traditional religion. Again, Sanneh's remarks resoundingly echo the transformation: "People sensed in their hearts that Jesus did not mock their respect for the sacred or their clamor for an invincible Savior, and so they beat their sacred drums for him until the stars skipped and danced in the skies. After that dance the stars weren't little anymore. Christianity helped Africans to become renewed Africans, not remade Europeans."[61] Ordinary people's reading helped set the tone for the nature of African Christianity, both of AICs, of the mainline churches (Catholic and Protestant), and of the charismatic and Pentecostal churches in Africa today.

---

59. Sanneh, *Whose Religion Is Christianity?*, 10.
60. Sanneh, *Whose Religion Is Christianity?*, 55.
61. Sanneh, *Whose Religion Is Christianity?*, 43.

IMPLICATIONS FOR AFRICAN CHRISTIANITY

Ordinary readers reflecting on the Bible contribute to the growth of the church by creating hymns, songs, music, and creative arts to depict biblical scenes, personalities, and messages; using African proverbs to instill morals; and imbuing contextual meanings to biblical stories. As Eric Anum observed: "Music, liturgy, proverbs, stories are indeed resources which are already being used by ordinary readers in their readings in most parts of Africa."[62] Gerald O. West gives examples of nonliterate Africans who become acquainted with the Bible stories and tradition orally through listening to public readings of the Bible in their languages.[63] Buoyed by biblical messages, they form groups and communities for the practical living of Christian life filled with love and support for one another spiritually and materially. Informed by a deepened faith drawn from the Bible, they bear witness to Christ through involvement in actions for social justice. They become part of nationalist movements for political independence from colonialism, participate in the processes of social reconstruction, and contribute to successful postindependent countries in Africa. These positive contributions to African Christianity could also be vitiated by a particular view of the Bible opposed to the social gospel inherited by some ordinary readers from their various churches.

Most popular readings of the Bible in Africa unquestioningly affirm the authority of the Bible as the word of God because of the belief in biblical inspiration. For those who hold to verbal inspiration, "everything is as the Bible tells it—creation in seven days, changing water into wine, the 969 years Methuselah lived, and so on—or else admit that one could not be Christian."[64] According to this view, Christianity is a scriptural religion; that is, it is one where the Bible's authority is all encompassing as the ultimate criterion of truth. The written Scripture displaces or diminishes the unwritten tradition from which it emerged, even though this was not the case for the culture from which the Bible emerged. Inspiration translates to inerrancy or infallibility of

---

62. Eric Anum, "Ye Ma Wo Mo! African Hermeneuts, You Have Spoken at Last: Reflections on Semeia 73 (1996)," in *Reading Other-Wise Socially Engaged Biblical Scholars Reading with Their Local Communities*, ed. Gerald O. West (Society of Biblical Literature, 2007), 15.

63. Gerald O. West, "(Ac)claiming the (Extra)ordinary African 'Reader' of the Bible," in West, *Reading Other-Wise Socially Engaged Biblical Scholars Reading with Their Local Communities*, 38.

64. James Barr, *The Scope and Authority of the Bible* (Westminster Press, 1980), 55.

canonized Scripture. "What fundamentalism has always insisted is not just that scripture should be received as authoritative . . . but that its authority should be grounded upon its infallibility and inerrancy and defined in these terms."[65] One has either to accept the Scripture as is or one becomes a heretic. The Bible becomes idolatrized. According to Barr, "The argument is easily stated: the Bible is authoritative, inspired, infallible and inerrant because it itself says so. The Bible 'claims' to be without error. Or, breaking it down into greater detail: Jesus says that the Bible is without error, Paul says so, Peter says so, and generally all biblical writers who are in a position to say anything about the matter say so."[66] The biblicist view makes Christianity a biblical religion whereby "the Bible is the voice of God and therefore speaks with His full authority. God's authority in Scripture can thus be described as original, unalterable, exclusive, permanent, ultimate, obligatory, and consequential. Scripture is to be authoritatively preached and submissively obeyed since the Author of and the authority within will reward righteous obedience and condemn those who disregard and disobey His authority in Scripture."[67] This biblicist view of Christianity, arising from the precritical approach of the ordinary people's reading of the Bible, is a big challenge that needs to be addressed by the academic scholarly reading of the Bible as scholars engage ordinary people's reading of the Bible.[68]

Armed with the Bible, many ordinary African readers fired with missionary zeal went out in droves to preach and to minister, to convert and to transform, to bear witness to the good news in all parts of Africa. Dissatisfied with the cold, unenergizing, moribund, and "ineffectual" liturgy of the mainline mission churches, coupled with their pompous clergy, many of these enthusiastic African readers of the Bible morphed from leaders of prayer groups into full-blown independent churches. In addition to numerous studies on AICs, Nathaniel I. Ndiokwere's focused study of the "Zionist," "Ethiopian," and "messianic" movements in South and East Africa, Kimbanguism in the former Congo, and the "Aladura" in West Africa capture this dynamic.[69]

> As the stories of Braide and Kimbangu illustrate . . . reading–or even simply hearing–the scriptures in one's own language was enough to

---

65. James Barr, *Fundamentalism* (Westminster Press, 1977, 1978), 163.
66. Barr, *Fundamentalism*, 72–73.
67. Richard L. Mayhue, "The Authority of Scripture," *The Master's Seminary Journal* 15, no. 2 (2004): 227–36.
68. Kīnyua, *Introducing Ordinary African Readers' Hermeneutics*, 292.
69. Nathaniel I. Ndiokwere, *Prophecy and Revolution*.

permit individual and corporate appropriations of the Christian message that radically challenged European preconceptions, even if, at least originally, they could plausibly claim to be direct and literal applications of the biblical text. As vernacular translations exposed the extent to which European Christianity had denuded the biblical text of its prophetic and miraculous elements, Africans . . . who had unusual charismatic gifts or mana sometimes assumed the mantle of the prophets and challenged their missionary mentors to join their many indigenous converts in believing their mighty works.[70]

The initial resorting to name-calling by mainline churches describing the new religious movements as "'mushroom Churches,' 'hand-clapping,' 'band-beating,' 'vision-seeing' Churches,"[71] did not diminish their appeal to African Christians. Rather, given their dynamic worship, prayer, and faith-healing and prophecy, they came to be appreciated as "African expression[s] of Christianity."[72]

Another explosive movement from ordinary African reading of the Bible in much of Africa happened in the 1980s with "the proliferation of new religious groups, churches and ministries, nearly all of them Pentecostal."[73] To study the phenomenon, in 1990 the All-African Conference of Churches (AACC) instituted a project under the leadership of Paul Gifford, a theologian dedicated to African Christianity. Gifford's AACC's project probes the Pentecostal phenomenon with questions on the denomination's attitude toward African cultures, metaphysics, and influence or not of Western literature, theology, technology, or media. These groups, through Bible reading, embraced holiness of life, "literal-minded biblicism, emotional fervour, puritanical mores, enmity toward ecclesiasticism, care for the poor and belief in the imminent second coming of Christ."[74] Members become referred to as "born-again" Christians, a term that denotes the central theme of redemption and transformation, on both the personal and structural level.[75] The impact was obviously observable in Ruth Marshall's apt description:

---

70. Stanley, *Christianity in the Twentieth Century*, 77–78.
71. Ndiokwere, *Prophecy and Revolution*, 274.
72. Ndiokwere, *Prophecy and Revolution*, 275.
73. Paul Gifford, introduction to *New Dimensions in African Christianity*, ed. Paul Gifford (All African Conference of Churches, 1992), 1.
74. Marius Nel, "A South African View of Pentecostalism as Another Response to Modernism," *In die Skriflig* 54, no. 1 (2000): 1.
75. Ruth Marshall, "Pentecostalism in Southern Nigeria: An Overview," in Gifford, *New Dimensions in African Christianity*, 9.

> The doctrinal stress in the "holiness" churches is placed on perfection, strict personal ethics, and biblical inerrancy. The ways of the "world" are the ways of sin, so believers are exhorted to shun all unnecessary material and carnal pleasures . . . One must not only repent, and give restitution for past wrongs, but radically transform one's daily practices. True converts do not lie, cheat, steal, quarrel, gossip, give or take bribes, drink, smoke, fornicate, beat their spouses, lose their tempers, or deny assistance to other members in need. Strict dress codes are enforced, and limited contact is allowed between members of different sexes. Marital fidelity is a central tenet, and divorce is not permitted.[76]

These strict moral codes, arising from reading the Bible in a particular way, have proven to be beneficial to youths and to society because it helped curb such bad habits as drug addiction, teenage sex, and unwanted pregnancy. It brought about honesty, character and integrity, zeal, and dedication to hard work among youths. Peace, tranquility, and reduction in crime reigned at the height of the holiness movements. Societal transformation was so glaring that everyone wanted in. The renewal moved to mainline churches, Catholic and Protestant, exhorting people to a life of repentance, trust in God, the power of the Holy Spirit, dedicated reading, and belief in the power of the word of God in the Bible, prayer, and faith healing, as well as prosperity through holiness of life and sowing of seed (donations) to the church and charitable groups.

Some members of the charismatic movements who became ordained as Catholic priests and even some priests who became fascinated with the progress of the movement conduct healing Masses and prayer centers both in their parishes and outside their jurisdiction upon invitation. Intense prayers dedicated to casting out evil spirits and all machinations of the devil distinguish these priests as more powerful than the regular priests, and they become known as "men of God" believed to be imbued with special powers by the Holy Spirit. The basis of these new dimensions of Christianity in Africa is belief in the authority of the Bible by the ordinary readers for whom the Bible as the word of God fulfills what it promises, particularly freedom of believers from forces of evil and divine blessings on the faithful.

While ordinary reading of the Bible by Africans appears to bring about conversion and transformation by its rigoristic ethical codes, its literal reading

---

76. Marshall, "Pentecostalism in Southern Nigeria," 10.

and its possible misinterpretation of some biblical passages and promises as reality (when they may have been originally merely symbolic) is problematic. It gives rise to sheer irrationalism, emotive behaviors, and unrealizable expectations. Sheer irrationalism promotes believing in magical powers of the prophets, men, and women of God; living in constant fear of malevolent forces believed to be capable of causing harm and threatening life; and attributing beauty and its accoutrements to the marine spirits and others. Emotive behaviors give rise to wanton credulity in the bizarre and action before thought, opening oneself to frauds and cheats ready to take advantage of the vulnerable. Unrealizable expectations include permanent righteousness, tremendous successes in life based on seed sowing, and belief in prosperity as God's gift to the faithful who tithe a certain percentage of their earnings to God through the priests, pastors, prophets, men, and women of God.

In the confusion, one finds oneself living a lie. To cover up from being branded a person of little faith, one is forced to superficial spirituality, which is nothing but hypocrisy. Every misfortune, including illness, heart disease, high blood pressure, stroke, diabetes, and HIV/AIDS, is misconstrued as the effects of the forces of evil, witches, wizards, and spirits, which must be exorcised. Necessary preventive measures and medical cures are not sought. Prophecies and predictions predicated on the whims and caprices of the man or woman of God are exalted above careful planning and measured strategies for success. Families, friends, and communities are divided when meanings are read into biblical passages as explanations of contemporary events and used to accuse some as witches and wizards, which leads to various forms of witch-hunting and violence against often-innocent victims. These make mockery of African Christianity nationally and internationally as shallow and bizarre, as products of enchanted imagination. They affect Christian engagement in the social gospel, in activism for good governance. They leave too much, virtually everything, to God and rob human beings of the creativity that God has given to humans to solve problems. Christians become pliable and docile, manipulable by frauds and charlatans who parade themselves as men and women of God. They become too easy to govern, unempowered to demand their rights in their countries under the law. Why? They believe God. In God's own time, everything will be okay.

Paul Gifford has studied the various dimensions of the impact of Pentecostalist groups in Africa. His latest study, published as *Christianity, Development and Modernity in Africa*, summed up the phenomenon as "enchanted

Christianity." He described the religious imagination of the Christianity he encountered in Zimbabwe (and other parts of Africa for thirty years) as one coming from "the worldview that sees spirits, demons, spiritual powers at play in all areas of life, and responsible for every ill. Spirits and witchcraft were said to be responsible for illness, misery, poverty, hunger and misfortune. One particular evil spirit was said to cause AIDS, and 'to put HIV blood in the veins' of one sufferer called up to be cured."[77] Even though Gifford attributes this enchanted Christianity to African cosmogony, which exalts spiritism, African cosmogony resonates with Judeo-Christian cosmogony; both are religious, believing in the supreme being as controlling the cosmos and having power to overcome the evils that threaten life. Both visions hold on to an enchanted universe, but Christianity believes that redemption comes only through Christ (Acts 4:12). One is reminded of Brian Stanley's counsel that "large-scale conversion to a new religion will take place only when the massive ruptures of customary practice intrinsic to such a change make sense within at least some of the categories of the existing world view."[78] The literalness and vividness of the depictions of the devil and spiritual realms in the Bible play into the African views of the enchanted world.

R. P. C. Hanson mentions such an oracular view of the Bible as predominating the belief systems of early Christians. According to him, "The age in which the early Church expanded from being a tiny Jewish sect to being a universal religion was one that was interested in oracles, and the early Church found no difficulty in deciding that the Bible—and especially the Old Testament—was full of them."[79] It is not surprising that these views of the Bible were handed down to Africans who correlated them with their traditional beliefs. The Bible is read and used as a proof text to build further edifices, ramifications, and typologies of the spirit world and to proffer solutions. These perpetuate beliefs in such worldviews, give jobs to self-acclaimed "experts" and exorcists, and at times with little credible proof, encourage literalism as normal Bible reading.

As we mentioned earlier, ordinary reading of the Bible in Africa gives rise to a *fuga mundi spirituality*, flight from the world spirituality, a preference for the promised bliss of the next life, because the image of the end of the world and future hope portrayed in the Bible is one where the just will

---

77. Paul Gifford, *Christianity, Development and Modernity in Africa* (Oxford University Press, 2016), 3–4.
78. Stanley, *Christianity in the Twentieth Century*, 59.
79. Hanson, "Biblical Exegesis in the Early Church," 420.

be rewarded with heaven and the wicked punished to eternal damnation in hellfire. Christian eschatology relates to last things, such as death, the end of the world, the judgment of humanity, and its ultimate destiny.[80] For the righteous, there is resurrection, immortality, and enjoyment of beatific vision; for the wicked, there is perpetual punishment in the hellfire. "Apocalyptism and millennialism, when Satan and all satanic powers will be annihilated during one thousand years of Christ's reign, are also forms of eschatology."[81] But there will be revival akin to the baptism of the Holy Spirit to prepare the whole world for the imminent return of Christ.[82] This is an invitation to every believer to participate in fulfilling the missionary mandate (Matt 28:18–20), to preach the gospel to all the world, so that everyone gets a chance to prepare and not be left behind. Beyond the positive impact of encouraging evangelization, to further make the kingdom of God a reality in this world, ordinary people's literal reading of the Bible on eschatological themes makes Africans prepare for the eschatological kingdom of heaven. This is because they do not envision the teachings of Jesus and the Bible on the last things to be figurative and requiring of further interpretations.[83] "Eschatology is not just concerned with what might happen at the end of the world; rather, it is essentially concerned with God's sovereignty and with all the different ways God does things, whether in peoples' lives, in society, or in the ultimate meaning of the entire cosmic process."[84] On the contrary, African's ordinary readers of the Bible understand eschatological symbols literally.

According to John S. Mbiti, "These eschatological symbols are certainly a vivid and rich method of conveying what otherwise is beyond physical realities. But the symbols are vehicles of theological meaning, and this is what the Akamba have failed to grasp on the conceptual level. Instead, they have come out with a purely materialistic image of eschatological realities, which in turn

---

80. John Arierhi Ottuh, "The Urhobo Traditional Theologumenon on Afterlife and Christian Theology of Eschatology: A Comparative Study," *Africology: The Journal of Pan African Studies* 10, no. 3 (2017): 212.

81. Matthew A. Ojo, "Eschatology and the African Society: The Critical Point of Disjunction," *Ogbomoso Journal of Theology* 11 (2006): 93.

82. Allan Anderson, "Spreading Fires: The Globalization of Pentecostalism in the Twentieth Century," *International Bulletin of Missionary Research* 31, no. 1 (2007): 8.

83. Joseph Ratzinger, *Eschatology: Death and Eternal Life*, 2nd ed., trans. Michael Waldstein, trans. ed. Aidan Nichols, OP (Catholic University of America Press, 1988).

84. Ezekiel Oladapo Aremu Ajani, "The Kingdom of God and Its Missiological Imperatives for the Contemporary African Christian Mission," *Ogbomoso Journal of Theology* 12 (2007): 118.

create a false spirituality in their Christian living."[85] Consequently, they seek to escape from this world into the world of the hereafter. Mbiti continues, "This false spirituality seems to have overtaken many Christians, not only in Ukambani, but also in other parts; they have discovered a future which, they expect, will suddenly bring them to a land of bliss, comfort and long life."[86] Such delusions to quicken eschatology, to begin to enjoy the beatific vision, and to attain salvation has led to mass suicides by some Christian sects in Africa and in different parts of the world. The most recent was in 2023 when Paul Mackenzie, a former taxi driver turned pastor who founded the Good News International Ministry, convinced more than three hundred families, up to one thousand people, that the world was coming to an end and their salvation lay in fasting and starving in the Shakahola forest. Most died in the forest; investigators discovered bodies in shallow graves.[87] According to a CNN report, "He drew in flight attendants and social workers; paramilitary police and professionals from all across Kenya."[88] In other words, it is not just hunger or poverty that draws people to such delusion but a firm belief that the end is near and that salvation and life in the hereafter is better than life here and now.

CONCLUSION

Ordinary readers of the Bible are not necessarily nonliterate. They include all those who read the Bible but are not trained as experts in biblical theology or Scripture scholars. This is why we also describe them as commonsense readers. By implication, most ordinary readers of the Bible read plainly, literally, and objectively, based on the preconceived notion of the Bible as inspired and consequently inerrant. Ordinary readers of the Bible also advert to the four senses of Scripture: literal, allegorical, tropological, and anagogical. "Literal" for most does not refer to the historical context of the text but the historical relevance of a text for every age, a form of futurism. "Allegory" implies their acceptance of the unity of the Old and the New Testaments, of the Old

---

85. Mbiti, *New Testament Eschatology in an African Background*, 183.
86. Mbiti, *New Testament Eschatology in an African Background*, 60.
87. David McKenzie and Bethlehem Feleke, "How Faith Turned Deadly for Kenyan Cult Followers Who Chose Starvation as Path to Salvation," June 19, 2023, https://www.cnn.com/2023/06/19/africa/kenya-starvation-cult-explained-intl-cmd/index.html.
88. McKenzie and Feleke, "How Faith Turned Deadly."

being fulfilled in Christ, and hence the Old being read in the light of Christ. The ordinary approach is tropological because the Bible is read as a guide for moral actions. And it is anagogical because the Bible is eschatological; it leads to life hereafter. We argued that it is wrong to classify ordinary readers of the Bible in Africa as conservative and fundamentalistic because the same terminologies are equally applicable to other readers of the Bible worldwide and because such broad strokes should not be used to paint everyone.

Ordinary readers of the Bible contribute to theology, evangelization, and church. Through their prayers, they invent the names of God appropriate to their contexts. Their reception of Jesus into the complex matrix of African meanings and values results in varieties of African Christologies, which scholarly theologians use to think through the many faces of Jesus in Africa.[89] They witness God's goodness and invite others to experience it. Their desire to fulfill the missionary mandate (Matt 28:18–20), so no one is left behind in the vision of God's glory, impels them to proclaim the good news. They take risks, spend money, take time to learn about the gospel to teach what they know, and share their encounters of God with people. They enhance the expansion of Christianity as a world religion. They build the church that they love by their tireless financial contributions, labor, and involvement in the various ministries of their parishes and churches. They sacrifice a lot to get things done for the church.

Popular reading of the Bible in Africa has implications for the nature of Christianity in Africa. Its quest for objective interpretation of Scripture not only leads to the forgetfulness of the subjects themselves, who are interpreting the scriptural texts, but it also results in futurism and dispensationalism. Contemporary events are interpreted as fulfillment of past events in the Bible. There is a constant expectation that current events have millennial, eschatological meaning. Hence, people live in the tension of *fuga mundi*, flight from the world spirituality, and crave for material success because of the prosperity gospel's belief in God's blessings of the righteous who pay tithes. Furthermore, it gives rise to enchanted Christianity, characterized by fear of the forces of darkness, evil, witches, and wizards. It leads to expectation of magical powers from the liturgy, undue attachment to miracles, and reliance on religious leaders who assume superhuman powers and hence makes them susceptible to cult worship/followership. It exposes African Christians

---

89. Robert J. Schreiter, *Faces of Jesus in Africa* (Orbis Books, 1980); Mugambi and Magesa, *Jesus in African Christianity*; Bediako, *Jesus and the Gospel in Africa*.

to the whims and caprices of charlatans and self-acclaimed healers, frauds, and cheats who hoodwink and defraud them of their possessions. It belittles the place of Africans in world Christianity, especially given the shift in the center of gravity of Christianity from the Global North to the Global South.

Commonsense engagement with the Bible offers numerous fruits, which redound to the benefit of African Christians. But common sense is not the answer to every question. When stretched beyond its domain of competence, a commonsense reading of the Bible leaves the believer vulnerable to superstition, delusion, self-deception, and predation. But these perils do not invalidate the commonsense approach. They establish the intellectual and moral exigences for a more theoretical approach to the Bible that can help Christians avoid these perils.

CHAPTER FOUR

Academic Reading of the Bible in Africa

INTRODUCTION

Academic study of the Bible in Africa has contributed much to contextual, inculturation/liberation hermeneutics, especially in the light of the patterns of the African worldview. This chapter explores the various dimensions of this academic study in Africa: the classical, inculturation, womanist, feminist, postcolonial, liberation, and biblical hermeneutics. It engages such significant African hermeneuts as Justin S. Ukpong, Musa W. Dube, Teresa Okure, and Gerald O. West. These scholars insist on an integrated reading of the Bible that recognizes the importance of the diachronic, historical-critical method and the contexts of the various African peoples, with the synchronic, theological reading of the Bible in its final form, as the word of God. Academic study of the Bible can be used to bridge the gap between the hermeneutical tendencies of ordinary African readers and formal scholarly methods of interpretation. This chapter argues that, to fulfill this work of mediation, academic biblical scholarship must not be divorced from the concerns of the ordinary African readers of the Bible. Each should inform the other. It therefore suggests changes in academic practices that could lead to more informed, critical study by ordinary readers of the Bible.

African biblical scholars are mostly trained in the classical, often Western methodologies of biblical hermeneutics.[1] Generally, they are influenced by

---

1. Gerald O. West alludes to the Western education of African biblical scholars, describing them as "trained within (Western/Euro-American) historical-critical method." Gerald O. West, "Towards an Inclusive and Collaborative African Biblical Hermeneutics of Reception and Production: A Distinctively South African Contribution," *Scriptura* 119 (2020): 3.

Western education and values. Musa W. Dube compares African biblical scholars with African indigenous church interpreters: "While most African biblical scholars have been trained in the West and resorted to Western ways of reading and analyzing social relations in the Bible, most African Indigenous Churches have always used African perspectives such as divination and storytelling in their biblical interpretation."[2] Using herself as an example, Dube observes that her Western training makes her cling to text-centric readings, leaving her less able to interrogate oral and indigenous interpretations of the Bible.[3] According to Eric Anum, African biblical scholars are textual, "objective/critical readers."[4] They are trained in literary and historical criticism, which interprets the Bible as literature, while other, faith-based interpreters advance the theological interpretation of the Bible as Scripture, as the word of God. Gerald O. West acknowledged that "while many, if not most, African scholars have been inducted into the modern scholarly guild by the hands of western trained whites, whether in Europe, the United States of America, or Africa, a significant proportion of these have (re)turned (either geographically or ideologically) to use the resources they have acquired to engage with African realities."[5]

The historical study of texts in their original contexts remain important for an understanding of biblical texts all over the world. As a piece of ancient literature, knowing the background of the biblical text, its sources, and its form of writing remain an essential element toward grasping the meaning of the text. This task requires rigor and skill—hence the need for a critical analysis. Justin S. Ukpong defends the necessity of the historical-critical method in theological interpretation of Scripture in Africa thus:

> In recent times, however, the historical critical method has come under heavy fire... In the African context, it has also been argued that since biblical studies in Africa are interested in the message of the text, historical criticism, which is interested more in the history of the text than in its message, should be abandoned. In view of the above, the question arises whether African biblical scholarship needs this method. In my view the answer is a qualified "yes."

---

2. Musa W. Dube, "The Subaltern Can Speak: Reading the Mmutle (Hare) Way," *Journal of Africana Religions* 4, no. 1 (2016): 55.
3. Musa W. Dube, "Readings of Semoya: Batswana Women's Interpretations of Matt 15:21–28," *Semeia* 73 (1996): 121.
4. Anum, "Ye Ma Wo Mo!," 10.
5. West, "(Ac)claiming the (Extra)ordinary African 'Reader' of the Bible," 29.

Ukpong offers three reasons for this endorsement. "The first reason," he notes, "is that in the contemporary post-Enlightenment age, it is no longer possible to return to an uncritical use of the Bible in the academy. Therefore, African academic reading of the Bible must be critical." But even if such a return were possible, it would not be desirable. He writes, "The second reason is that the lack of historical critical use of the Bible has, in the past, led to many abuses of the Bible in Africa, as for example in the apartheid system in South Africa in which ideological meanings were read into the biblical text. Historical critical reading of the Bible is therefore required to avoid such abuses." As we saw in the previous chapter, such abuses persist even in postcolonial contexts. "The third reason," argues Ukpong, "is that African biblical scholarship, unlike its western counterpart, is contextual in nature, that is, it links the biblical text to the African context. So that such a link may not be an imposition on the text, and for it to be credible, it is necessary to analyze the original context of the text to ensure that the two contexts are comparable and not completely divergent."[6]

Its use in African biblical scholarship is not in doubt. "Historical-critical methods, and redaction criticism in particular, provide resources for locating a biblical text within its historical period of production."[7] However, the historical-critical method is not construed or used as an end but as a means to arrive at the spiritual sense of Scripture. The hope is that the method does not limit itself to the historical reading of Scripture in the sense of being stuck only to the context of the text's formation but serves as a method toward an authentic, balanced interpretation of Scripture. Through critical history, this interpretation grasps the original context of the text and then, through proper theological interpretation, is also able to grasp the Scripture in its final form, as the word of God, inspired by the Holy Spirit, as God's word in human language relevant for all times and history. Dube observes, "It seems to me that to insist on dwelling on one historical time in this biblical drama, ignoring the continuing character of the story, is to do injustice to that very text."[8]

---

6. Justin S. Ukpong, "Can African Old Testament Scholarship Escape the Historical Critical Approach?," *Newsletter on African Old Testament Scholarship* 7 (1999): 4. See also Michael Prior, CM, "The Bible and the Redeeming Idea of Colonialism," *Studies in World Christianity* 5, no. 2 (1999): 129–55, for the ideological use of the Bible during the apartheid regime in South Africa and in colonialism as a whole.

7. West, "Towards an Inclusive," 8.

8. Musa W. Dube, "Toward a Post-Colonial Feminist Interpretation of the Bible," *Semeia* 78 (1997): 13.

Realizing the inadequacies of the Western exegetical methods in addressing African issues, and the importance of context, African biblical scholars are increasingly adopting African thought patterns in the reading of the Bible. Ukpong declared African academic study of the Bible to be primarily "about reclaiming the status of the Bible as word of God and classic, a guide to moral and spiritual life as well as an ancient literature worth attention beyond its time."[9] African biblical scholars uncover that the "Biblical texts are indelibly etched with the ideological markers of their sites of production."[10] Consequently, they pay special attention to "the ideological dimensions of redaction criticism."[11] This hermeneutic of suspicion is particularly articulated in the liberative biblical hermeneutics from South Africa, especially in the work of Itumeleng Mosala, which holds that struggle with dominant forces is inscribed in every text of the Bible itself. For this reason, Mosala argues that the question that should be at the heart of African biblical hermeneutics of liberation must be "the production of alternative significations."[12] "The task of a biblical hermeneutics of liberation," therefore, "is to go behind the dominant discourses [represented in the final form of the Bible] to the [co-opted] discourses of oppressed communities in order to link up with kindred struggles."[13]

Western exegetical methods emanate from the Western conceptual frame of reference. While it may be relevant to other contexts, African biblical scholars insist on working with the African contexts and patterns of thought, the diverse situations within which the Bible is read in various parts of Africa by both the ordinary people and by those trained as biblical scholars. This includes their social, political, economic, and religious conditions and how these impact the method one adopts in reading the Bible. In the light of the divide in African theology between inculturation and liberation perspectives, owing to differences of colonial policies and their impacts on the people as well as diverse responses to colonialism, academic reading of the Bible in Africa would emphasize inculturation and liberation hermeneutics, both responses to colonial hermeneutics. The conceptual frame of reference, according to Justin S. Ukpong (who popularized this notion), "is a mental

---

9. Ukpong, "Reading the Bible in a Global Village," 10.
10. West, "Towards an Inclusive," 3.
11. West, "Towards an Inclusive," 3.
12. Itumeleng J. Mosala, *Biblical Hermeneutics and Black Theology in South Africa* (William B. Eerdmans, 1989), 188.
13. Mosala, *Biblical Hermeneutics*, 188, cited in West, "Towards an Inclusive," 5.

apparatus. It refers to the type of understanding of the universe that informs the reading, that is, the mind-set that is at work in the reading operation. It comprises a particular world-view, values, disvalues, and basic assumptions about reality."[14] It is inescapable and central to any reading method one adopts for the Bible. An African conceptual frame of reference, or the pattern of life of Africans, consists in a unitive worldview whereby nature and supernature interacts cordially. It is a worldview that recognizes the place of sacredness in all aspects of life. Reading of the Bible in such an integrated worldview demands a recognition of the Bible as the word of God. In such reading, African contextual issues form the agenda.

JUSTIN S. UKPONG'S INCULTURATION HERMENEUTICS

Justin S. Ukpong, the doyen of Africa's biblical scholarship, indicates that contextual reading is Africa's major contribution to the development of biblical scholarship. According to Ukpong, "the term 'contextualisation' is a neologism coined by the Theological Education Fund in 1972 to express the process and practice of relating the gospel message to the people's concrete life situation."[15] Contextualization is carried out in young churches in different forms: liturgy, ministry, theology and culture, and liberation (political, economic, social, religious). As interactions between Christianity and the people's culture include both the religious and secular meanings and values, Ukpong advocates for a holistic approach to inculturation that incorporates the African worldview and life experiences. He believes the holistic approach accords with the integral nature of the African worldview over and against the Eurocentric dualistic worldview upon which classical theology is based. This means that "African traditional customs, contemporary political, economic, social and moral issues have also to be exposed to critical, pastoral and theological reflection in the light of Christianity."[16]

Ukpong calls for a sociological-anthropological approach to contextualization, "to articulate the Christian faith within the socio-cultural context of Africa in such a way that it becomes good news in all aspects of the lives of

---

14. Mosala, *Biblical Hermeneutics*, cited in West, "Towards an Inclusive," 14–15.
15. Justin S. Ukpong, "Contextualisation: A Historical Survey," *AFER* 29, no. 5 (1987): 278.
16. Justin S. Ukpong, "Inculturation: A Major Challenge to the Church in Africa Today," *AFER* 38, no. 5 (1996): 259.

Africans—religious, social, economic and political."[17] Since inculturation is "an attempt to give African expression to the Christian faith within a theological framework,"[18] inculturation biblical hermeneutic is the application of the methodology of inculturation theology to biblical interpretation.[19] "It is marked by a movement away from the context of the text and the text itself to the context of the readers."[20] "The goal of interpretation," Ukpong argues, "is the actualization of the theological meaning of the text in today's context so as to forge integration between faith and life, and engender commitment to personal and societal transformation."[21]

THE EVOLUTION OF INCULTURATION HERMENEUTICS

Ukpong divided the history of the development of biblical interpretation in Africa into three phases: phase 1 (1930s–70s), reactive and apologetic; phase 2 (1970s), reactive-proactive; and phase 3 (1990s), proactive, recognition of the ordinary reader, African context as subject of biblical interpretation, dominated by liberation and inculturation methodologies.[22] In the first phase, the African context was compared to the Old Testament and their relationship was emphasized. Some even argued for the Israelite origin of African communities on the basis of similarities between their cultural practices. Comparative studies asserted African traditional religious culture as preparation for the gospel.[23] In the second phase, with its two methods (Africa-in-the-Bible and

---

17. Justin S. Ukpong, "Towards a Holistic Approach to Inculturation Theology," *Mission Studies* 16, no. 2 (1999): 107.
18. Justin S. Ukpong, "Current Theology: The Emergence of African Theologies," *Theological Studies* 45 (1984): 501.
19. Justin S. Ukpong, "The Parable of the Shrewd Manager (Luke 16:1–13): An Essay in Inculturation Biblical Hermeneutic," *Semeia* 73 (1996): 190.
20. Justin S. Ukpong, "New Testament Hermeneutics in Africa: Challenges and Possibilities," *Neotestamentica* 35, nos. 1–2 (2001): 148.
21. Justin S. Ukpong, "Developments in Biblical Interpretation in Africa: Historical and Hermeneutical Directions," in West and Dube, *The Bible in Africa*, 24.
22. Ukpong, "Developments in Biblical Interpretation in Africa," 12
23. See Gerald West, "African Culture as Preparatio Evangelica: The Old Testament as Preparation of the African Post-Colonial," in *Postcolonialism and the Hebrew Bible: The Next Step*, ed. Ronald Boer (Society of Biblical Literature, 2013), 193–220; Eric Anum, "Comparative Readings of the Bible in Africa: Some Concerns," in West and Dube, *The Bible in Africa*, 457–73; Theo Witvliet, "Response to Lamin Sanneh, 'Domesticating the Transcendent: The African Transformation of Christianity," in *Bible Translation on*

evaluative approaches), African culture (context) was taken as the starting point for the reading of the Bible. The inculturation motif aimed at making Christianity relevant to African culture by asserting that Christianity should no longer be construed as a foreign religion in Africa. Interpreters in the liberative paradigm of the third phase emphasized deliverance from bondage and oppression and were suspicious of the Bible, even as they drew from the Bible to emphasize the God of the oppressed always being on the side of those at the margins.

Inculturation (Africa-in-the-Bible) hermeneutics aims at correcting negative impressions about Africans in the Bible, showing their presence in the Bible and their influence and role in the history of salvation and on the world stage. The de-emphasis of the role of Africa comes in the form of excluding Egypt from Africa and including it as part of the ancient Near East.[24] Evaluative studies are focused on the encounter between African religion, culture, and the Bible and their theological understanding. Its various approaches evaluate elements of African culture in the light of the biblical witness, look to the Bible in addressing the challenges of specific aspects of African culture, and interpret biblical themes in the light of African culture, life, and experience. It shows continuity between African culture and Christianity, as exemplified in the various formulations of African Christologies drawn from elements of African culture and tradition. Finally, it studies the biblical text to discover biblical models and practice in Africa. Ukpong's definition clarifies the scope of this methodology:

> An inculturation biblical hermeneutics is an approach that consciously and explicitly seeks to interpret the biblical text from socio-cultural

---

the Threshold of the Twenty-First Century: Authority, Reception, Culture and Religion, ed. Athalya Brenner and Jan Willem van Henten (Sheffield, 2002), 86–93; John V. Taylor, *The Primal Vision: Christian Presence Amid African Religion* (SCM Press, 1963).

24. Prominent authors in the comparative approach include David Tuesday Adamu, "The Place of Africa and Africans in the Old Testament and Its Environment" (PhD diss., Baylor University, 1986); Adamu, "The Table of Nations Reconsidered in African Perspective (Genesis 19)," *Journal of African Religion and Philosophy* 11 (1993): 138–43; Adamu, *Africa and Africans in the Old Testament* (Christian Universities, 1998); Teresa Okure, "Africans in the Bible: A Study in Hermeneutics," paper presented at the International Congress on the Bible in Africa, Cairo, August 4–20, 1987, and at the Society of Biblical Literature's seminar on the Bible in Africa, Asia, and Latin America, New Orleans, November 23–26, 1996, cited in Teresa Okure, SHCJ, "Jesus and the Samaritan Woman (Jn 4:1–42) in Africa," *Theological Studies* 70 (2009): 403n7.

perspectives of different people. This includes both their religious and secular culture as well as their social and historical experiences. This does not mean reading contemporary contexts into the biblical text; rather it means consciously and critically allowing different contemporary contexts to inform the interpretation positively and to influence the type of questions put to the text in the process of interpretation.[25]

Liberation hermeneutics of the reading of the Bible, just like the Latin American liberation theology, looks to the Bible "as a resource for struggle against oppression of any kind based on the biblical witness that God does not sanction oppression but rather always stands on the side of the oppressed to liberate them."[26] Black theology of South Africa and womanist theologies use a hermeneutics of liberation. Often the Exodus account of the liberation of the people of Israel is used as a model of God's liberative action for the oppressed. While the Bible was used for the political theology of liberation by the Black theology of South Africa in its fight against the apartheid regime's oppressive segregationist system, another liberative approach points to the possible subversive, oppressive, and elitist nature of the Bible itself, which allows for the hermeneutics of oppression exemplified by the apartheid system's misuse of the Bible to support its segregationist agenda against the Black people in South Africa. The womanist theologians critique the maleness of God both in Bible translations and in various hermeneutics of the Bible. They also attempt "a recovery of the forgotten and muted voices, the images and contributions of women in the biblical text."[27]

Despite the different points of emphasis across these paradigms, inculturation and liberative readings are complementary. "Issues of Africanness, ethnicity, and culture cannot be separated from the complex matrix they share with issues of race, class, and gender."[28] Africans read the Bible in the light of the daily challenges of their lives. This reading presumes a particular attitude to the Bible as the word of God, as the documentation of God's self-revelation. It sees the Bible as a nonideological text, as the norm and guide of Christian life, and hence as a corrective of culture. It is a dynamic rereading of the biblical text, one conscious of its historical past in the light of today's context.

---

25. Justin S. Ukpong, "The Parable of the Shrewd Manager," 191.
26. Ukpong, "Developments in Biblical Interpretation in Africa," 19.
27. Ukpong, "Developments in Biblical Interpretation in Africa," 22.
28. Joseph Ogbonnaya, "African Liberative Theologies," in *Introducing Liberative Theologies*, ed. Miguel A. De La Torre (Orbis Books,), 26–45.

In the third phase, both the contextual method and inculturation hermeneutics recognize the ordinary African (nonbiblical scholars) readers and integrate their perspective into the academic reading of the Bible. Through inculturation hermeneutics, the African context is made the subject of the interpretation of the Bible, and the various situations of African life become the subject of biblical interpretation in view of societal transformation envisaged through the Bible. Ukpong's erudite interpretation of the parable of the shrewd manager in Luke 16:1–13 connects the historical context of the text with other related Lukan texts on Jesus's attitude toward the rich. Ukpong analyzes the text and applies it to the context of the oppression of poor West African farmers. This method is indicative of the inculturation biblical hermeneutics' contextual reading centering on African context. It equally showcases the connection of inculturation hermeneutics with the present context of ordinary readers of the Bible, challenging hearers "to work towards the *reversal* of oppressive structures of contemporary economic systems."[29]

> The procedure involves interaction between academic and ordinary readers of the bible such that the ordinary readers are helped to develop critical awareness and identify and use local critical resources in their reading of the bible. In developing the hermeneutics for this approach to bible reading, the resources of the people's culture and historical life experience are used as complementary to conventional critical tools of biblical exegesis. This recognition, by the academic community, of the place of the ordinary readers in the scheme of things, regarding the appropriation of the biblical message, makes academic biblical scholarship relevant to the community of believers.[30]

Ukpong's summary above debunks positions like Paul Gifford's, which attempt to diminish and reduce African readings of the Bible to the comparative approach of responding to European views about Africa.[31] Paying attention to context is universally important to the interpretative process. Jonathan A. Draper argues that "to interpret a text without taking this [context] into account is to run a risk of self-deception ... This is not because the Bible does

---

29. Ukpong, "The Parable of the Shrewd," 207.
30. Ukpong, "Developments in Biblical Interpretation in Africa," 23.
31. Paul Gifford, "The Bible in Africa: A Novel Usage in Africa's New Churches," *Bulletin of SOAS* 71, no. 2 (2008): 203–19.

not confront us with the Word of God's revelation, but because we as readers and hearers of the Word are pre-disposed by our own social, economic, political and cultural contexts to read in a certain way."[32] For example, contextual interpretation of biblical texts on sexual morality enables European and North American Christian denominations to bless gay unions, marriages, and ordinations, despite those same denominations' steadfast opposition to LGBTQ inclusion in earlier eras and generations. The context changed and so, too, did the interpretation of the Bible. In Africa, contextual reading in its various forms is "trying to understand in what way the text may contribute to our life and our faith as Africans in a hostile global environment."[33] Inculturation hermeneutics remains the most popular reading of the Bible in Africa today, adopted by most scholars and relevant to nonbiblical scholars as well. Despite his criticism of certain aspects of inculturation reading of the Bible, David T. Ngong affirmed its popularity: "Even though there are other influential methods of reading the Bible in Africa, inculturation biblical hermeneutics is perhaps currently the most influential because it has the support of mainstream scholars, preachers, and ordinary Christians, being a central method of interpretation, especially in the current Pentecostalization of African Christianity."[34]

Ukpong advocates for a new way of reading the Bible in the light of inculturation, one that is distinct from the Western context by focusing on the contemporary communities rather than on the context that produced the text. He notes the yearning of African Christians in the mainline churches to experience the Jesus they read about in the Bible, the Jesus who healed the sick, raised the dead, and fed the hungry, deeds their churches claim were of the past and no longer needed in contemporary Christianity. Ukpong regrets the inability of African biblical scholars, who until recently had been unable to break away from the Eurocentric reading of the Bible they had been trained in, to apply the Bible to the lives and experiences of African Christians. The consequence is the gap between the scholarly reading of the Bible and the ordinary African Christian reading of the Bible.[35] Inculturation hermeneutics

---

32. Jonathan A. Draper, "Reading the Bible as Conversation: A Theory and Methodology for Contextual Interpretation of the Bible in Africa," *Grace and Truth* 19, no. 2 (2002): 16.

33. Draper, "Reading the Bible as Conversation," 19.

34. David T. Ngong, "Reading the Bible in Africa: A Critique of Enchanted Bible Reading," *Exchange* 43 (2014): 176.

35. Justin S. Ukpong, "Rereading the Bible with African Eyes," *Journal of Theology for South Africa* 91 (1995): 4.

simply aims to apply the messages of the Bible to challenge contemporary society and life of individuals and to give meaning to African sociocultural context. Inculturation hermeneutics

> designates an approach to biblical interpretation which seeks to make the African, and for that matter any socio-cultural context the *subject of* interpretation. This is different from making another context the subject of interpretation and then applying the result in the African context. It is also different from reading the context into the biblical text. Interpreting a text is a complex process. It involves an *interpreter* in a certain *context* making meaning of a *text* using a specific *conceptual framework* and its *procedure*. Every interpretation process has the above five components of interpreter, context, text, conceptual framework and procedure. Making a particular socio-cultural context the subject of interpretation means that the conceptual framework, its methodology and the personal input of the interpreter are *consciously* informed by the world-view of, and the life experience within that culture.[36]

Inculturation hermeneutics, Ukpong notes, is also cognizant of the sociocultural, political, and economic context of both the biblical texts and the context of the readers of the text. It advocates for an interpretation that advances social transformation of the society to promote integral development and well-being of the members. It insists on the praxis of the good news and the living out of the Christian message in the concrete situations of the people to bring about justice and equity, inclusion, and freedom of everyone. It advocates for the conversion of culture and the overcoming of any of its elements that hinder a peaceful, prosperous, and egalitarian society. In practical terms, the Christian message must be prophetic and promote social justice.[37]

THE ROLE OF THE ORDINARY READER IN INCULTURATION HERMENEUTICS

Even though ordinary readers "read" the Bible differently from trained scholars, African academic approaches are now integrating the ordinary people's

---

36. Ukpong, "Rereading the Bible with African Eyes," 5.
37. Ukpong, "Inculturation," 266.

perspective into the academic study. Ukpong identifies the ordinary people reading the Bible as the subjects, not the objects, of biblical interpretation. Their concern with existential issues in reading the Bible informs inculturation hermeneutics' emphasis on contextuality as central to biblical interpretation. And so, Ukpong's inculturation hermeneutics includes "the idea of reading with ordinary readers."[38] Reading "with" the people is indicative of the communitarian focus of African academic reading of the Bible. It is reading "from" the perspective of the community, directed to the community, for the community, and through the community's collaboration with African biblical scholars.

The outcome is a "mutual self-mediation," to use Bernard Lonergan's terminology, between academic biblical scholarship and ordinary people's reading of the Bible.[39] While academic reading learns from ordinary reading to read the Bible existentially, in the light of contemporary society and various challenges in life, ordinary people's reading of the Bible also learns to move away from fundamentalistic reading of the Bible to a critical reading. Contextuality is emphasized; knowledge of the conceptual framework of the community is presupposed; the voice of the poor is heard in the reading of the text.[40] But this collaboration and liberative focus can be pushed further. African academic biblical scholars' engagement with ordinary people is much more pronounced in Gerald O. West's liberative hermeneutics.

GERALD O. WEST'S CONTEXTUAL BIBLE STUDY

Gerald O. West is a South African biblical scholar engaged in liberative hermeneutics at the intersection of academic reading and ordinary people reading of the Bible.[41] He is convinced African biblical scholarship should be much more attentive, listening rather than prescribing, and much more observant than didactic, open to and respectful of the ordinary reader's hermeneutics.[42]

---

38. Ukpong, "Reading the Bible in a Global Village," 11.
39. Bernard J. F. Lonergan, "The Mediation of Christ in Prayer," in *Philosophical and Theological Papers, 1958–1964*, Collected Works of Bernard Lonergan 6, ed. Robert C. Croken et al. (University of Toronto, 1996) 160–82.
40. Ukpong, "Reading the Bible in a Global Village," 24–25.
41. Godwin I. Akper, "The Role of the 'Ordinary Reader' in Gerald O. West's Hermeneutics," *Scriptura* 88 (2005): 1–13.
42. West, "(Ac)claiming the (Extra)ordinary African 'Reader' of the Bible," 46.

ACADEMIC READING OF THE BIBLE IN AFRICA

For this reason, he is certain that African biblical scholarship is not neatly distinguished by the category "colonial" or "postcolonial" since the period of encounter with the Bible spans through periods prior to, during, and after colonialism. He opts for "a more detailed historical hermeneutical analysis of communities' biblical interpretation."[43] Thus, much of his work in South Africa has been to understand the alliance forged between the African biblical scholar and the ordinary African "reader" of the Bible.[44] This alliance has a history prior to colonialism, in the early encounters of Africans with the Christian missionaries who first presented to them the concept of text as a conveyor of meaning and as a powerful force that can be used positively or negatively.

West represented this historically in the early encounter, reception, and appropriation of the Bible by prominent South Africans: Mmahutu of the Tlhaping, who first encountered the Bible in the early 1800s; Isaiah Shembe in the late 1800s; and Trevor Makhoba in the late 1900s. He asserts: "The three (extra)ordinary interpreters of the Bible ... bear testimony both to the devastating impact of colonialism (including apartheid as a special form) and to the agency of indigenous Africans and the continuity that exists between their forms of African Christianity and African Religion. Their lives span two hundred years of biblical interpretation in South Africa and are more or less equidistant from each other."[45]

West advanced his view of African scholarly biblical interpretation by highlighting the hermeneutics of ordinary readers and taking practical steps to interface between them and academic readers of the Bible. He is influenced by Sharon D. Welch's *A Feminist Ethic of Risk*,[46] especially its emphasis of the ethics of solidarity. Welch's work leans heavily on Michel Foucault's epistemology, with its emphasis on solidarity and a communicative ethic. West is also drawn to the postmodern critique of the Enlightenment against the possibility of grand narratives and hence of claims to the universality of human experiences.[47] The Bible, for him, is a "site of struggle" for liberation from colonialism (and apartheid as a special form). The image of wrestling is drawn from Genesis 32:24, where Jacob struggled with God, a struggle

---

43. West, "(Ac)claiming the (Extra)ordinary African 'Reader' of the Bible," 46.
44. West, "(Ac)claiming the (Extra)ordinary African 'Reader' of the Bible," 29.
45. West, "(Ac)claiming the (Extra)ordinary African 'Reader' of the Bible," 32.
46. Sharon D. Welch, *A Feminist Ethic of Risk* (Fortress, 1990), 123–51.
47. Gerald O. West, *Biblical Hermeneutics of Liberation: Models of Reading the Bible in the South African Context*, 2nd rev. ed. (Orbis Books, 1995), 12–46.

that changed Jacob's relationship with God. According to West, "contextual Bible reading is not about understanding the Bible better. The Bible is read for change. The Bible as a site of struggle itself . . . is wrestled with (or re-read) until it contributes to real, substantive, systemic change . . . Key to our understanding of change is that personal relationships are rooted in socio-economic systems."[48] Elsewhere, he expatiates: "Like other forms of liberation hermeneutics, contextual Bible Study is dialogical, including not only the dialogue between context and the biblical text but also a dialogue between 'ordinary' and 'scholarly' readers as they together—in some way—dialogue with the Bible. It is a collaborative and communal process."[49] He brings this home by facilitating workshops on different books of the Bible with faith-based groups, including marginalized ones, like gay and lesbian communities.[50]

Contextual Bible study as a methodological approach goes a step beyond merely recognizing the contextual character of interpretation. It commits to the actuality of interpreting the Bible from the context of the poor. "So implicit in the notion of 'contextual' as it is used in the phrase 'contextual Bible study' is commitment to a particular context, the context of the poor and marginalized."[51] Considering his theology was articulated during apartheid, "contextuality" was used to veil liberation. His contextual Bible study, then, is liberation Bible study with an emphasis on being on the side of the poor, with the intention of bringing out the voice of the poor, the marginalized, and the oppressed in Bible interpretation. It arose in the harrowing days of the racist apartheid regime as ordinary people gathered with some socially engaged biblical scholars to use the Bible to make sense of the atrocities they were experiencing in their land, especially during the political crisis that was ongoing at KwaZulu-Natal, the epicenter of South African liberative hermeneutics.[52] In other words, West is not concerned with every ordinary reader

---

48. Gerald O. West, "Reading the Bible with the Marginalised: The Value/s of Contextual Bible Reading," *Stellenbosch Theological Journal* 1, no. 2 (2015): 240.

49. Gerald O. West, "Locating 'Contextual Bible Study' Within Biblical Liberation Hermeneutics and Intercultural Biblical Hermeneutics," *HTS Teologiese Studies/Theological Studies* 70, no. 1 (2014): 2.

50. Gerald O. West, "Facilitating Interpretive Resilience: The Joseph Story (Genesis 37–50) as a Site of Struggle," *Acta Theologica* 26 (2018): 17–37.

51. Gerald O. West, "Contextual Bible Study: Creating Sacred (and Safe) Space for Social Transformation," *Grace & Truth* 16, no. 2 (1999): 51.

52. Gerald O. West, *The Academy of the Poor: Toward a Dialogical Reading of the Bible* (Sheffield Academic Press), 34–35.

of the Bible.⁵³ He works specifically with Black South Africans. This means there are varieties of ordinary people reading the Bible: the literate, semi-illiterate, and illiterate who listen, whose hermeneutics is oral; and men, women, wealthy, poor, oppressed, marginalized, individuals, and groups, who hold the Bible in high repute and treasure its content as valid beyond its original context and as important for contemporary times.

The process of contextual Bible study began with a group inviting the Institute for the Study of the Bible (ISB)—later, the Ujamaa Centre for Community Development and Research⁵⁴—made up of biblical scholars with an interest in social activism, to reflect with them around a common project or to facilitate a theological reflection on a particular topic. They determined that the concern of the group was theological, to decipher the level of organization the groups had and urge them to collaborate with other groups like them, to broaden community collaboration. The biblical scholars collaborated with the people by bringing to bear their expertise in biblical interpretation, using the liberative paradigm of "See-Judge-Act processes."⁵⁵ The "See" was the participants getting to know each other by the sharing of their different realities. The "Judge" referred to the sharing of their experiences of contextual Bible studies. The "Act" was dedicated to theoretical and methodological reflection.⁵⁶ This enhanced the theological reflection of ordinary people reading of the Bible and helped them in their contestations against the various manipulative strategies of the apartheid regime and other forms of oppression in postapartheid South Africa. Contextual Bible study commits to a critical reading of the Bible whereby ordinary people move beyond what they learned about the Bible from their various Christian denominations to appropriation of diverse strategies of biblical interpretation, especially readings that

---

53. Gerald O. West, Introduction to *Reading Other-Wise Socially Engaged Biblical Scholars Reading with Their Local Communities*, ed. Gerald O. West (Society of Biblical Literature, 2007), 2.

54. "The Ujamaa Centre was established in 1989. It is located on the campus of the University of KwaZulu-Natal in Pietermaritzburg, South Africa," Gerald O. West and Sithembiso Zwane, "Re-Reading 1 Kings 21:1–16 Between Community-Based Activism and University-Based Pedagogy," *Journal for Interdisciplinary Biblical Studies* 2, no. 1 (2020). See also Gerald O. West, "Locating 'Contextual Bible Study,'" 2. It is also, he states, "the base from which I do much of my biblical studies work." Gerald West, "Reading the Bible with the Marginalised," 235.

55. West, "Reading the Bible with the Marginalised," 236–37.

56. West, "Reading the Bible with the Marginalised," 237.

are different from the missionary and colonial hermeneutics they had been exposed to earlier.

West insists that ordinary readers should be assisted by skilled, trained biblical scholars to a "behind the text" reading—that is, to knowledge of the historical and sociohistorical context of the text—to enable them to interpret the text in the light of their own contexts and to recognize when others want to use the text against them.[57] Critical reading of the text will also discourage selective use of the Bible by communities of ordinary readers.[58] This way, the dangers of "in-front-of-the-text" reading are forestalled. "Hence, West insists that biblical interpretation in Africa should take place within the matrix of accountability to the past and present communities of faith and the reconstruction for future communities of faith."[59] Finally, contextual Bible study is committed to action (that is, to praxis), accompanied with reflection, for the purpose of social transformation using the Bible. Thus, West has this to say about his signature biblical hermeneutics: "'Contextual Bible Study' is a form of praxis in which the Ujamaa Centre for Community Development and Research re-reads an already present (and significant) Bible with and within particular organized communities of the poor and marginalized, recognizing that theological change is required for sustained-systemic social change in contexts where the Bible is a sacred site."[60]

West is clear that trained biblical scholars are not involved in *educating* ordinary Bible readers. Primarily, they are engaged in *collaborating* with them. They facilitate workshops on topics a community or group is working with from the Bible. "Facilitating," West explains, is used deliberately as vital to the contextual Bible study aimed at "enabling active participation of each participant";[61] the socially engaged biblical scholar and the ordinary readers of the Bible benefit, are converted, in the process. He explains:

> We are not educating the community to read the Bible in our "trained" way. We are sharing the resources of biblical scholarship in particular social sites where there are already substantial local interpretive resources. Moreover, we quite deliberately share these interpretive

---

57. Gerald O. West, "The Relationship Between the Different Modes of Reading (the Bible) and the Ordinary Reader, *Scriptura* 9 (1991): 90–96.
58. West, "The Relationship Between the Different Modes of Reading," 96.
59. Akper, "The Role of the 'Ordinary Reader' in Gerald O. West's Hermeneutics," 8.
60. West and Zwane, "Re-Reading 1 Kings 21:1–16," 180.
61. West, "Reading the Bible with the Marginalised," 245.

resources in ways that do not foreground their academic framework. Our experience is that these additional reading resources are potentially empowering in enabling familiar texts to be read in unfamiliar ways and in enabling unfamiliar texts or literary units to be read, and in so doing to provide alternative lines of connection between local community contexts and biblical texts.[62]

This in no way implies that West, who is a white male who enjoyed the white privilege during the South African apartheid regime, is claiming for himself the same condition as Black ordinary readers of the Bible in South African. "Therefore, he sees his role as primarily that of reading 'with' the poor and oppressed and empowering them to 'read' for themselves. As a biblical scholar West is obviously not an 'ordinary reader,' because he has been trained to 'read' skillfully, differently, and critically, using resources and tools not available to the poor and marginalized 'readers' of the Bible."[63] Through such workshops—which emphasize resilience, the hallmark of liberation theologies—participants speak up, gain better perspectives on select scriptural passages, and read within their literary contexts.[64] They liberate themselves from oppressive popular misinterpretations, better appreciate the Bible as the word of God, and become capable of "building the religious-spiritual capacities required to live positively in a religious landscape dominated by theologies of retribution."[65]

LITERARY AND SOCIOHISTORICAL METHODS

West rejects the tension between what is African and what is not in biblical studies, the notion that "what is appropriate for African resources is not appropriate for biblical texts or what is appropriate for biblical texts is not appropriate for African resources."[66] He laments the slow pace of acceptance of literary methods by African biblical scholars and argues that ordinary African readers' narrative literary approach to the Bible predisposes them to literary methods. They only need to be availed of the necessary resources.

---

62. West, "Introduction," 2.
63. Akper, "The Role of the 'Ordinary Reader' in Gerald O. West's Hermeneutics," 1n1.
64. See, for example, West and Zwane, "Re-Reading 1 Kings 21:1–," 183.
65. West, "Facilitating Interpretive Resilience," 21.
66. West, "Facilitating Interpretive Resilience," 26.

He sees potential in the recent interest of biblical scholars in African orality as a possible path for literary methods within African resources. In his workshops, he leads participants to engage in a close reading of texts that narratively opens the contexts of the text, thus helping them make informed decisions on the text based on their contexts.[67]

The literary method is attentive to the historical context of texts of Scripture. It looks behind the text—that is, the original context of the text. It looks at the text, the reader in front of the text, how a text is perceived in the context of the reader, and its relevance or not, including possible reinterpretation in the light of the world of the reader. It is a critical reading of the text that goes beyond the final form of the text as presented to the reader and reaches back to the processes of the making of the text. It is the relationship between the diachronic, the processes through which the Bible as Scripture came to be, and the synchronic, the final form as the Bible, believed to be the word of God.

After initially opposing the link between the literary and sociohistorical methods, West acknowledges that in working with ordinary readers of the Bible, the interpretative skills of the African biblical scholars supplement and complement the resources they already have and enable them to find resonances between their sociohistorical contexts and those of the biblical traditions. He also came to the realization that "while many of their connections are with the biblical *text*, they also long to find lines of connection between their realities and the *historical* realities which lie behind the biblical text . . . they want to know that their lived realities are connected with the lived realities of those who have gone before them in the faith; and in both instances these lived realities have clear historical dimensions."[68] The oppressed, the enslaved, and those imprisoned unjustly look up to the Exodus story of Israel's liberation from Egypt with relief and hope. The poor and the hungry relish Jesus feeding the multitude. It matters a lot to the excluded, those afflicted with disease, and the innocent condemned to die to see continuity between them and Jesus. Those mourning look to the resurrection of Lazarus and to the resurrection of Jesus to be consoled over the death of their loved ones. West insists this historicity, which is sought by ordinary readers, must be based on the text to ensure that ordinary readers are not

---

67. West, "Facilitating Interpretive Resilience," 26.

68. Gerald O. West, "The Historicity of Myth and the Myth of Historicity: Locating the Ordinary African 'Reader' of the Bible in the Debate," *Neotestamentica* 38, no. 1 (2004): 128.

dependent on scholars. This means the biblical scholar must dismiss the myth of knowing what really happened behind the text by acknowledging honestly not knowing "what really happened."

West is in no way dismissing the distinction between historical narrative and fiction. He is not also presuming that ordinary readers do not make the distinction. He discovered, in fact, that they do, that "at times participants seem content to engage with biblical narratives as narratives that are meaningful, powerful, and true for them with no (overt) consideration of whether they are historical or fictional; at other times, participants continue to probe the narrative for its historical truth claims—they want to know the historicity of this myth."[69] West reminds the socially engaged African biblical scholars to always remember that sociohistorical biblical scholarship is always contested.[70] For this reason, they should always be guided by the experiences and questions of ordinary readers of the Bible they are working with. "Doing primary historical research or reading secondary historical works guided by the experiences of those we read 'with' will shape both what we find and what we fashion."[71] And it is important that recalling past ways of life in sociohistorical methods does not mean canonizing or adopting them, but they serve as guides to asking and answering questions about our own contemporary societies.[72]

MUSA W. DUBE'S FEMINIST HERMENEUTICS

Musa W. Dube advances liberative hermeneutics characterized by a hermeneutics of suspicion toward the Bible and solidarity of the oppressed for the achievement of liberation. Central to her scholarship is her question, "Given the role of the Bible in facilitating imperialism, how should we read the Bible as postcolonial subjects?"[73] Her response rings through her project: "In sum,

---

69. West, "The Historicity of Myth and the Myth of Historicity," 138.
70. His work on redaction criticism, using Itumeleng J. Mosala's work to argue on the Bible as a site of struggle, is instructive in this regard. See Gerald O. West, "Redaction Criticism as a Resource for the Bible as "a Site of Struggle," *Old Testament Essays* 30, no. 2 (2017): 525–45.
71. West, "The Historicity of Myth and the Myth of Historicity," 140.
72. Norman K. Gottwald, "Response to Contributors," in *Tracking the Tribes of Yahweh: On the Trail of a Classic*, ed. R. Boer (Sheffield Academic Press, 2002), 172–85, cited in West, "The Historicity of Myth and the Myth of Historicity," 141.
73. Musa W. Dube, *Postcolonial Feminist Interpretation of the Bible* (Chalice Press, 2000), 4.

the Bible as a Western book is bound to its imperialist history of subjugation and oppression. This imperialist history has constructed all of us, and its reality cannot be bracketed from our critical practice without perpetuating the history of unequal inclusion."[74] Postcolonial biblical interpretation interrogates the ethical responsibility Western imperialism lays on contemporary Western and non-Western biblical scholars. It includes the appropriation of African lands, race and gender issues, disempowerment of Africans, and their denigration in various forms under imperialistic ideology, including the ones showcased in the Bible's ways of telling their stories, claims to universality of the Western interpretive methods, contemporary history, and liberation, with focus "on how the meaning of biblical texts has shaped and continues to shape international relations of the postcolonial world."[75] She recognizes the varieties of reading the Bible, including inculturation hermeneutics, from above and from below as "acts of resistance, seeking decolonization and liberation."[76] She agrees the Bible must be read in the light of the culture and the meaning-making process of people. In this, gender matters must be incorporated into inculturation; there must be gender inclusive Christology and a critical study of both African traditional religions and of the biblical narrative.[77] In addition, the colonial origin of the Bible and its use as a weapon of domination and oppression must be emphasized.

Dube uses the symbol of the hare from African folklore to depict the power of resistance by the oppressed and the marginalized, the wisdom capable of navigating the complexities of the dominant and the subordinate that mark the relationship of the rich and the poor. The survival of the poor and the marginalized depends on the emulation of the Mmutle the trickster, the hare, in South African people's folklore.[78] Despite its small size, the Mmutle can defeat big, powerful animals like the elephant, the lion, and the whale. The poor must always be on their guard and make use of their intellect to survive

---

74. Dube, "Toward a Post-Colonial Feminist Interpretation of the Bible," 23, cited in Derek Alan Woodard-Lehman, "Through a Prism Darkly: Reading with Musa Dube," *Cultural Encounters* 4, no. 2 (2008): 39.

75. Dube, *Postcolonial Feminist Interpretation of the Bible*, 19.

76. Musa W. Dube, "Villagizing, Globalizing, and Biblical Studies," in Ukpong et al., *Reading the Bible in the Global Village*, 51.

77. Dube, "Villagizing, Globalizing, and Biblical Studies," 54.

78. For another use of the hare metaphor from African stories, see Tinyiko S. Maluleke, "Of Lions and Rabbits: The Role of the Church in Reconciliation in South Africa," *International Review of Mission* 96, nos. 380/381 (2007): 41–55.

in the world where the rich and the powerful reign. "Dedication to resistance should become an imperative way of life,"[79] even when it puts one's life in danger. This demands "dexterity and invention in the face of oppression"[80] and never giving the structures of the oppressor any ease but instead to consistently "challenge and subvert them."[81] The poor and the oppressed must remember they cannot achieve anything by themselves individually. They must be in solidarity with other oppressed and vulnerable members of society. They will stand alone at their own peril.[82] And this equally applies to feminist activists challenging and subverting structures of oppression of the patriarchal culture, religion, ecclesiology, society, and government. It is an imperative that must be pursued relentlessly until the structures of oppression are overcome, until gender justice is achieved. Perseverance is necessary, Dube argues, because women are doubly, even triply, oppressed. "They are doubly oppressed for they are under the yoke of colonialism and patriarchal oppression—of their own cultures and that of their colonisers. But it is also said they are triply oppressed for they are under the yoke of their national and foreign patriarchal cultures in addition to imperial oppression."[83]

Mmutle the trickster stories have implications for the reading of the Bible in Africa. They imply a reading from the side of the marginalized and the oppressed, a readiness to reconstruct the story from the point of view of survival and liberation. They demand Africans recognize they exist in the world as powerless among powerful nations. For this reason, they must remain wise, conscious of the possibility of being exploited and oppressed, yet engaged with the powerful, confident, and independent-minded and in solidarity with one another.

> The analysis of the Mmutle trickster discourse highlights four postures of reading for liberation. First, the vulnerable and oppressed should keep a permanent vigil toward the powerful and always watch out for their interests without fail. Second, the vulnerable and oppressed should

---

79. Musa W. Dube, "On Becoming a Change Agent: Journeys of Teaching Gender and Health in an African Crisis Context," *Journal for Interdisciplinary Biblical Studies* 21 (2020): 15.
80. Dube, "On Becoming a Change Agent," n7.
81. Dube, "On Becoming a Change Agent," 16.
82. Dube, "The Subaltern Can Speak," 68.
83. Musa W. Dube, "Boleo: A Postcolonial Feminist Reading," *HTS Teologiese Studies/Theological Studies* 76, no. 3 (2020): 3.

be willing to be in solidarity with other vulnerable and oppressed members of the society and to use teamwork. Third, sharp and transgressive thinking skills are vital weapons of resistance, survival, and liberation. Fourth, the Mmutle trickster philosophical framework demands skills of rewriting and redirecting a story toward new and unexpected ends in the service of resistance, survival, and liberation.[84]

Dube insists the colonized must remain to reposition their countries; they must persist to redress the injustices not only of the colonizers but also of those of the African leaders who have taken over the reins of power and continue oppressing their own people like the colonizers had done. "It also underlines the multiplicities of identities within each country and the importance of being able to recognize and live with the Other who is different within our boundaries."[85] These accord with the Ubuntu philosophy according to which Africans identify themselves in the other.[86]

Because the New Testament emerged in the setting of imperialism, feminist hermeneutics must be suspicious of imperialist hermeneutics that excludes colonialism and thus legitimize imperialism. Texts should be read to decipher how they present women, whether they are used as agents of subjugation and promoters of imperialism. This is important because "the use of female gender to describe the colonized serves the agendas of constructing hierarchical geographical spaces, races, and cultures, but it also comes to legitimate the oppression of women in societies where these narratives are used."[87] Their gendered roles should also be investigated no matter how highly placed in the imperialist ladder, like the pharaoh's and Pilate's wives. They remained "subject to male constructions in the maintenance of male power."[88] Dube insists that reading for decolonization entails noting that the consciousness of the imperialist setting of the biblical texts must be integrated into feminist hermeneutics of liberation. This way, the reality of the

---

84. Dube, "The Subaltern Can Speak," 54.
85. Musa W. Dube, "A Luta Continua: Toward Trickster Intellectuals and Communities," *Journal of Biblical Literature* 134, no. 4 (2015): 899.
86. Engelbert Mveng, "Impoverishment and Liberation: A Theological Approach for Africa and the Third World," in *Paths of African Theology*, ed. Rosino Gibellini (Orbis Books, 1994), 154–65; Augustine Shutte, " Ubuntu as the African Ethical Vision," in *African Ethics: An Anthology of Comparative and Applied Ethics*, ed. Munyaradzi Felix Murove (University of KwaZulu-Natal Press, 2009), 85–99.
87. Musa W. Dube, "Reading for Decolonization (John 4:1–42)," *Semeia* 75 (1996): 42.
88. Dube, "Toward A Post-Colonial Feminist Interpretation of the Bible," 20.

women of biblical religions belonging also to their traditional religions and cultures, which are suppressed by imperialism, will inform their practice of Christianity. They will form the bulwark of resistance against the destruction of their cultures, narratives, and values. "To read for decolonization, therefore, is to consciously resist the exploitative forces of imperialism, to affirm the denied differences, and to seek liberating ways of interdependence in our multi-cultural and post-colonial world."[89] It is also not enough to deconstruct imperialist constructions in biblical narratives; feminist decolonizing reading "must demonstrate awareness of imperialism as a persistent and exploitative force at a global scale, they must demonstrate a conscious adoption of resistance to imperialism, and they must struggle to map liberating ways of interdependence in our multi-cultural world."[90] Dube's is indeed a hermeneutics of suspicion toward the biblical text. Anything short of decolonization of biblical texts is tantamount to "maintain[ing] the imperial strategies of exploitation and subjugation and to hinder building the necessary 'political coalitions' among feminists of different cultures, nations, colors, classes, and sexuality."[91]

Since the society and religion is patriarchal, the Bible is gendered in favor of men, and the idea of God is constructed using male titles like "Shepherd, King, Lord, Mighty Warrior, Father, but hardly ever as Bakerwoman, Midwife, Mother, Friend." "Fortunately," Dube attests, "many Christian and non-Christian readers, communities and institutions agree that God is neither father nor mother. The use of the word 'father' only reflects a particular culture and time as well as the limitation of human language in representing God. Massive gender research, however, has shown that the metaphorical use of male language to represent realms of power does in fact reinforce the exclusion and subordination of women in society."[92] For this reason, she insists, women must name Christ themselves "beyond what is written in the Bible or what we have heard in our churches."[93] Christ, the liberator of the "culturally downtrodden," is the one women must embrace to free themselves from oppression today. Just as Jesus respected the Scriptures

---

89. Dube, "Toward A Post-Colonial Feminist Interpretation of the Bible," 21.
90. Dube, "Toward A Post-Colonial Feminist Interpretation of the Bible," 22.
91. Dube, "Toward A Post-Colonial Feminist Interpretation of the Bible," 22.
92. Musa W. Dube Shomanah, "Praying the Lord's Prayer in a Global Economic Era," *The Ecumenical Review* 49, no. 4 (1997): 444.
93. Musa W. Dube, "Who Do You Say That I Am?," *Feminist Theology* 15, no. 3 (2007): 347.

but rejected their oppressive use, so it is not acceptable to use the Bible to oppress women in the church or outside the church, to deny them positions both of power and of authority or any form of inclusion both in society and in the church or religion. Jesus is the healer of all gender injustices; he frees all the oppressed, including abused children, the lonely, maltreated and ignored elderly people, and women marginalized, disempowered, and robbed of "power of leadership, property ownership and decision-making [that] are largely in the hands of men,"[94] reduced to the lower class of simply bearing children, restricted from performing certain roles and being at certain places, and expected to bear different forms of oppression. Dube argues that gender roles are the result of the fall. Their grip is broken by the redemptive work of Christ.[95]

Dube laments that most biblical texts are written from the perspective of the fall. Hence, women are discriminated against and disempowered by their gender and reduced to the role of being mothers (female children are not mentioned, but only sons are given prominent place in the Bible). The gospel's depiction of Jesus, however, is a notable exception to the Bible's lopsided gender perception. Numerous passages evince his positive relationship with women, including with his mother (John 2:1–11; John 19:25–27), the woman at the well (John 4), the hunchbacked woman (Luke 13:10–17), the woman caught in the act of adultery (John 8:3–11), the woman with the issue of blood (Matt 9:20–22), an so on. Jesus's focus was liberative, affirmative, and healing. These stories, Dube argues, provide models of breaking gender injustice stereotypes. "From these examples it is clear that Jesus came to a world of gender imbalance, a world that sentenced many women to violence and to the disease of gender injustice. However, he undertook to announce liberation, to undermine gender inequality and to begin charting the path of gender justice. He sent women to preach, giving them public leadership roles: it causes them to leave their water-pots behind and to proclaim the word in public."[96] Jesus as healer and liberator demands radical restructuring of the laws, the ethics, and our ways of being a church to reflect "Christ, the one who empowers and sends women and men to go and preach the liberating gospel of Christ."[97] The implications demand rereading of the biblical texts in

---

94. Dube, "Who Do You Say That I Am?," 353.
95. Dube, "Who Do You Say That I Am?," 354.
96. Dube, "Who Do You Say That I Am?," 361.
97. Dube, "Who Do You Say That I Am?," 365.

the light of the goodness of creation, gender justice, and equality as humans created in the image and likeness of God (Gen 1:27).[98]

Dube's field work on women in leadership in churches, which had participants from mainline churches and the AICs, continues the theme of gender equality by chronicling the struggles of ordained women in the exercise of power among predominantly patriarchal churches. These women leaders recount their experiences of being dehumanized because church members expected their work to reflect that of men. Some leave their leadership positions in their churches to run charitable organizations because of their "negative experiences of discrimination."[99] One ordained woman, a deacon of the Lutheran Church, shared her experience of patriarchy embodied in the women she served. "As she says, 'Women seem to be their own oppressors. They are always fighting amongst themselves. When we are having a meeting, women will be jealous of one another, and they will choose a man. So, I usually sit down with them, trying to motivate them that they can do it without men, but time and again they go back to their habits.'"[100] This internalized perspective shows the scope of the difficulty women experience in churches due to the patriarchal, cultural interpretation of the Bible, an interpretation that is skewed against women. Women who founded their own churches and administer and minister in them navigate the written text's prescription for male gender ordination by claiming oral divine call through visions and dreams. They are called by God to their ministries. In the famous words of Bishop Virginia Lucas: "I always tell people that when God spoke to me through the Spirit, God never opened the Bible to me. Instead God's Spirit told me to begin a church and heal God's people, which is what I am doing."[101]

THE BIBLE AS A SITE OF POSTCOLONIAL CONTESTATION

Dube's hermeneutics of suspicion is anchored in postcolonial discourse. She depicts the pervasiveness of colonialism, independence, neocolonialism, globalization, and the AIDS epidemic as a continuous story of subjugation,

---

98. Musa W. Dube, "'And God Saw that it was Very Good': An Earth-Friendly Theatrical Reading of Genesis 1," *Black Theology* 13, no. 3 (2015): 230–46.
99. Musa W. Dube, "'God Never Opened the Bible to Me': Women Church Leaders in Botswana," *Studies in World Christianity & Interreligious Relations* 48 (2014): 322.
100. Dube, "'God Never Opened the Bible to Me,'" 324.
101. "'God Never Opened the Bible to Me,'" 318.

conquest, oppression, and appropriation of African lands, resources, and personnel for various imperial powers, to the detriment of Africa. African identity was distorted to sow seeds of endemic hate and ethnocentrism that later was responsible for genocidal killings that continue to divide Africans against themselves. Dube's feminist reading of the African story through "Mama Africa" is a quest for healing, a vision of an inculturated Christianity respectful of the autochthonocity of each cultural expression of religion. "Mama Africa is standing up. She is not talking. She is not asking. She is not offering any more money—for none is left. Mama Africa is coming behind Jesus. She is pushing through a strong human barricade of crowds. *Weak and still bleeding but determined, she is stretching out her hands. If only she can touch the garments of Jesus Christ.*"[102]

Using the prologue of John's Gospel, Dube plotted the difference between the powerful travelers who come and dominate their hosts, take their lands, and rule over them and the weak travelers who cannot go beyond their limited confines in foreign lands and who are always reminded of their status as foreigners. Her reference was to the white people who visited Africa, took over its lands, and colonized its peoples; and even after independence, they were begged to come back to rule and dominate Africa through trade. Dube identifies the word of John's prologue with the powerful traveler and John the Baptist as a symbol of the powerless travelers often subjugated by the powerful. The resistance against the powerful travelers are reminiscent of the resistances against colonialism, neocolonialism, and other forms of imperialism. One must not accept collaborating with the powerful travelers to be given power, as that would only make one inferior. She concludes and admonishes, "As readers of biblical texts, we are also invited to travel. Since travel remains central to our lives, nationally and internationally, biblical readers need to examine the power relations authorized by narratives and interpreters. Readers of biblical texts as fellow travelers may need to examine the journeys they undertake. Readers may need to take different paths, to plot new journeys, and to draw new maps and to establish new rules for travelling and hosting others."[103]

For Dube, it is impossible to read the Bible outside the prism of colonialism. She argues that the Bible is both a colonizing text as well as a postcolonial

---

102. Musa W. Dube Shomanah, "Fifty Years of Bleeding: A Storytelling Feminist Reading of Mark 5:24–43," *The Ecumenical Review* 51, no. 1 (1999): 17 (italicized in the original).

103. Shomanah, "Fifty Years of Bleeding," 88–89.

one. It is colonial because Christian religion has used the Bible to sponsor imperialism and authorize subjugation of nations and lands. It is a postcolonial book because the New Testament and some Hebrew texts were born in imperialist settings. According to Derek Alan Woodard-Lehman, who has studied Dube, "Stated directly, the Bible is a site of postcolonial contestation. That is, all readings (lay clerical, and/or academic) are biased for or against colonization even if these remain unconscious and unarticulated."[104] Because the Bible facilitated imperialism, Dube asks how it should be read by colonial subjects.[105] She focuses on the distortion of the languages of Africans by colonialism to make it serve not the people but the colonial administration and the Christian missionaries. She is referring to the politics of Bible translations and their use of words and meanings portrayed in their dictionaries.[106] "The Bible and dictionaries are treated together for they are closely interconnected: the dictionaries drew their vocabulary from the Setswana Bible. They were also produced by the same institution and personalities."[107] The Setswana Bible had translated the word *demon* with the Setswana word for ancestors, *Badimo*. The impression given is that African peoples had been worshipping demons prior to the coming of Christianity. Dube laments the devastating impact:

> The translation is a minefield planted in the Setswana cultural spaces, warning every Motswana Christian believer and reader of the Bible to stay away from the dangerous and deadly beliefs of Setswana. It marks boundaries and designates the Setswana cultures as a "dangerous, devil and death zone", to be avoided at all costs. The translation invites us, the Batswana biblical readers, to distance ourselves from *Badimo*, the demons, and to identify ourselves with Jesus, a Christian divine power. It achieves its aims through literary techniques of writing and characterization. The characterization maintains Jesus' holy role, but *Badimo* are given a new role, that of demons . . . Be that as it may, the Christian tradition hardly lost anything central to its faith in this translation,

---

104. Woodard-Lehman, "Through a Prism Darkly," 39.
105. Dube, *Postcolonial Feminist Interpretation of the Bible*, 4, 9.
106. For an in-depth analysis of the politics of Bible translation and postcolonial hermeneutics, see J. Kabamba, *Kiboko, Divining the Woman of Endor African Culture, Postcolonial Hermeneutics, and the Politics of Biblical Translation* (T&T Clark, 2017).
107. Musa W. Dube, "Consuming a Colonial Cultural Bomb: Translating Badimo into 'Demons' in the Setswana Bible (Matthew 8.28–34; 15.22; 10.8)," *Journal for the Study of the New Testament* 21, no. 73 (1999): 36.

while the Setswana tradition lost its very center. The translation is, therefore, a structural device of alienating natives from their cultures.[108]

One wonders about the distorting influence of such mistranslation in the minds of the ordinary reader who relies only on the Setswana Bible. A crisis of identity sets in because they will be torn between their cultural values and the Christian faith. Colonial textuality is designed to control the minds of the colonized and turn them, from the inside, against themselves and their values. "Their translations seized the symbols that are central institutions of Setswana cultures and equated them to the evil powers."[109] Dube recognizes the difference between colonial administration and the missionaries but insists they remained part of the colonizing adventure. The schools, hospitals, and trade centers established by the missionaries were structures aimed at establishing the commonwealth of global Christianity on the graves of indigenous cultures, to make room for European consciousness. Dube uses the AIC's resistance to such a colonial cultural bomb against the culture and life of Setswana as ideal. She emphasizes the successful efforts of the AIC to resist the colonization by incorporating the Bible as one of the tools of divination. "The Setswana Bible that was once used to champion the degradation of *Badimo*, became now one of the divining sets, used to get in touch with *Badimo* and Jesus among the AICs' Bible readers. This method of reading among the AICs resists the suppression of diversity and cultivates liberating interdependency between the Christian and Setswana world views."[110]

Dube argues that texts are written to capture the mind of the colonized, to present the colonizer as superior and as actually doing a good thing for the colonized. The decolonization of colonizing texts is an imperative that must be embarked upon by the colonized. They do so by rereading these texts and writing their own "new narratives that assert the adequacy of their humanity, the reality of global diversity, and their right to independence."[111] Dube did just that in her reading of Matthew's Gospel from the point of view of Batswana women belonging to the AICs, of the despised but assertive and independent African church women for whom "Moya is regarded as an ever-present and new word of God."[112] Dube highlighted four aspects of the AIC

---

108. Dube, "Consuming a Colonial Cultural Bomb," 41–42.
109. Dube, "Consuming a Colonial Cultural Bomb," 43.
110. Dube, "Consuming a Colonial Cultural Bomb," 58.
111. Dube, "Consuming a Colonial Cultural Bomb," 43.
112. Dube, "Readings of Semoya," 116.

women interpretation of the text of Jesus's encounter with the Canaanite woman in Matthew 15:21–28: "the framework of Semoya, the wisdom of a creative integration of different religious traditions, a feminist model of liberation, and healing as a political struggle."[113]

A Semoya reading is a framework that resists discrimination and promotes healing and freedom. The Semoya reading spotlights that it was the Spirit that led Jesus to the scene to meet with the Canaanite woman to heal her daughter. It does not interpret the Canaanite woman as an outsider but as part of the people of God for whom Jesus came. Jesus resisted and overcame the inclination to exclude others based on race. A Semoya framework of reading, thus, "is a reading that confronts a story that has been extensively used to justify imperial imposition and apartheid to articulate a reading that affirms liberating interdependence and healing between different races."[114] Their integration of various cultures and religions in their practice of Christianity as a result of their rejection of the imperial imposition of Christianity as the only true form of religion is an exercise in cross-cultural encounter that restores the dignity of African religious culture. It is not syncretism but a stepping stone to inculturated Christianity.

The Semoya strategy not only resists religious imperialism, but it also offers a feminist model of liberation because women can now lay claim to divine calling outside the often patriarchal-oriented word of God in the Bible.

> Through listening to the word of the Spirit, the AICs women offer a feminist strategy that breaks free from the patriarchal and canonical constraints of biblical traditions. It allows them to claim divine empowerment and leadership despite their gender. Moreover, this feminist model of reading is by no means ungodly or less biblical. It is biblically grounded, since such books as John provide for a direct dependence on the Spirit (Jn 14:26). It is also godly because it is guided and justified by whether the word of the Spirit empowers one with the responsibility to restore and enhance life through leadership and healing.[115]

The Semoya strategy is a postcolonial feminist liberative approach because it not only seeks the agency of women and gender justice, but it is also committed "to dismantling the structures of empire and colonialism."[116]

---

113. Dube, "Readings of Semoya," 123.
114. Dube, "Readings of Semoya," 125.
115. Dube, "Readings of Semoya," 126.
116. Dube, "Boleo," 3.

BIBLE READING IN AN HIV AND AIDS CONTEXT

Dube was the World Council of Churches' HIV/AIDS theological consultant for the region of Africa. She organized several conferences, edited books, wrote articles, and engaged in distance tutorials to direct the church's responses to the HIV/AIDS pandemic and to reorient biblical hermeneutics of HIV/AIDS, which is one of the contexts of African biblical hermeneutics. HIV and AIDS were products of the oppression that threw many people, especially women, into poverty, a situation exacerbated by gender injustice that made women into objects rather than subjects. And so, Dube described HIV/AIDS as "a disease of social injustice."[117] Even though primarily a medical issue, HIV/AIDS became a moral issue when it became perceived as divine punishment for sexual immorality because it spread initially among gay partners and sex workers. It later assumed a psychological dimension when the victims were stigmatized and their dignity as human beings was questioned as a result.

The rash of theories about the "cure" complicated an already tense situation as flurries of rape and abuse mounted, leaving mothers fearful of leaving their daughters, even with their fathers and relatives. It spread to the majority of the world, the Two-Thirds World, and among the youths, the poor, the socially marginalized, the migrants, and so on.[118] The disease became a symbol of the relationship between the colonized and the colonizer. Hence, it became a postcolonial issue as well. "Consequently in the 1990s it had become undeniable that HIV and AIDS was a medical issue as it was a social justice issue. It became evident that it is about individual morality as it is about the structural morality of our institutions, our relationships, our histories; indeed our whole world. It was as physical as it was psychological."[119]

The initial biblical interpretations of HIV/AIDS led to stigmatizations as the texts used invoked divine punishments on victims. Dube, alongside other biblical scholars like Gerald O. West,[120] recommend reading with people living with AIDS (PLWHA) as a biblical hermeneutics, to break the stigma and discrimination and to build compassionate communities.[121] Such readings insist on exposing structural oppression as the leading cause of situations that

---

117. Musa W. Dube, "Go Tla Slama. O Tla Fola: Doing Biblical Studies in an HIV and AIDS Context," *Black Theology* 8, no. 2 (2010): 212.
118. Dube, "Go Tla Slama," 218.
119. Dube, "Go Tla Slama," 219.
120. West, "(Ac)claiming the (Extra)ordinary African 'Reader' of the Bible," 29–47.
121. Dube, "Go Tla Slama," 230.

inflict hardship and poverty on people, leaving them (especially women) with no option but to sell the only thing they have, which is sex.[122] Dube observes:

> The experience of the HIV and AIDS epidemic has been an apocalyptic text, revealing multiple ethical fractures in social structures and institutions, thus underlining the imperative for birthing new ethics, theology, church, nations, and world. The dominance of HIV and AIDS in the African continent gives the African church the identity of an HIV and AIDS positive church, an identity that implicates the whole church worldwide. The ecumenical theology and ethics of an HIV positive church is characterized by a listening, vulnerable, healing, compassionate, woman and child-friendly church that remembers those who died of AIDS and lives positively in the resurrection agenda of birthing and nurturing just societies.[123]

An HIV-positive church demands a compassionate response and hence must be, according to Ezra Chitando, "an HIV competent church."[124] Such a church identifies with the vulnerabilities of not only PLWHA but with everyone's vulnerability, and as such, it acknowledges that we all are HIV positive, considering our vulnerabilities. Dube proclaims that the church has HIV.[125] And so the major theological challenge for Christians is to recognize the face of Jesus in every individual with HIV/AIDS, in the light of Paul's statement in 1 Corinthians 12: 12–27 to the effect that if one member of the body suffers, all members suffer.[126] And so, all are called to practice the mission of care central to the gospel (Mark 10: 13–16, Matt 19: 13–15, 25). Thus, "an HIV positive church accepts that harsh light that has fallen upon its eyes—highlighting that its structures, institutions, policies, theologies, and ethics are based on faulty and sinful foundations that betray the quality of life on God's Earth."[127]

---

122. Musa W. Dube, "Twenty-Two Years of Bleeding and Still the Princess Sings!" in *Grant Me Justice!*, ed. Musa W. Dube and Musimbi Kanyoro (Cluster Publications, 2004), 186–200.

123. Musa W. Dube, "Let There Be Light! Birthing Ecumenical Theology in the HIV and AIDS Apocalypse," *The Ecumenical Review* 67, no. 4 (2015): 531.

124. Ezra Chitando, *Living with Hope: African Churches and HIV and AIDS*, vol. 1 (WCC, 2007), cited in Dube, "Let There Be Light!," 537.

125. Musa W. Dube, "Theological Challenges: Proclaiming the Fullness of Life in the HIV/AIDS & Global Economic Era," *International Review of Missions* 91, no. 363 (2002): 539.

126. Dube, "Theological Challenges," 539.

127. Dube, "Let There Be Light!," 539.

Such a church knows it has to work for holistic liberation, a total overhaul of structures of societies that keep people poor, oppressed, excluded, hungry, and in penury, if it is to beat the deadly virus. Such a church knows it cannot sacrifice gender justice at the altar of patriarchy and masculinity. The HIV-positive church can only remain a prophetic church if it perpetually searches for healing in solidarity with others.

TERESA OKURE'S CONTEXTUAL BIBLICAL HERMENEUTICS

New Testament scholar Teresa Okure specializes in appropriating the Bible in a variety of contexts for the purpose of liberation from forces of oppression, gender inequality, race, and sexism and for the suggestion of a proper ecclesiology for Africa. On the question of where to find the truth of Scripture, Okure outrightly answers, "Clearly, our cultures influence our reading and shape our understanding of the Bible. In Scripture God's word is communicated in limited and at times archaic human language and idioms, with all their inevitable cultural moorings, and we hear that word through the lens of a particular culture and life context."[128] Okure contends that the Bible is a community book, and as such, it disavows private interpretation (2 Pet. 1:19–21) and favors intercultural interpretation. "We need to read together to be able to help one another see with new eyes; what our cultures may blind us from seeing, people from other cultures can help us to see more clearly in the light of the gospel."[129] This simply means that the Scriptures, because they are cultural texts, are spoken and heard in every language and culture. There is no other way of receiving the words of Scripture, given that to be human is to be cultural. Culture can be seen as "the DNA or inalienable, distinctive character and stamp of a given people."[130] It also means that we must transcend the limitations of our cultures in reading, interpreting, or translating the Bible. "We need the transcendence of the gospel to help us get out of these cultural ghettos."[131]

---

128. Teresa Okure, SHCJ, "What Is Truth?," *Anglican Theological Review* 93, no. 3 (2011): 405.

129. Okure, "What Is Truth?,", 405–6.

130. Teresa Okure, SHCJ, "Africa: Globalization and the Loss of Cultural Identity," in *Globalization and Its Victims*, ed. Jon Sobrino and Felix Wilfred, *Concilium* 2001/5 (SCM Press, 2001), 67.

131. Okure, "What Is Truth?," 407.

One such ghetto is that of not recognizing the need to use inclusive language in translations of texts of Scripture. This reluctance goes to the heart of patriarchy and gender injustice that marginalizes women in Scripture, in theology, and in self-understanding as members of a community of believers, as the body of Christ.

> We want to reject a culture that excludes and marginalizes people on the basis of race, color, language, religion, class, and their God-given sex, when God has included them in Christ and in the divine self. A culture of "me, myself, and I" (the false trinity), a culture in which God has to be grateful to me, a culture in which money is everything, a culture in which God has been reduced to our disciple and in which we check in or check out, pick and choose from God's injunctions as it suits us—you and I are the ones to confront that culture, with its shopping mall-inspired mentality, so that the gospel can be proclaimed, and can liberate everybody the way it wants, for our sole good.[132]

Okure delves into the relationship between exegesis and hermeneutics. She raises the questions of whether they are the same, in what areas they are different, and how both are harmonized. Dismissing the claim often made by white male theology to universality, objectivity, and all-inclusiveness, which has been exposed by Global South and women theologians to be a lie, Okure points to the contextuality and subjectivity of all interpretations.[133] "In view of this, not only is the claim to pure interpretation or pure chronicle out of the question, one cannot help interpreting every situation in life on a daily basis... This applies to method as well as to content. Open admission of this natural limitation invites us to explore its implications for our personal and communal readings of the Bible in our diverse socio-cultural locations."[134] This is equally true of the Bible, which has also been described contextually from the Western civilizational perspective as "cultural heritage."[135] It is also the same for other contexts. Texts, including biblical texts, are received in the light of their historical contexts, the readers' cultural contexts, denominational

---

132. Okure, "What Is Truth?," 413.
133. Teresa Okure, SHCJ, "'I will open my mouth in parables' (Matt 15.55): A Case for a Gospel-Based Biblical Hermeneutics," *New Testament Studies* 46, no. 3 (2000): 445–63.
134. Okure, "'I will open my mouth in parables,'" 449.
135. Wim Beuken et al., eds., *The Bible and Its Readers*, Concilium 1995/1 (SCM Press, 1991).

creedal beliefs, education, specialty, training, experiences, and ideological leanings. In other words, in biblical interpretation, a lot depends on whose desk the interpretation falls or on the presuppositions of the person interpreting the text.

> If the text falls on the mind of a fundamentalist, it will be cut from its cultural and historical moorings, and fitted into the interpreter's religio-cultural straitjacket . . . If the text falls on the desk of a historical-critical scholar eager to discern its prehistory, it will be dismembered, rearranged chapter and verse (as in the classic case of John 5, 6, 7), and relocated historically and theologically in hypothetical contexts. The text's place in the canon may be affected. If the text falls on the mind of a scholar with a genius for inventing detective stories, it will be "historically" situated in very "highly imaginative" and "daringly bold" social locations, with hardly any substantial evidence to support the "historical" reconstructions. A "benediction" may then become a "curse", or "red herring" for a gospel of life. The text then loses its own voice, identity and right to be heard on its own terms and becomes subject to the scholar's reigning theories . . . If the text falls on the heart of a committed disciple, it will be received with enlightened faith and Christological humility. That disciple will read and submit self to be read by the text. His/her entire life will form the fertile soil in which the word grows and bears lasting fruit: now thirty-, now sixty- and now a hundredfold. That disciple will not think that he/she has definitively understood or given a final response to the word, or see his/her localised response as normative for all disciples in their own locations.[136]

Okure thinks what most do in reading the Bible is hermeneutics—that is, giving meaning in new contexts to past events. "To be technically an exegete, one has to be an eyewitness. NT Christians were strict on this, and therefore on who could qualify as an eyewitness reporter."[137] This is all the more true since what is prevalent in New Testament scholarship is "not a reporting on the extant text, but a tearing apart of these texts in search of their pre-literary forms."[138] She doubles down, citing E. E. Elis in *International Bible*

---

136. Okure, "'I will open my mouth in parables,'" 449–50.
137. Okure, "'I will open my mouth in parables,'" 451.
138. Okure, "'I will open my mouth in parables,'" 450.

Commentary, "All scripture is interpretation or hermeneutics where life issues hold the key to new insights for each generation. The history of interpretation within scripture and of patristic exegesis testifies to this."[139]

Okure regrets the division within biblical scholarship into three unrelated areas: biblical science, biblical studies, and biblical theology. She accuses biblical scholarship of becoming "the chief bearer of separation, if not of the secularisation of biblical interpretation itself. As a result biblical criticism has been largely like the barren fig tree, full of leaves, season after season, but with little or no fruit to nourish God's people hungry for the word of life."[140] She suggests biblical scholars adopt the example of Jesus, who knows the Scripture well but begins with the life of ordinary people and their needs and places the Scripture "at the service of life, his own and that of the people (cf. Luke 24.12-27), and life questions gave him the hermeneutical key for interpreting the scriptures anew."[141] Hence her call for a "gospel-based biblical hermeneutics" characterized by respect for the ancient authors of the biblical texts, grounded in contemporary life, and centered on the life and person of Jesus.[142] She emphasizes the need to relate hermeneutics to life situations and stories for proper interpretation of the Bible and its relevance to life. "NT scholarship needs to promote a parabolic method of reading that encourages placing one's stories alongside the gospel stories. This awareness invites us to mine our total, human reality as resources for understanding the gospel for our own time."[143]

Whatever method used in interpretation must not be conceived as universal, applicable to everyone, because people of other cultures and contexts relate their meaning-making process and life situations to the Bible and come up with alternative methodologies suitable to their life questions. "Equally, people whose socio-cultural locations differ from ours will see the same text differently. No reading in any age or context exhausts the possibilities of meaning of a given text."[144] Finally, Okure concludes and takes position on biblical hermeneutics centered on attending to varieties of contexts:

> No reading is value free or context free. Equally no reading is purpose free and effect free. Each exegetical hermeneut needs to honestly

---

139. Okure, "'I will open my mouth in parables,'" 451.
140. Okure, "'I will open my mouth in parables,'" 454.
141. Okure, "'I will open my mouth in parables,'" 459.
142. Okure, "'I will open my mouth in parables,'" 461.
143. Okure, "'I will open my mouth in parables,'" 461.
144. Okure, "'I will open my mouth in parables,'" 461.

discern why he or she reads, for as we perceive the biblical texts, so we derive meaning from them. Perhaps only when we learn to read from the context of our lives, to meet our challenges of discipleship, will we fully understand or reap the fruit of God's gospel and experience it as God's power to mend our broken lives and world.[145]

In her writings, Okure makes conscious effort to relate the Scripture to various life situations and contexts. She locates the theme of reconciliation in the complex world of diversity,[146] highlights the use of the Bible in *Laudato si'*,[147] advances conversion and commitment in Africa,[148] and reiterates the importance of spirituality in biblical hermeneutics,[149] all centered in an all-inclusive Christology amenable to the religiously pluralistic world.[150]

FEMINIST HERMENEUTICS

In "Jesus and the Samaritan Woman (Jn 4:1–42) in Africa," Okure brings out the marginality and subsequent rejection of Jesus by his Judean people (because he came from Galilee, a town despised as not fit for anything good) and the racial prejudice and hatred of the woman because she is a Samaritan, as well as her marginalization simply because she is a woman.[151]

Jesus and the Samaritan woman "share the experience of rejection, prejudice, and isolation."[152] But Jesus enabled her "to transcend the barriers of prejudice and the stigmas of racism and sexism, and to know and accept God's free gift in himself, who offers to all who believe in him salvation,

---

145. Okure, "'I will open my mouth in parables,'" 463.
146. Teresa Okure, SHCJ, "'The Ministry of Reconciliation' (2 Cor 5:14–21): Paul's Key to the Problem of 'the Other' in Corinth," *Mission Studies* 23, no. 1 (2006): 105–21.
147. Teresa Okure, SHCJ, "The Use of Scripture in *Laudato Si'*," *Grace & Truth* 37, no. 1 (2021): 6–15.
148. Teresa Okure, SHCJ, "Conversion, Commitment: An African Perspective," *Mission Studies* 10, nos. 1–2 (1993): 109–33.
149. Teresa Okure, SHCJ, "The Life-Giving Spirituality of the Syro-Phoenician Woman (Matt 15:21–28 and Mark 7:24–30)," *Grace & Truth* 37, no. 2 (2021): 40–51.
150. Teresa Okure, SHCJ, "'In Him All Things Hold Together': A Missiological Reading of Colossians 1:15–20," *International Review of Mission* 91, no. 360 (2002): 62–72.
151. Okure, "Jesus and the Samaritan Woman," 407.
152. Okure, "Jesus and the Samaritan Woman," 409.

'living water,' and the Holy Spirit (4:7–10; 7:37–39)."[153] Okure draws attention to the gender inequality in people's assessment of women in relation to men. "Nothing is said about the sixth man who is not her husband, though it is worth noting that in cases of sexual immorality, the woman is always at fault (see Jn 8:1–11)."[154] She regrets the misinterpretation of mission as specifically reserved for men, with the excuse that Jesus did not send women. This erroneous and one-sided perception of mission forgets that Mary Magdalene, a woman, was the first person Jesus appeared to after the resurrection. "In the church, the commissioning has been tied to apostleship. This has been seen as the sole prerogative of men, since it is argued that Jesus did not choose women among his twelve apostles. Apostleship itself has been defined primarily in terms of governing, ruling and teaching. Women have been excluded from these activities, and divine intention has been cited to justify the practice (cf. I Tim. 2:11–12; I Cor. 14:33–36)."[155]

In Africa, women are excluded from church leadership and suffer other forms of inequality coupled with injustices and marginalization facing Africans, including the discriminations caused by ethnicity among Africans. "On the global scene, both in the church and in society, Africans have only to appear and their color disqualifies them—'Can anything good come from Africa?' Discriminations based on sex and class, though not peculiar to Africans, take a distinctive twist where Africans are concerned."[156] The passages call attention not only to ecclesiology, missiology, ecumenism, dialogue, and inculturation of the gospel in Africa but also to changes in attitudes to women in church, from derogatory disregard toward celebration of their gifts, for their good as persons, and for the good of all.[157] Particularly, there is the mere tokenism offered to women just to save face: "The attitude of the hierarchical church, which continues to legislate for the exclusion and silencing of women or gives them only token considerations that are subject to the 'sensitivity of the faithful' in any local church, is antigospel and anti-Christos."[158] The call for reconsideration of what it means to be a church despite the theme

---

153. Okure, "Jesus and the Samaritan Woman," 409.
154. Okure, "Jesus and the Samaritan Woman," 408.
155. Teresa Okure, SHCJ, "The Significance Today of Jesus' Commission to Mary Magdalene," *International Review of Mission* 81, no. 322 (1992): 178.
156. Okure, "Jesus and the Samaritan Woman," 411.
157. Okure, "Jesus and the Samaritan Woman," 415.
158. Okure, "Jesus and the Samaritan Woman," 416n24.

of the synod of Africa, *Ecclesia in Africa*[159] and *Africae Munus*,[160] is a result of the continuing prevalence of patriarchy in the ways of being a church in Africa. Women theologians in Africa identify this "as an anti-gospel reality that has entrenched itself in the life of the Church as it has in society, in its organization as well as its liturgical life."[161]

CONCLUSION

We have argued that African scholars trained as biblical scholars focus on contextual interpretation of Scripture. They hold that contextuality is central because the Bible is a cultural heritage appropriated according to the cultural framework and is relevant to people's various life situations. Contextual hermeneutics applies to the diverse forms and methodologies of inculturation and liberation motif interpretations of the Bible. It includes colonial, postcolonial, feminist/womanist, as well as ordinary people readings of the Bible. Justin S. Ukpong favors inculturation hermeneutics while recognizing feminist and ordinary people's hermeneutics. His hermeneutics equally segues to the liberation hermeneutics since inculturation aims at autochthonocity and social, political, and economic transformations of society. Gerald O. West focuses on reading with and for ordinary people—that is, the nonspecialist readers of the Bible. His writings and the workshops he facilitates are not so much education of ordinary readers as they enable people to respond adequately to the religious questions they have because of the oppressions, segregation, and sufferings they undergo, especially in South Africa under the apartheid regime. West recognizes the importance of scientific study of the Bible but cautions against its possible nonacceptance of the Bible as the word of God. He also promotes the feminist hermeneutics and agrees with Musa Dube that HIV/AIDS is a social justice issue.

---

159. Pope John Paul II, *Post-Synodal Apostolic Exhortation Ecclesia in Africa*, accessed April 4, 2024, https://www.vatican.va/content/john-paul-ii/en/apost_exhortations/documents/hf_jp-ii_exh_14091995_ecclesia-in-africa.html.

160. Pope Benedict XVI, *Post-Synodal Apostolic Exhortation Africae Munus*, accessed April 20, 2024, https://www.vatican.va/content/benedict-xvi/en/apost_exhortations/documents/hf_ben-xvi_exh_20111119_africae-munus.html.

161. Teresa Okure, SHCJ, "Guest Editorial: Ecclesiology in Africa," *International Journal for the Study of the Christian Church* 8, no. 4 (2008): 272.

Dube concentrates on feminist, colonial, and postcolonial hermeneutics. Her hermeneutics of suspicion demands rereading the Bible to expose the influences of patriarchal culture and power dynamics skewed against women, which are still perpetuated in churches and societies that marginalize and exclude women in many and in various ways. She moves for the decolonization of the Bible from Western accretions promoting Western imperialism and undermining African cultural values as well as impeding the appropriation of Christianity in local African cultures. Dube's contextual biblical hermeneutics equally emphasizes reading the Bible within the context of HIV/AIDS, a disease she says spreads more among the poor and women because of the structures of society that exclude many in favor of a few. HIV/AIDS is therefore a social justice issue that must be addressed by measures aimed at engendering gender justice, bridging the rich/poor divide, and employing a Christic biblical hermeneutics that follows the liberative example of Jesus toward all.

Teresa Okure's contextual hermeneutics highlights and problematizes the arrogance of the historical-critical method's claim to neutrality, objectivity, and universality and as the only genuine appropriate biblical hermeneutics. While recognizing its contribution in liberating biblical scholarship from dogmatic exegesis and the excesses of allegorical exegesis, Okure condemns the fissure historical criticism created in biblical scholarship. Contrary to the abstractness of historical criticism and its being out of touch with reality, she insists that the reader's sociocultural location and perspective affect not only interpretation but the text itself. She contends that every interpretation is hermeneutical and not exegetical because the events being interpreted are two thousand years removed from every interpretation. For this reason, Okure calls for a radical review of biblical, especially New Testament, methodologies that would integrate exegesis into hermeneutics, what she calls "exegetical hermeneutics," that emphasize hermeneutics and place exegesis at its service. Exegesis would then become a faith-filled scholarly activity that would reveal the meaning of extant texts in their own contexts, using every available concrete resource. Okure's contextual hermeneutics is also liberative, with emphasis on gender justice in church and society.

The contextual hermeneutics of African biblical scholars recognizes the validity of the scientific diachronic historical criticism with its emphasis on the original context of the biblical texts. They just do not limit "context" only to the extant texts of the Bible. Context includes the sociocultural location of the interpreter or the reader of the text. Context equally incorporates the contemporary contexts within which the text is read and applied. Because of the polyvalence of contexts—those of the texts, of the reader, and of the appropriation and application of the texts—the academic reading of the Bible by African biblical scholars also recognizes the ordinary readers of the Bible as members of the community of readers or interpreters, as their readings point to the life situations within which the Bible is relevant and applicable. Ordinary people's reading needs the expertise and skill of the academic readers of the Bible to grasp the riddles of life and to bring to action various strategies for gender and social justice, cultural revival, and social transformation. In the same way, the academic readers of the Bible need the experience of the ordinary readers to recognize the importance of the variety of contexts within which the Bible is interpreted.

The question remains one of the relations of the diachronic and the synchronic reading of the Bible and the future of Bible reading in Africa. Does reading the Bible through African eyes compare with the position of Vatican Council II and the Catholic teaching on the interpretation of the Bible in the church? In what way or ways could African reading of the Bible impact biblical interpretation? What needs to change in African reading of the Bible in the light of the teaching of the church and Christianity? These questions we leave to subsequent chapters on the ecclesiological foundation of biblical interpretation and the future of reading the Bible through African eyes.

CHAPTER FIVE

Ecclesiological Foundations of Biblical Interpretation

INTRODUCTION

Ordinary African reading of the Bible and the academic reading by African biblical scholars are both enabled and constrained by various Christian denominations' official statements on biblical interpretation. Ordinary readers rely on what they learn from their churches, schools, seminaries, institutions, education, and organizations they belong to. Most recognize the Bible primarily as Scripture, as the word of God, as revealing God. The authority of the Bible is dependent on its inspiration; it is trusted as leading to the truth, to God. Most ordinary readers open themselves to the Bible as a divine instrument, not only to guide their actions but also to cure and to liberate them from suffering and pain. The Bible is the book of life through which human beings communicate with God in prayer. African biblical scholars agree that the Bible witnesses God's revelation. African academic readings presuppose the official positions of their traditions on biblical interpretation. They problematize the inadequacies of these ecclesial positions with their emphasis on contextual hermeneutics.

This chapter investigates the developments in African Christian hermeneutics, especially African Catholic hermeneutics, in the light of Vatican II's Dogmatic Constitution on Divine Revelation, *Dei Verbum*, and the Pontifical Biblical Commission's *The Interpretation of the Bible in the Church*. It lays out the presuppositions of African biblical scholarship and ordinary person's reading to the extent that they have been educated through their denominations. Reading the Bible through African eyes is not exotic. It is not some strange excursion outside the framework of other Christian hermeneutics. The uniqueness of African reading lies in the distinctiveness of the sociocultural contextual framework in which it occurs. This chapter focuses on some of the difficult demands of *Dei Verbum*, especially on the appropriate interpretation of Scripture that holds together in tension the context of scriptural texts and their relevance for Christian life. It emphasizes the complementarity of historical criticism and theological interpretation of Scripture, in relation to the variety of viewpoints on biblical interpretation, with particular focus on African ordinary readers and the academic reading by African biblical scholars.

DOGMATIC CONSTITUTION ON DIVINE REVELATION (*DEI VERBUM*)

One of the most remarkable achievements of Vatican II is the constitution on the word of God, *Dei Verbum* (*DV*). In it, the council fathers fulfilled their intent to anchor church teachings on Scripture. Not surprisingly, it is also one of the most received of the documents of Vatican II.[1] Robert Murray says that it is "the most theologically concentrated" of the four major constitutions (on the liturgy, the church, divine revelation, and on the modern world) "but in its wider relevance it both undergirds and touches most of the Council documents."[2] What most people like about it, and which is revolutionary of the Catholic conception of revelation, was the shift away from propositional view of revelation to a personal one in which Christ is rightly understood as "a divine human being, not a set of bullet points."[3] It states:

> In His goodness and wisdom God chose to reveal Himself and to make known to us the hidden purpose of His will (see Eph. 1:9) by which

---

1. Anthony Towey, "*Dei Verbum*: Fit for Purpose?" *New Blackfriars* 90, no. 1026 (2009): 206–18. Towey observed that *Dei Verbum* is "arguably one of the most well received of the documents of Vatican II" (p. 206). See also Richard J. Clifford, "The Achievements and Challenges of Vatican II on Scripture: The Gift of the Word," *America* 209, no. 14 (2013): 14–19.

2. Michael Barnes, SJ, "Opening Up a Dialogue: *Dei Verbum* and the Religions," *Modern Theology* 29, no. 4 (2013): 12.

3. Towey, "*Dei Verbum*?," 12.

through Christ, the Word made flesh, man might in the Holy Spirit have access to the Father and come to share in the divine nature (see Eph. 2:18; 2 Peter 1:4). Through this revelation, therefore, the invisible God (see Col. 1;15, 1 Tim. 1:17) out of the abundance of His love speaks to men as friends (see Ex. 33:11; John 15:14–15) and lives among them (see Bar. 3:38), so that He may invite and take them into fellowship with Himself. (*DV #2*)

Dei Verbum reechoes the divine and the human authorship of Scripture with its implication of inspiration and inerrancy regarding salvific intention (*DV #11*) and charged biblical exegetes to engage both the divine and the human in biblical interpretation.[4] That is, the interpretation of Scripture should not emphasize the human critical element without acknowledging the divine authorship that makes the Scripture possible in the first place. Specifically, the critical study of the Bible should be conscious of authorial intention (*DV #12*). In addition, biblical exegetes must not forget that the Bible is the word of God in human language (*DV #13*). Thus, *Dei Verbum* emphasizes the unity of Scripture. That is, even though the Bible is a collection of writings, it is the one God who is responsible for inspiring the human authors. While historical biblical critical approaches oversee the human level of Scripture, the spiritual sense of Scripture remains important since the Bible is the book of God's self-revelation in history, for which reason we identify Scripture as the Word of God. The goal of Scripture is to pass on the message of God's revelation and salvation to humankind, to deepen the God-human relationship. The unity of Scripture equally implies the unity of the Old and the New Testaments as well as the tradition as Scripture (*DV #9*).

Finally, *Dei Verbum* examines the sacred Scripture in the life of the church. First, the word of God has been part and parcel of the life of the

---

4. This position is shared by other Christian denominations, such as the Orthodox and Protestant (Baptists). Myk Habets rightly expressed the lopsidedness of emphasizing either the divine or the human authorship above the other: "Where Scripture is treated exclusively as a divine work, it takes on a Docetic stamp and is read in woodenly literal ways; this is a significant critique of classic Dispensationalism. Where the human involvement in the writing of Scripture is overly emphasized, an Ebionite approach to the Bible results; this is a significant critique of classically liberal Christianity. According to classic Christianity—Catholic, Orthodox and Protestant—both Divine and human authorship need to be acknowledged adequately in rightly interpreting God's Word." Myk Habets, "Theological Interpretation of Scripture," *International Journal of Systematic Theology* 23, no. 2 (2021): 236.

church, in the liturgy and other devotional practices, for "the spiritual nourishment of the members of the people of God, the source for them of a life of faith, of hope and of love—and indeed a light for all humanity."[5] Second, it approves measures to disseminate the Bible through translations into various languages. All are enjoined to read the Scripture for "ignorance of Scripture is ignorance of Christ" (*DV* #25).[6] Third, the Scripture is the soul of sacred theology. Hence, "sacred theology rests on the written word of God, together with sacred tradition, as its primary and perpetual foundation" (*DV* #24).[7]

INTERPRETATION OF THE BIBLE IN THE CHURCH

The Pontifical Biblical Commission, in its document *The Interpretation of the Bible in the Church (1993)* (*IBC*),[8] reaffirmed the human and divine authorship of the Bible. The first of the twenty principles of Catholic biblical interpretation states: "Sacred Scripture is the word of God expressed in human language. The thought and the words belong at one and the same time both to God and to human beings in such a way that the whole Bible comes at once from God and from the inspired human authors."[9] Because the Bible is the work of human authors, it can be read like any other ancient text. And for this reason, the *IBC* endorses the use of historical criticism and other tools of science, including the use of philosophical hermeneutics, philologies, literary methods, analysis, rhetoric and semiotics, that help determine the presuppositions of the interpreter, which is subjective; the object of interpretation,

---

5. Pontifical Biblical Commission, *The Interpretation of the Bible in the Church* (henceforth *IBC*), March 18, 1994, https://archive.org/details/InterpretationOfTheBible/mode/2up?view=theater. See *Dei Verbum* #21.

6. This quotation is drawn from the Second Council of Orange and referenced in the First Vatican Council, Second Council of Orange, Canon 7: Denzinger 180 (377); First Vatican Council, Second Council of Orange, Canon 7: Denzinger 1791 (3010). See also Heinrich Denzinger, ed., *Compendium of Creeds, Definitions, and Declarations on Matters of Faith and Morals*, 43rd ed. (Ignatius Press, 2012).

7. *IBC*, 1.

8. Pontifical Biblical Commission, *The Interpretation of the Bible in the Church (1993)*, The Holy See, https://www.vatican.va/roman_curia/congregations/cfaith/pcb_documents/rc_con_cfaith_doc_19930415_interpretazione_sw.html.

9. Peter S. Williamson, "Catholic Principles for Interpreting Scripture," *The Catholic Biblical Quarterly* 65, no. 3 (2003): 332 (italicized in the original). Williamson constructed the principles from his analysis of the *IBC*.

what the human author intended; and the plurality of meanings, including meanings beyond the historical context of the text.

However, it is mindful of the possible dangers of this method, especially excluding the divine component of Scripture. "The search for the original can lead to putting the word back into the past completely so that it is no longer taken in its actuality. It can result that only the human dimension of the word appears as real, while the genuine author, God, is removed from the reach of a method which was established for understanding human reality."[10] Hence it warns that historicism and historical positivism must be avoided. Historicism limits biblical texts merely to their original contexts, while historical positivism opts rather for "objective" methods and sources that discount religious faith, which it considers biased. Scattered in the *IBC* are various descriptions of the use of the historical-critical method, which Peter S. Williamson brought together as the fifteenth principle:[11]

> The historical-critical method is the indispensable tool of scientific exegesis to ascertain the literal sense of a text in a diachronic manner. In order for this task to be completed, it must include a synchronic study of the final form of the text, which is the expression of the word of God. The historical-critical method can and must be used without philosophical presuppositions contrary to Christian faith. Despite its importance, the historical-critical method cannot be granted a monopoly, and exegetes must be conscious of its limits. Exegetes must recognize the dynamic aspect of meaning and the possibility that meaning can continue to develop.[12]

This position of the *IBC* is affirmed by Richard Simon. As articulated by James A. Sanders, "Richard Simon had said that while he agreed with Spinoza that original moments were important in discerning the truth about Scripture,

---

10. Pontifical Biblical Commission, *The Interpretation of the Bible in the Church*, CatholicFidelity.com, accessed December 29, 2023, https://www.catholicfidelity.com/apologetics-topics/bible/the-interpretation-of-the-bible-in-the-church-by-the-pontifical-biblical-commission-to-pope-john-paul-ii/.
11. It is important to note Joseph Fitzymer's view of Williamson's work, which he praised as successful, noting that it "succeeds well . . . as a whole in identifying, describing, and discussing the twenty principles of the Catholic interpretation of the Bible which are found in the 1993 document of the Biblical Commission." Joseph A. Fitzymer, "Catholic Principles for Interpreting Scripture: A Study of the Pontifical Biblical Commission's *The Interpretation of the Bible in the Church*," *Biblica* 83, no. 3 (2002): 437.
12. Williamson, "Catholic Principles for Interpreting Scripture," 343 (italicized in the original).

the work of the Holy Spirit was also important all along the formative path of Scripture through to closure, precisely because God has never withdrawn the authority he gave Moses and the Elders in the first place."[13]

Pope John Paul II articulated this truth about Scripture in his address during the reception of the *IBC* thus: "Indeed, [the true meaning of the Scriptures] is inseparable from their goal, which is to put believers into a personal relationship with God."[14] For this reason, the basic question and the criteria for evaluating interpretations of Scripture texts should be on whether "the given interpretation reveal the meaning of a text as the word of God for Christian faith."[15] In doing this, *Dei Verbum* and other Catholic statements on biblical interpretation expect biblical exegetes to listen to the magisterium of the church.

Since the Bible is the word of God, attention must also be paid to the faith experience of the readers of Scripture that the text provokes. Biblical exegetes have tended to focus only on the text and the text's human authors rather than on the religious experience of the readers to whom the text was written. Renowned American biblical scholar William K. Kurz, SJ, points to this discrepancy in the interpretation of the Bible skewed against the revelation of Scripture manifest in the biblical scholars' disregard of the twofold nature of Scripture in the practice of biblical interpretation. The focus, he states, has been more on "what the sacred writers actually intended," disregarding "what God wanted to manifest by means of their words."[16]

> Methodologically, contemporary critical approaches to scripture are directed primarily if not exclusively toward understanding the Bible on the human level. Because of this focus on only the human level, not enough attention has been given to a more basic root problem at the level of faith and of metaphysical presuppositions about the nature of the Bible. Since the Enlightenment, both modernistic and now post-modernistic underpinnings of critical approaches to Scripture have been averse to beliefs and to metaphysical presuppositions that the Bible is in actual reality the Word of God written in human words.[17]

---

13. James A. Sanders, "Scripture as Canon for Post-Modern Times," *Biblical Theology Bulletin* 25, no. 2 (1995): 61.
14. Cited in Williamson, "Catholic Principles for Interpreting Scripture," 340.
15. Cited in Williamson, "Catholic Principles for Interpreting Scripture," 340.
16. *Dei Verbum*, #12.
17. William Kurz, "*Dei Verbum*: Sacred Scripture Since Vatican II," Theology Faculty Research and Publications 24 (Marquette University, 2007), 176.

Hence, Kurz shared Williamson's "frequent complaints about historical-criticism's failures to meet the needs of Catholics."[18] He praises Williamson's book, especially its recognition of a pastoral need: "I judge his effort to be an urgent pastoral necessity in view not only of communication failures between Catholic exegesis and pastoral catechesis but also of the many Catholics leaving the Church because 'they are not being fed' with Bible teaching as rival congregations are."[19] Kurz's emphasis rhymes with the demands of *Dei Verbum* about attending to the spiritual sense of Scripture as the word of God. But this worry is peculiar to scholarship and is not the concern of the everyday, commonsense, ordinary reader of the Bible who interprets Scripture and applies it to their everyday life as the word of God. In this commonsense reading, one encounters problems of futurism (reading current events in the light of Bible passages),[20] literalism (reading the Bible completely outside its original context), and finally, fundamentalism, which "implicitly holds that what [one] believes corresponds to a single, underlying code that explains everything about the world, in its totality."[21]

THE LITERAL SENSE OF SCRIPTURE

"Literal sense of Scripture" here does not mean the biblical literalism often drawn from belief in biblical inerrancy, a belief considered necessary because of biblical inspiration.[22] It means the historic, diachronic approach of Scripture whereby the context, the author, and the world of the text; the intended audience; and so on are taken into consideration. According to the *IBC*, "The literal

---

18. William Kurz, review of *Catholic Principles for Interpreting Scripture: A Study of the Pontifical Biblical Commission's* The Interpretation of the Bible in the Church, by Peter S. Williamson, *Theological Studies* 64, no. 1 (2003): 156.

19. Kurz, "Review," 156.

20. For more on futurism, preterism, historicism, and general eschatology, see Ron J. Bigalke Jr., "The Revival of Futurist Interpretation Following the Reformation," *Journal of Dispensational Theology* 13, no. 38 (2009): 43–56.

21. J. Pickering, *Turn Neither Right Nor Left* (Wipf & Stock, 2019), cited in Bradley M. Trout, "The (Mis)interpretation of the Bible in South Africa: Towards a Better Hermeneutic,' *In die Skriflig* 55, no. 3 (2021): 1–8.

22. On the link, distinctions, and split within conservative Protestants between evangelicals and fundamentalists, see John Bartkowski, "Beyond Biblical Literalism and Inerrancy: Conservative Protestants and the Hermeneutic Interpretation of Scripture," *Sociology of Religion* 57, no. 3 (1996): 259–72.

sense of Scripture is that which has been expressed directly by the inspired human authors."[23] As Joseph A. Fitzymer explains, literal sense demands attention to the historical, "which is particularly attentive to the ancient meaning of the biblical text and its underlying sources and traditions."[24]

The literal sense of Scripture, and indeed all interpretations of Scripture, seeks the meaning of scriptural texts and draws out implications for the present. When necessary, one may extrapolate morally from the meaning of scriptural statements, their universal applicability beyond their original local contexts.[25] The meaning of Scripture raises questions about the author's intention and the meanings to be deciphered beyond what the biblical authors originally meant, to what the divine author meant, since God is equally the author of the Bible. The following questions come to mind. Is the human intention different from the divine intention? Do the human authors understand fully God's revelation they had written down? Can the statements of the authors of the books of the Bible be understood outside and beyond what they have written? How extensive are the applications of these statements, limited to the author's original audience-reference, or extensive to other referents, including contemporary audience-referents despite differences both in history and culture, between biblical meaning and the issues of today? Is the Old Testament relevant for the church as the recipient of the New Testament? Should the Old Testament be read in the light of the New Testament, or should each be read independently?[26] What is the meaning of the complex

---

23. *IBC*, 79.

24. Joseph A. Fitzmyer, SJ, *The Interpretation of Scripture: In Defense of the Historical-Critical Method* (Paulist Press, 2008), 78.

25. Ramesh E. Richard, "Methodological Proposals for Scripture Relevance, Pt 2: Levels of Meaning," *Bibliotheca Sacra* 143, no. 570 (1986): 128. Fitzmyer says of historical critical method, its stages, and techniques: "All such critical techniques, historical and literary, are geared to one end: to determine the meaning of the sacred text as it was intended by the human author moved long ago to compose it and to ascertain what it is saying to us today." Cf. Fitzmyer, *Scripture, The Soul of Theology* (Paulist Press, 1994), 23.

26. For more on the relationship of the Old and the New Testaments, see Richard, "Methodological Proposals for Scripture Relevance, Pt 4," 302–13; Benjamin Sargent, "One Meaning or Many? A Study in New Testament Interpretation of Old Testament Texts," *Churchman* 124, no. 4 (2010): 357–65; Lewis Foster, "Realgeschichte: Old and New in Interpretation," *Journal of the Evangelical Theological Society* 28, no. 2, (1985): 153–68; Geoffrey W. Grogan, "The New Testament Interpretation of the Old Testament: A Comparative Study," *Tyndale Bulletin* 18 (1967): 54–76; Franz Delitzsch, "Must We Follow the New Testament Interpretation of Old Testament Texts?" *The Old Testament Student*, 6, no. 3 (1886): 77–78; C. van der Waal, "The Continuity Between the Old and

human-divine authorship of the Bible, and what are its implications for the meaning of Scripture? Statements, implications, and extrapolations help in determining the meaning of scriptural statements, their implications, and what moral imperatives could be drawn from them.

Dei Verbum's emphasis on the divine and the human authorship of the Bible, its insistence on the unity of Scripture and of Scripture and tradition forming the word of God, as well as its push for historical-critical method and for the spiritual sense of Scripture can be summed up under the umbrella of the diachronic and the synchronic readings of Scripture. That is, it can be summarized by the relationship between the processes through which the Bible as Scripture came to be and its final form as word of God. It is about the processes of reading a text as a movement in time into the world of the biblical authors, their intentions and meanings, and a movement that occurs as the present reader of the biblical text appropriates the text and applies it to the various contemporary challenges of life. This is the method recognized by the *IBC* as historical criticism: "The historical-critical method, as its name suggests, is particularly attentive to the historical development of texts or traditions across the passage of time—that is, to all that is summed up in the term *diachronic*."[27]

Joseph Ratzinger (Pope Benedict XVI) highlights its importance for biblical interpretation. In fact, he made it central to the broad outlines of his book *Jesus of Nazareth* and defends its use:

> The first point is that the historical-critical method—specifically because of the intrinsic nature of theology and faith—is and remains an indispensable dimension of exegetical work. For it is of the very essence of biblical faith to be about real historical events. It does not tell stories symbolizing suprahistorical truths, but is based on history, history that took place here on this earth. The *factum historicum* (historical fact) is not an interchangeable symbolic cipher for biblical faith, but the foundation on which it stands: *et incarnatus est*—when we say these words, we acknowledge God's actual entry into real history.[28]

New Testaments," *Neotestamentica* 14, (1980): 1–20; S. Burnham, "The Value of the Old Testament for a Correct Knowledge of the New," *The Old Testament Student* 5, no. 4 (1885): 157–61.

27. *IBC*, 3.

28. Joseph Ratzinger (Pope Benedict XVI), *Jesus of Nazareth II*, trans. Adrian J. Walker (Doubleday, 2007), xv.

Ratzinger was a member of the Pontifical Biblical Commission and wrote the preface to the *IBC*. He rejected the draft proposal by the Preparatory Commission that would have prioritized tradition over Scripture, arguing such a position would have posed an obstacle to biblical scholarship.[29] His endorsement of historical critical method is not surprising because it is indispensable to biblical interpretation.

Rowan Williams emphasizes the importance of the diachronic (historical) method for the interpretation of Scripture:

> One way of seeing how the relation between literal and non-literal senses of Scripture has been worked out in doctrinal history is to see it as a tension between what I shall call "diachronic" and "synchronic" styles of reading... If diachronic reading is a reading which can show me something of a text's intentionality (in the widest sense—its internal direction and its consciously envisaged audience), it will put to me questions about the writer's world, questions about history, even if only the history of the process of composing. And such questions are not necessarily a way of disregarding the specificity of the writing as it presents itself, to the extent that they genuinely arise from the act of reading with attention and patience.[30]

The literal sense of Scripture, therefore, involves a reading that emphasizes not only the Scripture in its final form but also one that includes the different stages in the production of each book of the Bible. Unfortunately, diachronic reading has been reduced to merely academic and scholarly reading, such that it is placed beyond the reach of the nonscholar. As Teresa Okure observes, the impact was the spread of false knowledge under the guise of truth from the hands of biblical scholars trusted as experts: "The biblical scholar thus becomes the expert over the word of the biblical author, and many of God's people (who cannot discern *hypotheses* from *peristases*) perish through false knowledge, while we scholars may ply our trade through the land and lack divine wisdom (cf. 1 Cor 1.18–25; 1er 8.8–9)."[31] The *IBC* even notes, "Instead of making for easier and more secure access to the living sources of God's

---

29. See Alan Bernard McGill, "Reading the Bible Through Stained Glass: Postliberal Resistance to the Historical-Critical Method," *New Theology Review* 30, no. 2 (2018): 33.

30. Rowan Williams, "The Literal Sense of Scripture," *Modern Theology* 7, no. 2 (1991): 120–21.

31. Okure, "'I will open my mouth in parables'," 454.

word, it makes of the Bible a closed book. Interpretation may always have been something of a problem, but now it requires such technical refinements as to render it a domain reserved for a few specialists alone."[32]

The synchronic approach becomes the favored reading because it appears more relevant to the variety of stories and the drama characteristic of our lives as human beings. Biblical stories are appropriated as our own stories; moral readings are favored because "the text is read as something requiring change in the reader, change of a kind depicted in the text itself."[33] Yet, the synchronic reading is not primary,[34] as it presupposes the diachronic—that is, "that the time of the text is recognizably continuous with my time. The movements, transactions and transformations of the text are not different in kind from the movement of my own experience, from how I tell my own story."[35] Analogically, Williams's view is simple; there is a connection between the time of the Bible and our own time. We make sense of our own time analogically in the light of the biblical times even though both are different in many ways.

---

32. *IBC*, 4. Fitzymer mentions the two preliminary steps of historical-critical method to be borrowed from classical philology to include "(1) introductory questions and (2) textual criticism. The first step raises introductory questions and deals with: (a) the authenticity of the writing (e.g., Did David compose the psalm? Did Paul write the Epistle to the Ephesians?); (b) the integrity or unity of the writing (e.g., Is chapter 16 an original part of the Pauline letter to the Romans?); (c) the date and place of composition; (d) the content of the writing, analyzed according to its structure, outline, style, and literary form (Is it a letter, a narrative, an apocalypse, a sermon?); the occasion and purpose of the writing (i.e., the author's intention in composing it, as this is evident in the writing); and (f) its literary background (Has the author being influenced by Assyrian, Egyptian, Canaanite, Palestinian Jewish, or Hellenistic ideas?) . . . The Second step, textual criticism . . . deals with the transmission of the biblical text in its original language and in ancient versions: In what manuscripts is the best form of the text preserved? What is the best family of manuscripts? Does an ancient version reflect a better reading, one possible superior to the transmitted Hebrew, Aramaic, or Greek text?" Fitzymer, *Scripture*, 20.

33. Williams, "The Literal Sense of Scripture," 125.

34. The priority of a diachronic approach is contested by some theologians for whom theological reading of Scripture is the centerpiece of interpretation because the Bible is primarily the word of God and a property of the church and is at the service of the church. Brad East, for one, insists on the priority of the community reading of the text of Scripture: "My more polemical point is that reading within the community of the church and in accordance with its commitments has fundamental priority over against other communities and other commitments, and that this way of reading engenders a relationship to the biblical text that is hermeneutically superior to all others." Brad East, "What Are the Standards of Excellence for Theological Interpretation of Scripture," *Journal of Theological Interpretation* 14, no. 2 (2020): 154.

35. Williams, "The Literal Sense of Scripture," 125.

Thus, the connection between the diachronic and the synchronic reading, with the diachronic as primary, saves us from fundamentalistic exegesis: "that our diachronic reading assumes a continuity between the time(s) of the text and what we recognize as movement and production in our own lives. We are able to make time now for the performance of canonical narrative and argument because it is the kind of thing that takes time in our own 'narrative'; and we are able to enter the time of the canonical text because we see it as a possible movement or process for the kind of beings we are."[36] According to Williams, there is actually no other way of entering into the inner life of Scripture other than the literal reading or diachronic approach as primary. It recognizes that Scripture is relevant today because of the close links between its original context and the contemporary contexts. Williams asserts:

> What I am suggesting here is that it is "diachronic" reading of Scripture that gives us the "interiority" of the text, and that this interiority is not a point of hidden clarity and security but a complex of interwoven processes: a production of meaning in the only mode available for material and temporal creatures. Synchronic reading of whatever kind relies on that suspicion of "surface" phenomena that can make interpretation a systematic exercise in losing or ignoring the object, seeking the "spirit" through the absence of the "letter."[37]

The disregard of the diachronic, historical sense of Scripture, in favor of simplifying the application of the word of God in Scripture to concrete moral issues, only results in a misunderstanding of the literal sense of Scripture, reading the Bible at surface level, and supporting this commonsense reading with multiple quotations of other texts of Scripture. Ramesh E. Richard, a leading evangelical hermeneut thinking alongside Williams's view, argues that "Scripture relevance without the *sensus literalis* aborts the undertaking of hermeneutics at its earliest stages."[38] One cannot abort the historical sense for the sake of the scriptural relevance. According to Ratzinger, "If we push this history aside, Christian faith as such appears and is recast as some other religion . . . indeed, faith itself demands this . . . The historical-critical

---

36. Williams, "The Literal Sense of Scripture," 127.
37. Williams, "The Literal Sense of Scripture," 129–30.
38. Ramesh E. Richard, "Methodological Proposals for Scripture Relevance, Pt 1: Selected Issues in Theoretical Hermeneutics," *Bibliotheca sacra* 143, no. 569 (1986): 15.

method—let me repeat—is an indispensable tool, given the structure of Christian faith."[39]

According to the *IBC*, the historical-critical method is important for four reasons. First, as a historical method, it helps in shedding light to the historical processes that gave rise to the biblical texts. "At the different stages of their production, the texts of the Bible were addressed to various categories of hearers or readers living in different places and different times."[40] Second, as a critical method, through each of its steps from textual to redaction criticism, it provides a precise, scientific method that helps provide meaning of Scripture to the modern reader. Third, as an analytic method, it studies biblical text as any other ancient text "and comments upon it as an expression of human discourse."[41] Finally, and "above all in the area of redaction criticism, it does allow the exegete to gain a better grasp of the content of divine revelation."[42]

At the same time, however, just as Okure, West, Dube, and Ukpong have argued, one cannot forsake scriptural relevance just to protect the historical, diachronic, and literal senses of Scripture. In fact, as Ukpong notes, the past reconstructed in the literal sense is meaningful only in the light of the present: "For, since the past can only be reached and communicated through our situatedness in the present, the meaning we get of the past is not a meaning of what happened in the past *pure and simple*, but of what happened in the past filtered through the present; that is, the meaning that we, from the present standpoint, are able to make of the past."[43] Okure agrees with Ukpong and dismisses the difference often made between exegesis and hermeneutics in favor of integrating exegesis into hermeneutics, what she labelled "exegetical hermeneutics," a technique that "lays emphasis on 'hermeneutics,' the applied meaning of a text, and places exegesis at its service. Exegesis here would be

---

39. Ratzinger, *Jesus of Nazareth*, xv, xvi. The historical-critical method is indispensable because its various stages—textual criticism, literary criticism, form criticism, and editorial criticism—make Scripture clearer. The *IBC*'s summary aptly clarifies the interconnectedness of the stages: "From textual criticism one progresses to literary criticism, with its work of dissection in the quest for sources; then one moves to a critical study of forms and, finally, to an analysis of the editorial process, which aims to be particularly attentive to the text as it has been put together. All this has made it possible to understand far more accurately the intention of the authors and editors of the Bible as well as the message which they addressed to their first readers." *IBC*, 6.
40. *IBC*, 7.
41. *IBC*, 7.
42. *IBC*, 7.
43. Ukpong, "Reading the Bible in a Global Village," 18.

understood as a faith-filled scholarly effort to reveal the meaning of the extant texts in their own contexts, using all available concrete resources."[44] Thus, "depicting the reader and the text in historical terms, is necessary but not sufficient for a satisfactory account of scriptural interpretation. Theological categories are also needed and should become fully operative."[45] Scripture in its final form and Scripture in its formative stages go together. Both promote genuine scriptural hermeneutics, "for it is the text in its final stage, rather than in its earlier editions, which is the expression of the word of God. But diachronic study remains indispensable for making known the historical dynamism which animates sacred Scripture and for shedding light upon its rich complexity."[46] Any of the approaches taken to the extreme, excluding the other, is catastrophic for biblical interpretation. Diachronic approach alone results in historicism. Synchronic (canonical) approach alone gives rise to fundamentalism. Neither is acceptable.

FUNDAMENTALISM

The *IBC* rejects the fundamentalist biblical interpretation for its refusal to use the historical-biblical method or any other scientific method, preferring as it does the literalist approach based on the principle that "the Bible, being the word of God, inspired and free from error, should be read and interpreted literally in all its details."[47] The *IBC* traced the literalist interpretation of the fundamentalists to the five statements, or tenets, adopted at the North American Niagara Bible Conference in 1895, which include "the verbal inerrancy (i.e. infallibility) of Scripture, the divinity of Christ, his virginal birth, the doctrine of vicarious expiation, and the bodily resurrection at the time of the second coming of Christ."[48] The *IBC* does not reject these beliefs but contests

---

44. Okure, "'I will open my mouth in parables'," 456.
45. Darren Sarisky, *Scriptural Interpretation: A Theological Exploration* (Wiley & Sons, 2013), 4, cited in D. Christopher Spinks, "Catching Up on a Conversation: Recent Voices on Theological Interpretation of Scripture," *Anglican Theological Review* 99, no. 4 (2017): 775.
46. Sarisky, *Scriptural Interpretation*, 9.
47. Pontifical Biblical Commission, *"The Interpretation of the Bible in the Church* [1993]," in *The Biblical Commission's Document*, Subsidia Biblica 18), ed. Joseph Fitzmyer (Pontificio Istituto Biblico, 1995), 101.
48. Pontifical Biblical Commission, *"The Interpretation of the Bible in the Church* [1993]," cited in Peter Beckman, "The Interpretation of the Bible in the Church and the

the fundamentalist ideology surrounding them, including half-hearted acceptance of the incarnation manifest in the fundamentalist denial of God's use of the human authors and hence their preference for dictation word by word by the Spirit of the Bible. It states:

> Fundamentalism also ignores or denies problems concerning original Biblical languages in the text, and in the case of the development of the Gospel tradition, confuses the final form with the initial words of Jesus... It tends to adopt a narrow point of view which includes an out-of-date cosmology and fosters prejudices such as racism, which are contrary to the Gospel. It also adopts a principle of "Scripture alone" which separates the Bible from the divinely guided tradition. It frequently places itself in opposition to church, creeds, doctrines, and/or liturgical practices in its privatized interpretation.[49]

Peter Beckman has offered a series of corrections to the *IBC* with regards to the fundamentalist verbal inspiration and the scientific nature of the Bible as a belief of both Catholics and Protestants prior to the modern scientific historical-critical approaches to the Bible.[50] But according to Beckman, the Catholic Church has advanced beyond its previous anti-historical study of the Bible and is ready to correct its mistakes and to warn of the dangers of fundamentalist interpretation of the Bible.

Fundamentalism is a complex phenomenon associated broadly with religion as it struggles to adhere to its beliefs in the face of secularization and modernity's attempt to displace religion through various demystifications aimed at restricting religion to the private sphere and away from public life. And so, fundamentalism is bandied about to describe those who attempt to remystify society in the face of Enlightenment reason's attempts to destroy religious faith.[51] At times, fundamentalism is used to describe people who strive to conserve their values (especially religious ones), those who cite,

---

Fundamentalist Interpretation," *Theoforum* 50 (2020): 72. The error of *IBC* on these statements and its source has been corrected by Peter Beckman (p. 73n8).

49. Beckman, "The Interpretation of the Bible in the Church," 73.
50. Beckman, "The Interpretation of the Bible in the Church," 73–75.
51. For instance, Edward Farley argues a theory that fundamentalism is just religion's ways of contending with attempts by modernity to reduce its influence: "Fundamentalism is the Response of Religion to Modernity." Edward Farley, "Fundamentalism: A Theory," *Cross Currents* 55, no. 3 (2005): 379.

maintain, and justify the role of the supernatural, both in the founding and in the giving of their preferred religious texts and scriptures. According to Michael O. Emerson and David Hartman, "Fundamentalism is such a commonly and loosely used term, thrown around like a baseball in the media, backyard arguments, and political arenas. Sometimes the term fundamentalist is used to describe any group that takes religion seriously or that views religion's role in public life to be greater than the labeler would wish it to be. The term also might be used for those who are too religiously confident or who engage in any sort of action out of religious conviction."[52] Here, we use *fundamentalism* as it "was first used to describe a conservative strain of Protestantism that developed in the United States roughly from 1870 to 1925,"[53] marked especially by a literalistic approach to the Bible. For this reason, strictly speaking, fundamentalism is a point of view, an approach, and not a method of biblical interpretation.[54]

According to James Barr, fundamentalism is characterized by "a very strong emphasis on the inerrancy of the Bible, the absence from it of any sort of error; a strong hostility to modern theology and to the methods, results and implications of modern critical study of the Bible; an assurance that those who do not share their religious viewpoint are not really 'true Christians' at all."[55] Barr contends that fundamentalism is anchored in the religious experience of Evangelical Revivals, according to which a distinction is made between nominal Christians and the true Christians, depending on one's witness of faith in the Gospels and in the Bible. Nominal Christians distrust the authority of the Bible and presume salvation based on belonging to the church. True Christians, through the evangelical revival, are renewed through the Gospels, are converted, and begin to trust in salvation in Christ through the Scriptures. "Central to fundamentalism is the correlation between two pairs of contrasts: on the one side the contrast between the true Christian and the nominal Christian, on the other side the contrast between the more

---

52. Michael O. Emerson and David Hartman, "The Rise of Religious Fundamentalism," *Annual Review of Sociology* 32 (2006): 126.

53. Emerson and Harman, "The Rise of Religious Fundamentalism," 131.

54. For the view of fundamentalism as a point of view, see Diane Begant, "Fundamentalism and Biblical Commission," *Chicago Studies* 34, no. 3 (1995): 209–21.

55. James Barr, *Fundamentalism* (SCM Press, 1977), 1. "Conservatives have often argued that, with the rise of biblical criticism, biblical truth is being betrayed into the hands of the intellectuals, who arrogate to themselves the right to decide and who seek to impose their esoteric schemes upon the church" (p. 129).

conservative theological opinions and the more 'liberal.'"[56] The criteria for determining the true from the nominal Christian is the abiding fidelity or not to the Bible, the authoritative God-given way for all who profess him to know him.

Christianity becomes a biblical religion in the hands of fundamentalists. Its inspiration and consequent inerrancy place the Bible at the center of the faith. The authority of the Bible as Scripture summarizes Christianity as a religion. In it is contained not only the truths of faith but also God's requirements for the true Christian. Right doctrine, which must be faithfully taught and adhered to, is "salvation from sin [metaphysical than personal] through the blood of Christ and through personal faith in him"[57] and is not separable from the Bible. Thus, while it could refer to religious, theological positions, found also in other religions, fundamentalism is more apropos for biblical scholarship, in the conflict between biblical conservatism and biblical criticism, more so with regards to "conservative attitudes to the Bible, *within Christianity*."[58]

Fundamentalism strongly defends the divine authorship of the Bible, holding on to verbal inspiration, but disregards the human authorship. Its preference for dictation as the form of divine inspiration therefore has no place for God's use of human authors in the composition of texts of Scripture. The implication, therefore, is literalistic interpretation, including acceptance of the seven-day creation account of Genesis.[59] It advocates the unity of Scripture, by which it means that Christian faith is an assent to a system of beliefs based on the Bible and that alteration of any of these body of beliefs would imply the collapse of the entire Christian doctrinal system. Hence,

---

56. Barr, *Fundamentalism*, 14.
57. Barr, *Fundamentalism*, 25.
58. Barr, *Fundamentalism*, 7.
59. However, a fundamentalist approach to the Bible is a variation of literally and nonliterally interpretation. According to James Barr, "This variation is made necessary by the real guiding principle of fundamentalist interpretation, namely that one must ensure that the Bible is inerrant, without error. Inerrancy is maintained only by constantly altering the mode of interpretation, and in particular by abandoning the literal sense as soon as it would be an embarrassment to the view of inerrancy held." Barr, *Fundamentalism*, 46; cf. p. 51, "Inerrancy is the constant factor in all fundamentalist interpretation. Literalness is not a constant factor, but may vary up and down" and p. 53, "The inerrancy of the Bible, the entire Bible including its details, is indeed the constant principle of rationality within fundamentalism. Seen from outside, it distorts and deranges all sorts of relations which to the student of the Bible seem quite obvious; but, seen from within, it is a constant and dependable principle which applies equally at every point."

fundamentalists engage in harmonization of the various scriptural texts to account for apparent contradictory accounts of biblical events.[60] At the same time, it admits "a certain grading of biblical materials" so that some books are more central than others.[61] Dianne Begant sums up the fundamentalist approach to the Bible thus:

> Fundamentalism claims that because the Bible is inspired, it is not subject to any historical limitations. Fundamentalism opposed any critical biblical interpretation, and so it rejects fiercely the various conclusions that flow from any such use. It contends that there is only one interpretation that is correct, the interpretation that comes from a literal reading of the text... Therefore, Fundamentalists insist: there are no fanciful tales, myths or legends that distort the truth; there is no biblical doctrine that is incompletely formulated or inadequately expressed; there is no thought of future reinterpretation of the teaching and no need for further theological development... The basic premise of Fundamentalist biblical interpretation is inerrancy or the full truth of scripture.[62]

Fundamentalists hold that everything narrated in the past tense necessarily corresponds to ancient reality and that everything put on the lips of Jesus was necessarily uttered by him.[63] For example, scholars speak of three stages of the development of gospel tradition: (1) what Jesus did and said; (2) what

---

60. For instance, Edward Josiah Young once wrote that if the Bible cannot be trusted with small matters, it cannot be trusted with bigger matters: "If the evangelists were guilty of trifling errors and evidences of carelessness in so-called minor matters, we simply cannot escape the conclusion that they may have been just as careless in more important things. If the writers of the Gospels cannot even agree as to the number of those whose eyes were opened by the Lord, we may very rightly ask how we can know whether the eyes of any were opened? Since the accounts are so garbled, there may not have been any miracle performed at all." Edward Josiah Young, *Thy Word is Truth*, 131–35, cited in Barr, *Fundamentalism*, 347n24.

61. Barr, *Fundamentalism*, 61–69.

62. Begant, "Fundamentalism and Biblical Commission," 211–13. Notice the difference between the fundamentalist use of the word *literal* and the historical-critical method's use of it. Fundamentalists mean by *literal* that the Scripture means what it says and says what it means. In other words, the meaning of the words remain the same today as they were understood by the original authors, editors, and communities. The historical-critical method, on the other hand, uses *literal* in the sense of the way the original authors of the Bible used it. They do not presume that the meaning has remained the same "over time and across cultures" (pp. 211–13).

63. Fitzmyer, *Scripture*, 23.

the disciples preached about him; and (3) what the evangelists wrote by synthesizing the tradition of what was said about him. While the historical-critical method is concerned with relating stage 3 with stages 1 and 2, the fundamentalist equates stages 3 and 1.[64] While fundamentalists hold that "the Bible actually tells you what Jesus said," James Barr argues that "it doesn't. It tells you what Matthew or Mark, who were not reporting verbatim, intended the reader to understand."[65] Okure asserts that the New Testament's Greek composition (rather than Aramaic, the probable language Jesus spoke) shows the readiness of the early Christians to share the gospel with their neighbors: "The survival of the NT only in Greek shows to what extent the NT Christians were more eager to transmit the gospel to their Greco-Roman audiences than to preserve the *ipsissima verba* of Jesus. This awareness calls for respect for their work and concerns within their personal and historico-cultural limitations."[66] Thus, fundamentalism, which the *IBC* calls "dangerous," stands at the opposite pole of another approach to Biblical interpretation the *IBC* objects to. The other is historicism, which denies the divine authorship and hence also the theological interpretation of Scripture.[67] Fundamentalism and historicism stand against *Dei Verbum*'s position that the Bible is God's word in human language.[68]

Even though fundamentalism is deemed dangerous, it shares much in common with the *IBC* and *Dei Verbum*. Both accept the inspiration of Scripture and its inerrancy.[69] They all accept the divine authorship of the Bible and affirm it as the word of God. None denies the Bible's authority as the rule of faith and guide to Christian life. All therefore accept the truth of Scripture. The major difference lies in the authority of Scripture and its interpretation. Based on the Reformation's tenet of *sola scriptura*, fundamentalists view the Bible as the only source of truth and its meaning as self-interpreting. For *Dei Verbum* and the *IBC*, the Bible and church tradition is Scripture. For the Catholic Church, the authoritative interpretation of the Bible is the church's

---

64. Fitzmyer, *Scripture*, 24.
65. Barr, *Fundamentalism*, 59.
66. Okure, "'I will open my mouth in parables'," 452.
67. See Jacob Runyon, "A Spiritual Application of the Historical-Critical Method," *Assembly: A Journal of Liturgical Theology* 37, no. 1 (2011): 10–13.
68. *Dei Verbum*, #13.
69. In fact, "Roman Catholics were until recently bound to a quite strictly fundamentalist position, and only with some difficulty have their scholars in more recent years been able to extricate themselves from it." Barr, *Fundamentalism*, 105.

magisterium, which preserves and thus interprets the deposit of faith. The final authority of biblical interpretation therefore is the church. "The evangelical tradition of religion is from the beginning the accepted framework within which the Bible is interpreted, and no interpretation is carried out in such a way as to question this tradition."[70]

THE PURIST IDEAL

Barr criticizes positions like Karl Barth's, which asserts the sufficiency of Scripture to interpret itself, leading to the universal rule of interpretation that "a text can be read and understood and expounded only with reference to and in light of its theme." Barr refers to such a position as the "purist" ideal—that is, the view that "the ideas and categories used in interpretation must themselves be taken from 'within' the biblical material; to use the usual phrase, the Bible has to be interpreted 'in its own terms.'"[71] The great New Testament scholar Rudolf Schnakenberg would agree with Barr in rejecting the position that the Bible interpret itself.

> Let it be immediately stated that the revelation of the New Testament did not come out of the blue: Jesus' starting point was the Old Testament and many of the current Jewish concepts; and Christianity, too, in its early stages did not ignore the world around it, but revealed its message to it by means of an intellectual exchange. There can be, then, no theology of the New Testament without research into the history of religion and without a comparison with the ideas of other religious currents. It is only in this way that the particular and unique nature of Christianity becomes clearer. For this reason too, an attempt to build up a theology of the New Testament purely and directly from the Bible, merely presenting the ideas that are already present and seeking to use biblical terms as exclusively as possible, is doomed to failure. This leads to a study of the Bible which is in itself unfruitful and fails wholly to appeal to the people of today.[72]

---

70. Barr, *Fundamentalism*, 107.
71. Barr, *Fundamentalism*, 171.
72. Rudolf Schnackenburg, "The Position in the Theology of the New Testament," in *The Bible in the New Age*, ed. Ludwig Klein (Sheed & Ward, 1965), 38.

The features of the purist position include acknowledgment of the relation between the Old and the New Testaments, discomfort with a historical-critical study of the Bible, emphasis on the centrality of the Bible, biblical assumptions as key to biblical interpretations, and an ideal of objectivity based on these assumptions, with other presuppositions viewed as external and thus disregarded and discredited. The position stresses obedience and attentiveness to the Bible, which should be allowed to "speak" to us in its own way while we are to "listen." This was manifest in the neoorthodox movement of the First World War period, with its strong emphasis in the Bible over and against the historical-critical interpretive trends of mainline liberal Protestantism. The Bible is the word of God in three senses: in Jesus Christ the word incarnate, in the Bible as inspired by the Holy Spirit, and in the proclamations of the church.[73] For this reason, "it is uncomfortable if men begin to let their conceptions operate actively on the Bible, acting critically, reconstructing historical data, judging that theological elements are contradictory, analyzing according to canons thus worked out."[74] The purist ideal assumes that the Scripture is the property of the church, which the church expounds to the world. It defends the inspiration of the Bible as the authority of Scripture.

Inspiration distinguishes the Bible from other books, scriptures, and writings. It states God's authorship of the Bible through the human authors of its various books, and as such makes the Bible, in its verbal form, authoritative for questions of faith and morals (2 Tim 3:16). By implication, the Bible is infallible, or inerrant. "The point then is that the Bible, being from God, cannot be wrong; it cannot be in error and cannot lead into error."[75] Two implications follow: The Bible is theological truth and historical fact, so it is theologically infallible and historically correct; Scripture is normative for all matters concerning faith and morals because God is the author. The Bible becomes the highest authority, binding on Christians. According to some interpretations of the normativity of Scripture, this demands rejection of the historical-critical method and any other form of interpretation, including patristic allegorical interpretation and the medieval fourfold sense of Scripture.

Inspiration and inerrancy of the Bible is common to Protestant orthodoxy and the Roman Catholic Church. Both are ways of expressing the Christian belief that the Bible comes from God, that God speaks through the Bible as

---

73. James Barr, *The Bible in the Modern World* (SCM Press, 1973), 18–22.
74. James Barr, *Old and New in Interpretation* (SCM Press, 1982), 181–82.
75. Barr, *The Bible in the Modern World*, 14.

Scripture, and thus that the Bible owes its origin from God, by God in some way, guiding the human authors. Both Protestant orthodoxy and the Roman Catholic Church recognize literal interpretation of the Bible because of their acknowledgment of history and the variety of contexts of the stories and the content of the Bible as Scripture. However, this in no way means that both the Protestant and the Catholic churches accord similar authority to the Bible. For the Catholic Church, the Bible and tradition are both Scripture. For the Protestant orthodoxy, tradition is subordinated to the Bible. However, both distance themselves from bibliolatry expressed in the fundamentalistic view of inspiration, which denies historicity and advocates theological infallibility of the Bible.[76] "The fundamentalist denies that there is any historical error in the Bible; he does this because he feels that, if any historical error were admitted, it would open the way to assertions of theological error as well. His characteristic argument is 'Where do you stop?' If the Bible is 'wrong' about the age of Ishmael when he was expelled with his mother from Abraham's camp, or about the historicity of Daniel, then it can be wrong about the love of God or about justification by faith."[77]

THE SUFFICIENCY OF SCRIPTURE

Noel Weeks[78] advances a version of biblicism, an extreme conservative fundamentalistic view of Scriptural authority, as superior to all advances in modern scholarship, science, and technology. According to Weeks, the authority of

---

76. Bibliolatry is treating the Bible as an idol—that is, mistaking the symbol for the reality. It is an attitude toward the Bible informed by an interpretation of inspiration and inerrancy of the Bible that negates any interpretation of the Bible outside of the texts of the Bible as erroneous. It is the view that the Bible contains everything and treats every subject matter in the world. The basic principles of modern science, psychology, mathematics, business, marketing, and so on are all contained in the Bible because everything comes from God, who is the author of the Bible. Bibliolators cling idolatrously to the letter of the word. Characteristically, for them, "the most difficult and unnatural explanation of a passage is always to be preferred, inasmuch as the glory of God is thereby seen more clearly. These interpreters find miracles where none were intended. Indeed, they find everything everywhere, and anything anywhere." Editorial Note, "Bibliolatry," *The Old Testament Student* 3, no. 3 (1883): 92–93, accessed October 13, 2023, http://www.jstor.org/stable/3157116.
77. Barr, *The Bible in the Modern World*, 15.
78. Noel Weeks, *The Sufficiency of Scripture* (Banner of Truth Trust, 1988).

Scripture is exhaustive and therefore cannot be relativized "by reducing its authority to its immediate context."[79] For Weeks, the Bible's claim of inspiration (2 Tim 3:16–17) is sufficient evidence of biblical infallibility. Further evidence is the lordship of Jesus over creation and the Holy Spirit's inspiration and illumination of Scripture. For this reason, the Bible is transcultural and beyond relativism.[80] His view opens a window into the whole spectrum of arguments, opinions, and approaches, into the form of theological interpretation of Scripture based on the evidence of Scripture itself as sufficient, complete, absolutely true, and therefore "an unerring guide of conduct."[81]

John MacArthur articulates the sufficiency of Scripture in terms of its comprehensiveness and superiority. He writes,

> God's Word is sufficient to meet every need of the human soul as David verifies frequently in his psalms. Psalm 19:7–14 is the most comprehensive statement regarding the sufficiency of Scripture. It is an inspired statement about Scripture as a qualified guide for every situation. Scripture is comprehensive, containing everything necessary for one's spiritual life. Scripture is surer than a human experience that one may look to in proving God's power and presence. Scripture contains divine principles that are the best guide for character and conduct. Scripture is lucid rather than mystifying so that it enlightens the eyes. Scripture is void of any flaws and therefore lasts forever. Scripture is true regarding all things that matter, making it capable of producing comprehensive righteousness. Because it meets every need in life, Scripture is infinitely more precious than anything this world has to offer.[82]

In a similar way, Harold Lindsell, in his *The Battle for the Bible*,[83] combatively defends the inevitability of biblical inerrancy. Lindsell argues that inerrancy is central to biblical authority and is the test for true Christian conservative evangelical faith. He even claims inerrancy has eschatological implications;

---

79. Gerald Bray, review of *The Sufficiency of Scripture* by Noel Weeks," *Churchman* 102, no. 3 (1988): 262.

80. Terry G. Hiebert, review of *The Sufficiency of Scripture*, by Noel Weeks, *Journal of the Evangelical Theological Society* 33, no. 2 (1990): 249.

81. Albert Barnes, *Notes on the Old Testament: Psalms*, vol. 1, cited in John MacArthur, "The Sufficiency of Scripture," *The Master's Seminary Journal* 15 no. 2 (2004): 168.

82. John MacArthur, "The Sufficiency of Scripture," 165.

83. Harold Lindsell, *The Battle for the Bible* (Grand Rapids Zondervan Publishing House, 1976).

it is one of the things revealed at the second coming of Christ. Hence, "when biblical inerrancy is abandoned, other defections, some heretical, inevitably follow."[84] Lindsell claims that unfaithfulness to the inerrancy of Scripture is responsible for the myriads of problems bedeviling the Lutherans, the Southern Baptists, Fuller Theological Seminary, and many colleges and institutions.[85]

The controversial reception of Lindsell's book cautions us from painting all evangelicals as fundamentalists. Distinctions among evangelicals regarding the inspiration, and inerrancy of the Bible are numerous. We must distinguish between the fundamentalist-evangelical and progressive-evangelical. The position of progressive evangelicals, which stands between inerrantists and extreme liberals, is a much more balanced theological interpretation of the Bible. According to George Marsden,[86] "Progressive evangelicals stood somewhere in between. They wanted to affirm the divine origins of Scripture but give more practical weight than did the inerrantists to understanding it as also the product of human cultural circumstances."[87]

Dennis W. Jowers asserts that the sufficiency of Scripture satisfies four conditions: "First, it contains all of the articles one must believe in order to attain salvation. Second, it contains all precepts one must obey in order to live piously before God. Third, it is sufficiently perspicuous to convey this information to an attentive reader; and fourth, it is self-authenticating."[88] The Bible's testimony to itself is central to conservative theological interpretation of Scripture. It ties in with the doctrine of inspiration and hence of the absolute trustworthiness of God through his word in the Bible. The Evangelical Theological Society (ETS) adopts the inerrancy of Scripture as its theological ethos: "The Bible alone, and the Bible in its entirety, is the Word of God written and is therefore inerrant in the autographs."[89] Inspiration and inerrancy

---

84. Charles Caldwell Ryrie, review of *The Battle for the Bible*, by Harold Lindsell. *Bibliotheca Sacra* 133, no. 532 (1976): 356.
85. William L. Hendricks, review of *The Battle for the Bible*, by Harold Lindsell, *Southwestern Journal of Theology* 19, no. 1 (1976): 113.
86. Grant Wacker, "Reckoning with History: Richard Bushman, George Marsden, and the Art of Biography," *Journal of Mormon History* 43, no. 2 (2017): 21–45.
87. Wacker, "Reckoning with History," 14.
88. Dennis W. Jowers, "The Sufficiency of Scripture and the Biblical Canon," *Trinity Journal* 30 no. 1 (2009): 49.
89. Article 3 of the Constitution of the Evangelical Theological Society (adopted December 28, 1949, and amended in 1950, 1951, 1959, 1976, 1985, and 1990), cited in Denny R. Burk, "Is Inerrancy Sufficient? A Plea to Biblical Scholars Concerning the

confers authority to the Bible as Scripture. Every statement in the Bible is accurate and true "because God Himself is true and cannot lie."[90] The Bible is authoritative "because God Himself is authoritative."[91] The implication is that the Bible commands obedience in everything in the life of the Christian. "As the Chicago Statement itself affirms, 'Holy Scripture . . . is to be believed, as God's instruction, in all that it affirms; obeyed, as God's command, in all that it requires; embraced, as God's pledge, in all that it promises.'"[92] Inspiration, inerrancy, and the sufficiency of Scripture go together in the evangelical Christian conception of the Bible. As Denny R. Burk, a conservative evangelical theologian and one of the architects of the 2017 Nashville Statement (which argues LGBTQ rights and inclusion),[93] explains: "The classic biblical text on the nature of Scripture not only addresses the Scripture's own inspiration, but also its own sufficiency. This text indicates that the written Word of God, Scripture (γραφή), is totally sufficient for everything that the Christian (and thus the church) needs."[94]

According to Kevin J. Vanhoozer, the sufficiency of Scripture means that Scripture, by itself, is enough, "that the Bible alone is enough for ruling the church's social imaginary, especially as this concerns the story of what God is doing in creation and redemption. Scripture is sufficient for understanding extrabiblical knowledge in the framework of biblical narrative and for perceiving reality as sustained and directed by the triune God."[95] Rejecting naive biblicism, according to which the sufficiency of Scripture means the self-sufficiency and the omnicompetence of Scripture, Vanhoozer distinguishes between material and formal sufficiency. Material sufficiency means sufficiency in a particular subject matter. "The material sufficiency of Scripture means that the Bible tells us everything we need to know to be saved, not necessarily everything we want to know."[96] The Bible is sufficient for salvation, not sufficient for every form of knowledge in every academic discipline.

Authority and Sufficiency of Scripture," *Southwestern Journal of Theology* 50, no. 1 (2007): 76.

90. Burk, "Is Inerrancy Sufficient?," 80.
91. Burk, "Is Inerrancy Sufficient?," 80.
92. Burk, "Is Inerrancy Sufficient?," 80.
93. Denny R. Burk, "Why Nashville and Why Now?," *Eikon: A Journal for Biblical Anthropology* 4, no. 2 (2002): 7–23.
94. Burk, "Is Inerrancy Sufficient?," 83.
95. Kevin J. Vanhoozer, "The Sufficiency of Scripture: A Critical and Constructive Account," *Journal of Psychology and Theology* 49, no. 3 (2021): 218.
96. Vanhoozer, "The Sufficiency of Scripture," 221.

We cannot use the Bible to interpret scientific laws or teach mathematics.[97] "The Bible does not provide us with enough knowledge to cure cancer, plot the orbit of the moon, or get rid of crabgrass from your lawn."[98] The formal sufficiency of Scripture means that Scripture interprets itself because it contains its own clarity. This means that parts of Scripture are interpreted in the whole of the rest of Scripture. "The canon is the most important context for interpreting Scripture, because the parts interpret the whole and the whole interprets the parts, and because what needs to be known is clearly taught in some places even if not in others."[99] Vanhoozer explains further that Scripture interpreting itself does not mean that Scripture is the sole source, resource, and norm: "Everyone agrees that Scripture is the primary source for learning about what God was doing in Jesus Christ. But there are secondary sources for learning about God," including reason, experience, and church tradition.[100]

Unlike the extreme ultraconservative position of Weeks, Lindsell, MacArthur, and Jowers, according to whom Scripture provides answer to all questions, Vanhoozer limits the sufficiency of Scripture to the domain of theology and soteriology, "where the topic is God and the gospel."[101] The Protestant principle of *sola scriptura* means Scripture first but not Scripture only. So, the Scripture makes use of various other resources in serving as the medium of God's revelation, including the human language, the Church's proclamation

---

97. Vanhoozer warns that this should not lead to bibliophobia, by which we become afraid to invoke the authority of Scripture in any other thing or discipline outside soteriology. Vanhoozer, "The Sufficiency of Scripture,"227. He writes: "On the one hand, then, the sufficiency of Scripture never meant that the Bible ought to be the exclusive source in every domain of knowledge. There are some matters, like jet propulsion, which seem to fall outside the parameters of Scripture's authority, in the sense that Scripture does not explicitly address the domain of rocket science. On the other hand, Scripture is clearly the primary source in domains like theology and soteriology, where the topic is God and the gospel. Still other fields, however, like anthropology broadly conceived—the study of human nature and behavior—are 'mixed' domains: both Genesis and the Human Genome Project have something to contribute. The Bible is not a handbook of science, to be sure, but 'that does not mean it will have nothing to say which touches on the realm of the scientist'. . . . It may not be able to instruct us in the finer points of nuclear physics or addictive behaviors, but it does not follow that it has nothing to teach us about metaphysics, ethics, and psychology. For example, Scripture is sufficient to rebut reductionism, the idea that only the material world is truly real" (p. 227).
98. Vanhoozer, "The Sufficiency of Scripture," 229.
99. Vanhoozer, "The Sufficiency of Scripture," 222.
100. Vanhoozer, "The Sufficiency of Scripture," 222.
101. Vanhoozer, "The Sufficiency of Scripture," 227.

through various ministries in the service of the word, and of course, the Holy Spirit, who enlightens the people. "'Scripture alone' does not mean 'Scripture abstracted from the economy of grace' or 'Scripture apart from the community of faith' or even Scripture independent of church tradition."[102] So, the Spirit inspires, and illuminates.[103] Scripture's sufficiency equally implies that the Scripture controls our social imaginary and prevents a one-dimensional material conception of the universe, one that obstructs self-transcendence and grace. In other words, the formal sufficiency of Scripture means that while Scripture is self-interpretive, it makes use of other resources in the work of interpretation. "First, while Scripture alone is the supreme norm, it is not alone as a source or resource; even the Reformers acknowledged the role of the Holy Spirit, church tradition, and scholarly tools. Second, Scripture is its own interpreter in the sense that it provides the primary context for its interpretation (the canon)."[104]

Vanhoozer's reconstruction of the sufficiency of Scripture accords the Bible its authoritative place in doctrine and in the spiritual life of Christians. It corrects the extreme conservative positions that present the Bible as sufficient for all aspects of life. It explains fairly and much more broadly the Protestant principle of *sola scriptura* as not excluding the church and its hermeneutical traditions, ministry, worship, and sacraments. Vanhoozer indirectly draws attention to the multiplicity of churches within Protestantism and the different conceptions of the authority of the Bible as Scripture, including those of the "charismatic Enthusiasts, whose main form of spiritual authority is direct, unmediated inspiration,"[105] and hence the infallibility, complete harmony, and noncontradiction among all the passages of the Bible.[106] Vanhoozer's critical construction of the sufficiency of Scripture recognizes the place of the critical study of the Bible introduced during the Enlightenment, which advanced the modern historical-critical method of the study of the Bible by the recognition of the importance of the context of the scriptural texts and their relations

---

102. Kevin J. Vanhoozer, *Biblical Authority After Babel: Retrieving the Solas in the Spirit of Mere Protestant Christianity* (Brazos Press, 2016), 111.

103. Vanhoozer, "The Sufficiency of Scripture: A Critical and Constructive Account," 228.

104. Vanhoozer, "The Sufficiency of Scripture," 231.

105. Knut Alfsvag, "These Things Took Place as Examples for Us: On the Theological and Ecumenical Significance of the Lutheran Sola Scriptura," *Dialog: A Journal of Theology* 55, no. 3 (2016): 205.

106. Alfsvag, "These Things Took Place as Examples for Us," 205.

to their surrounding cultures and peoples. Thus, one will readily agree with Norwegian Lutheran theologian, Knut Alfsvag:

> Presented in its historical context, the principle of sola Scriptura does not appear as naive, but as a meaningful attempt at retrieving positions and practices that from the outset defined the self-understanding of the Christian church. It does not suggest reading the Bible in a room void of context; neither does it entail the idea of infallibility either in relation to the Bible, the church, or the teaching ministry. But it does entail the ability and willingness of the Christian community to find its own existence defined and described in the biblical texts.[107]

The sufficiency of Scripture does not mean sufficiency for everything but *sufficiency for everything for which it was divinely given*.[108] Vanhoozer argues that the Protestant principle that Scripture interprets Scripture means that "the parts interpret the whole and the whole interprets the parts" and "the parts that are less clear must be read in the light of those that are more clear."[109] According to Vanhoozer, "These are crucial principles, but they apply to the interpretation of any text. We must be careful not to let 'Scripture interprets Scripture' become an excuse for naïve biblicism."[110] What Luther meant by the principle that Scripture is interpreting itself is that it is not the church that interprets Scripture but that Scripture interprets the church. "The church understands its nature and function only in the light of Scripture."[111] In other words, the principle of the sufficiency of Scripture does not mean that Scripture rejects human interpretation, or for that matter, the place of church tradition in Scriptural interpretation. It does not mean that historical criticism is not allowed. While we must avoid negating transcendence, and limiting humanness to mere immanence, we must eschew "bibliolatry—viewing the Bible itself as somehow divine. God is divine, not the Bible! Hard-core fundamentalism and literalism, born in extreme reaction to contextual study of the Bible, have so idolized the Bible as to abuse it."[112]

---

107. Alfsvag, "These Things Took Place as Examples for Us," 207.
108. Vanhoozer, *Biblical Authority After Babel*, 114.
109. Vanhoozer, *Biblical Authority After Babel*, 116.
110. Vanhoozer, *Biblical Authority After Babel*, 116.
111. Vanhoozer, *Biblical Authority After Babel*, 117.
112. James A. Sanders, *From Sacred Story to Sacred Text* (Fortress Press, 1987), 5.

HISTORICISM

Even though he was an ardent supporter of the historical-critical method, Jospeh Ratzinger was not oblivious to its dangers. Its major weakness is leaving the context of the text, its history, audience, and so on, in the past. It considers the biblical words as human words only. It fails to integrate the events and by extension the messages of the books of the Bible as the one word of God, because it considers them as separate events that has meaning only within their limited contexts. This is historicism. For this reason, it is insufficient as a method in and of itself. Laurence Lerner defines historicism as "the view that literature is not for all time, but of an age."[113] True to their task, the historian is obliged to preserve the memory of the past.[114] But "historicism assumes that the truth of history or theory is time-dependent. Carried to a logical extreme, historicism is self-destructive and can lead to solipsism."[115] Ratzinger warned that historical-critical method, is limited by its very method, and in this sense, could result to historicism:

> For the time being, it is important . . . to recognize the limits of the historical-critical method itself. For someone who considers himself directly addressed by the Bible today, the method's first limit is that by its very nature it has to leave the biblical word in the past. It is a historical method, and that means that it investigates the then-current context of events in which the texts originated. It attempts to identify and to understand the past—as it was in itself—with the greatest possible precision, in order then to find out what the author could have said and intended to say in the context of the mentality and events of the time. To the extent that it remains true to itself, the historical method

---

113. Laurence Lerner, "Against Historicism," *New Literary History* 24, no. 2 (1993): 273.
114. Dwight W. Hoover, "The New Historicism," *The History Teacher* 25, no. 3 (1992): 355.
115. Hoover, "The New Historicism," 355–56. Postmodern approaches to historicity move against what it considers as the anchor of historicity; its base in foundationalism, by which it means objectivity independent of the subject; and in literary studies, a meaning embedded in a text which the interpreter finds, supposedly without consideration of the prejudices and biases of the interpreter. See F. W. Dobbs-Allsopp, "Rethinking Historical Criticism," *Biblical Interpretation* 7, no. 3 (1999): 235–71; Jonathan Rée, "The Vanity of Historicism," *New Literary History* 22, no. 4 (1991): 961–83; Hoover, "The New Historicism," 355–66.

not only has to investigate the biblical word of the past, but also has to let it remain in the past. It has to glimpse points of contact with the present and it can try to apply the biblical word to the present; the one thing it cannot do is make it into something present *today*—that would be overstepping its bounds. Its very precision in interpreting the reality of the past is both its strength and its limit."[116]

The limit of critical history Ratzinger points to above is related to Leopold von Ranke's view of the task of the historian as "simply to show how it really was, (*wie es eigentlich gewesen*)."[117] That is, the focus of the historian should be with the values of the past, without any concern with the present. The role of the historian is therefore to reconstruct history "into a *unified, coherent, meaningful whole.*"[118] The implication is a rejection of the transcendental aspect of the Bible. According to B. H. McLean, "As its name implies, 'historicism' limits its object of study to historical entities, excluding such ideal or transcendental principles as God, providence, or the Hegelian progress of the spirit (Geist). Historicism views biblical history as an historical phenomenon, comprised of unique, unrepeatable acts, arising from mundane material causes. Under the growing influence of the natural sciences, the biblical world was viewed as an 'interconnected nexus of causes, a self-contained and autonomous whole whose laws had the lucidity and validity of mathematical axioms, thus emptying the world of the need for special interventions of the divine (i.e., miracles).'"[119] Unfortunately, the past the historian seeks to critically analyze does not exist in its pristine state. What exists is the past reconstructed in the text, and in the case of translated texts, by the interpretations of the translator, a fact emphasized by Okure and West in their contextual hermeneutics.[120]

A multiplicity of contexts should also be taken into consideration in the course of the work of critical history. So, the task of the historical-critical method is complicated both by the method itself and by the past that it

---

116. Ratzinger, *Jesus of Nazareth*, xvi.
117. Cited in David Jasper, "The New Testament and Literary Interpretation," *Religion & Literature* 17, no. 3 (1985): 1.
118. B. H. McLean, "The Crisis of Historicism: And the Problem of Historical Meaning in New Testament Studies," *Heythrop Journal* 52, no. 2 (2012): 219 (italicized in the original).
119. McLean, "The Crisis of Historicism," 218.
120. Gerald O. West, "Some Parameters of the Hermeneutic Debate in the South African Context," *Journal of Theology for Southern Africa* 80 (1992): 3–13; Okure, "'I will open my mouth in parables'," 445–63.

seeks to study. Outside of the past, as reconstructed by the perspective of the historian under the influence of the ideologies and prejudices, and the power dynamics of the context of the historian, the factual reality of the past is hard to find. Ukpong draws out the consequences: "What we achieve in the historical exercise is making meaning of (reconstructing) the past with the insights (tools and wisdom) of our present situatedness. (There is hardly 'recovering' the past *as it was*)."[121]

The historical-critical method that recognizes the theological faith-filled sense, the spiritual sense, of the Bible as the word of God and hence that does not leave the Bible only in the past of their original contexts, remains important for scriptural interpretation. But the historical-critical method that interprets the Bible just like any other text and fails to recognize its surplus of meaning as the word of God remains stuck in the past and is historicism. Such a method is of no value to Christian hermeneutics.

THE UNITY OF SCRIPTURE

Dei Verbum #12 emphasizes both the divine and the human authorship of Scripture, the unity of the Old and the New Testaments of the Bible. It lays out biblical hermeneutics as requiring consideration of not only the diachronic, historical, and literal senses of Scripture but also the synchronic, spiritual, and allegorical sense. It states:

> However, since God speaks in sacred Scripture through men in human fashion, the interpreter of sacred Scripture, in order to see clearly what God wanted to communicate to us, should carefully investigate what meaning the sacred writers really intended, and what God wanted to manifest by means of their words.[122]

DV further mentions church tradition as the sphere of divine revelation (*DV* #10). For the interpretation of Scripture to be in accordance with the spirit of the unity of Scripture, "the living tradition of the whole Church must be taken into account along with the harmony which exists between elements of the faith" (*DV* #12). Thus, the interpretation of Scripture must be cognizant of

---

121. Ukpong, "Reading the Bible in a Global Village," 18.
122. Walter M. Abbott, SJ, *The Documents of Vatican II* (Guild Press, 1966), 120.

church tradition and the faith of the community. Reflecting on the historical-critical method, Ratzinger emphasized that though it is an indispensable tool for biblical interpretation, "it does not exhaust the interpretative task for someone who sees the biblical writings as a single corpus of Holy Scripture inspired by God."[123]

This interpretive key accords with the church's long tradition of recognizing the spiritual and the literal senses of Scripture. Patristic and medieval biblical scholars, including the early African biblical hermeneuts, read the Old Testament in the light of the value it has in the gospel and in the light of faith in Christ and the Christian hope in the resurrection. It portrays the continuing relevance of the Old Testament as the word of God and hence its contemporaneity.

Cardinal Henri de Lubac, after a careful reading of the patristics, concluded that "spiritual exegesis" or allegory is not a borrowing of literary techniques from the Greeks but rather a distinctly Christian approach to the Old Testament developed in the New Testament, particularly in the letters of St. Paul: "The allegory is not in the text, but in the realities of which the text speaks; not in history as narrative, but in history as event; or, one can say, allegory is in the narrative only inasmuch as this relates a real event."[124] De Lubac highlights Jesus Christ as not only the unity of Scripture but as the central figure of the Bible. For this reason, the spiritual sense of Scripture is giving spirit to the letter of Scripture, the Old Testament, expounding its meaning in the light of Christ and the Christian faith and hope in the resurrection.

De Lubac observes that despite its importance, a number of historians don't recognize what seems clear in St. Paul, that "the spiritual sense of the Old Testament is the New Testament."[125] Such historians attribute allegory to Philo; others think it a product of Platonic prejudice; for many more, it's a way of maintaining the relevance of Scripture until the human mind attained maturity; still others condemn the spiritual sense of Scripture as Greek invention at the same level as Greek "dogma" of the councils and Greek "mysticism" of the monks. In the final analysis, in the view of historians unfavorable toward an allegorical or spiritual sense of Scripture, it amounts to the corruption of the gospel; in the period of Protestant Reformation, the

---

123. Ratzinger, *Jesus of Nazareth*, xvi.
124. Robert Edwin McNally, "Medieval Exegesis," *Theological Studies* 22, no. 3 (1961): 452.
125. De Lubac, *Medieval Exegesis*, xiv.

corruption was attributed to "the very spirit of Catholicism."[126] Nor is this rejection of the spiritual sense limited to non-Catholics as it includes in its fold Scholasticism's rationalizations. What begs for answers is how all the doctors of the church and Christian thinkers of the first centuries could altogether stray to the path of error.

According to de Lubac, the twelfth century set the stage for systematization of the various ways of reading Scripture following Tyconius's rules. These rules in medieval exegesis are about the relation between the Old Testament and the New Testament. These much-talked-about rules were summed up in poems, starting with Augustine of Darca, whose distich gave rise to the four senses of scripture: history, allegory, morality, and anagogy. There were separate rules for each of the senses, as the rule for allegory is different from those of history, from those of the moral sense, and from anagogy, the rule for a foretaste of the future heavenly state.[127] These rules guide the scope of the use of each sense and restrain exegetes from abusing them during interpretation. Keeping to the rules of interpretation in each of the senses not only sustains the relationship of the senses to one another, to the context, but it also guides the method of interpretation, preserves the relationship between literal and allegorical senses of Scripture, and reduces haphazard movement from one sense to another by merely skimming Scripture, which results in a betrayal of the spiritual sense.[128]

John Cassian—who in the fifth century propounded this fourfold sense of Scripture—used Jerusalem to illustrate it: "According to history, Jerusalem is a city of the Jews. According to allegory, it is the church. According to tropology, it is the human soul. According to anagogy, it is the heavenly city of God."[129] Medieval exegesis provides a window into an interpretation of Scripture that unifies the historical-critical method and the spiritual

---

126. De Lubac, *Medieval Exegesis*, xv.
127. De Lubac, *Medieval Exegesis*, 15.
128. It is interesting to note that the four senses of Scripture are shared also by Jewish scholars. "In the Middle Ages, Jews and Christians elaborated a four-fold method of scriptural interpretation. Jews called it *PaRDeS*. This word, meaning 'paradise-garden,' is an acronym for four layers, often simultaneously present, in the biblical text: there is *Peshat*, the literal meaning; *Remez*, the allegorical meaning; *Derash*, the tropological and moral meanings; and *Sod*, the mystical meaning." Michael Fishbane, "The Teacher and the Hermeneutical Task: A Reinterpretation of Medieval Exegesis," *Journal of the American Academy of Religion* 43, no. 4 (1975): 710.
129. Christopher Ocker, "Medieval Exegesis and the Origin of Hermeneutics," *Scottish Journal of Theology* 52, no. 3 (1999): 339.

sense of Scripture as the word of God, a point both Ratzinger and Kurz emphasize in scriptural interpretation. As de Lubac observed, and as Robert Edwin McNally notes, unfortunately, the spiritual sense of Scripture has been neglected: "More often than not it has been misstated, misunderstood, forsaken in favor of a unilateral, literal, scientific hermeneutic which in many respects seems less theological and spiritual than its venerable ancestor. One notes too frequently nowadays an absence of concern for Holy Scripture as a spiritual book."[130]

Yet, whatever method used in reading the Bible, it will be meaningless if the Bible is not read as Scripture, as the text of Christian revelation. The senses of medieval exegesis fulfill Scripture as a spiritual book. "These three spiritual senses, comprising the mystical order, involve a *conversio*, allegory from the past to the present Christ, tropology, a reform of each life by the act of Christ, anagogy, a reform of the present by the future. Allegory signifies a conversion of intellect, tropology of morals, anagogy of desires. Allegory builds up or edifies faith, tropology charity, anagogy hope. Allegory is the sense of dogma, tropology of moral, anagogy of mysticism."[131] These senses of Scripture make sense because "the purpose of biblical exegesis, implicit and explicit, was to form the practice and belief of Christian people, individually and collectively."[132] This aligns with the purpose of *Dei Verbum* and the *IBC*: "The aim is that the word of God may become more and more the spiritual nourishment of the members of the people of God, the source for them of a life of faith, of hope and of love—and indeed a light for all humanity (cf. *Dei Verbum* #21)."[133]

The recalling and extolling of medieval exegesis is not borne out of a desire to promote the earliest form of hermeneutics or what the *IBC* calls "a pre-critical level of interpretation,"[134] which does not differentiate biblical

---

130. McNally, "Medieval Exegesis," 448.
131. McNally, "Medieval Exegesis," 453.
132. Frances M. Young, "Biblical Exegesis and the Formation of Christian Culture," cited in Edwina Murphy, *The Bishop and the Apostle: Cyprian's Pastoral Exegesis of Paul* (De Gruyter, 2018), 1.
133. IBC, 3–4.
134. IBC, 3. Ian Christopher Levy's *Introducing Medieval Biblical Interpretation: The Senses of Scripture in Premodern Exegesis* corrects some of the impressions the modern reader of the Bible has about medieval exegesis: "Medieval exegesis speaks to us today not because it is similar to contemporary exegesis but because it is rooted in certain hermeneutical assumptions that view the reader of a text as a participant in the creation of a text's meanings. The reader, so the medieval understood, was not to aspire to an objective,

commentary from theology and scriptural interpretation.[135] For one, the medieval hermeneutics promoting the allegorical reading of the Old Testament from the point of view of Christ based on the canonicity of Scripture raises the question whether that is the actual intent of the collection of books of the Hebrew Bible (the Christian Old Testament).[136] This is because it is not always so easy to affirm the unity of Scripture and yet keep the Old and the New Testaments separate to preserve their specificity. Yet "that all Scripture is to be read in the light of Christ is patristic and traditional Christian doctrine."[137] According to Hugh of St. Victor, "All divine Scripture is one book, and this one book is Christ, speaks of Christ and finds its fulfilment 'in Christ.'"[138] The point is to highlight the importance of the literal sense and the spiritual sense of Scripture. It is to emphasize the unity of Scripture, the role of history and the Spirit in its interpretation, and hence the reading of Scripture that is conscious of history and its nature as the word of God. This is the intent of *Dei Verbum* #12 and that of the Pontifical Biblical Commission's *IBC*: to ensure "a symphony of many voices."[139]

---

presuppositionless interpretation, as Enlightenment thinkers naively argued, but to an interpretation that is actively formed and shaped by a tradition." Craig S. Farmer, review of *Introducing Medieval Biblical Interpretation: The Senses of Scripture in Premodern Exegesis*, by Ian Christopher Levy, *Review of Biblical Literature* 24 (2022): 494.

135. James M. Vosté reminds us that "the exegete who at the same time reads the Fathers soon recognizes that the majority of the medieval commentators do nothing more than copy or summarize the great exegetes of the first five centuries of the Church. The present-day exegete, therefore, cannot afford to tarry with the medieval interpreters, who were but tiny rivulets, but they must trace the stream back to its sources in the Fathers." James M. Vosté, "Medieval Exegesis," *The Catholic Biblical Quarterly* 10, no. 3 (1948): 229.

136. The impression created of the pre-modern interpretation of Scripture was that it was precritical and thus in error. Stephen Fowl confessed as much of the impression he got from his graduate studies about medieval exegesis: "The way I was taught by virtually all of my professors, at least implicitly, was that premodern biblical interpretation was simply a form of error." Stephen Fowl, "Theological Interpretation of Scripture and Its Future," *Anglican Theological Review* 99, no. 4 (2017), 672.

137. James Okoye, "The Pontifical Biblical Commission, the Old Testament, and Christ as the Key to All Sacred Scripture," *Catholic Biblical Quarterly* 80, no. 4 (2018): 671. According to Okoye, "St. Augustine enshrined this conviction in the phrase, *Novum Testamentum in Vetere latet, et in Novo Vetuspatet* ("The New Testament lies hidden in the Old, and the Old Testament is unveiled in the New"; p. 671).

138. Hugh of St Victor, *De Arca*, cited in Henry Wansbrough, OSB, "The Bible in the Church Since Vatican II," *Scripture Bulletin* 43, no. 1 (2013): 10.

139. *The Interpretation of the Bible in the Church*, III, A,3, cited in Armand Puig i Tàrrech, "Interpreting the Scripture from a Catholic Point of View, *Sacra Scripta* 15, nos. 1–2 (2017): 34.

The harmony is achieved by emphasizing the unity of Scripture in Christ. This is not a misreading of the Old Testament since Christianity acknowledges that salvation is mediated through God's choice of the Jews from whom the word took flesh. Armand Puig i Tàrrech, a Spanish Scripture scholar and president of the Holy See's Agency for the Evaluation and Promotion of Quality in Universities and Ecclesiastical Faculties (AVEPRO) notes:

> The Christological reading of the entire Scripture naturally and seamlessly integrates God, whose Son is Jesus, the one anointed as Lord. It is therefore evident that the Scripture cannot be understood outside of Christ and Christ cannot be understood outside of God. The Scripture rests, in its entirety, on a fundamental affirmation that includes God, the source and origin, and the Logos Word: "all things came into being through him" (John 1,3; see Gn. 1,1–2) and it is he who has rescued humanity in the plenitude of the times (Gal 4,4–5). Consequently, the Old or First Testament and the New Testament, the expression of the two moments of a single salvation economy, cannot be antagonistic.[140]

For Tàrrech, the love of God and God's desire for human salvation, which is fulfilled in Christ, anchors the christological reading of the Bible, of the Old and the New Testaments, not as separate books unrelated to each other but as books related by the salvation history initiated by God and fulfilled in the paschal mystery.

Joseph Ratzinger, while endorsing the christological reading of the Bible, recommends the method spearheaded by American scholars called "canonical exegesis." According to Ratzinger, canonical reading is "reading the individual texts of the Bible in the context of the whole."[141] This reading is informed by the church position that Christ is the center that informs Scripture. And so, "a canonical reading evaluates passages in their relationship to the fullness

---

140. Tàrrech, "Interpreting the Scripture from a Catholic Point of View," 37. Yet a caveat is in order. As John Bright points out, "To say that the Old Testament can retain its place in the Church only if specifically Christian meanings can be found in its texts comes perilously close to saying that it can be regarded as canonical Scripture only when given a meaning other than the one it plainly intended." John Bright, *The Authority of the Old Testament* (Abingdon, 1967, 91), cited in Philip Culbertson, "Known, Knower, and Knowing: The Authority of Scripture in the Episcopal Church," *Anglican Theological Reviewer* 74, no. 2 (1992): 164n103.

141. Ratzinger, *Jesus of Nazareth*, xix.

of revelation in the person and work of Jesus."[142] Canonical exegesis implies reading every passage of the Bible as inspired and as playing a part in the whole narrative of God's salvation history. Ratzinger notes that canonical reading "does not contradict historical-critical interpretation, but carries it forward in an organic way toward becoming theology in the proper sense."[143] Canonical exegesis is therefore a rereading, a reconstruction of Scripture that brings out the "deeper value," or in Ricoeur's terminology, the surplus of meaning embedded in texts, as "any human utterance of a certain weight contains more than the author may have been immediately aware of at the time."[144] Ratzinger draws out the three interacting subjects of Scripture: the author, the receiving community (the Church), and God.

> First of all, there is the individual author or group of authors to whom we owe a particular scriptural text. But these authors are not autonomous writers in the modern sense; they form part of a collective subject, the "People of God," from within whose heart and to whom they speak. Hence, this subject is actually the deeper "author" of the Scriptures. And yet likewise, this people does not exist alone; rather, it knows that it is led, and spoken to, by God himself, who—through men and their humanity—is at the deepest level the one speaking.[145]

Canonical exegesis is favored in Ratzinger's apostolic exhortation *Verbum Domini*. There, the pope asserts the demand of *Dei Verbum* for the interpretation of Scripture in the light of the spirit in which it was written as the word of God. To do this, it must abide by three fundamental criteria: "1) the text must be interpreted with attention to *the unity of the whole of Scripture*; nowadays this is called canonical exegesis; 2) account is to be taken of the *living Tradition of the whole Church*; and, finally, 3) respect must be shown for *the analogy of faith*. Only where both methodological levels, the historical-critical and the theological, are respected, can one speak of a theological exegesis, an exegesis worthy of this book."[146] Canonical exegesis makes Scripture relevant to every

---

142. Okoye, "The Pontifical Biblical Commission," 676.
143. Ratzinger, *Jesus of Nazareth*, xix.
144. Ratzinger, *Jesus of Nazareth*, xix.
145. Ratzinger, *Jesus of Nazareth*, xx–xxi.
146. Pope Benedict XVI, *Post-Synodal Apostolic Exhortation Verbum Domini*, #34, The Holy See, accessed September 4, 2023, https://www.vatican.va/content/benedict-xvi/en/apost_exhortations/documents/hf_ben-xvi_exh_20100930_verbum-domini.html.

age. It is not stuck in the past, as the historical-critical method alone tends to limit scriptural texts. Canonical exegesis promotes the typological sense of Scripture, as the Old Testament, the Prophets, and the Writings, events, and persons of the Old Testament are seen as types fulfilled in the New Testament. These interpretations of Scripture were employed with ease by the fathers of the church. As Ratzinger points out, texts have deeper value beyond the words employed by the author. This deeper meaning or value arises because some texts transcend their times and contexts.

> When a word transcends the moment in which it is spoken, it carries within itself a "deeper value." This "deeper value" pertains most of all to words that have matured in the course of faith-history. For in this case the author is not simply speaking for himself on his own authority. He is speaking from the perspective of a common history that sustains him and that already implicitly contains the possibilities of its future, of the further stages of its journey. The process of continually rereading and drawing out new meanings from words would not have been possible unless the words themselves were already open to it from within.[147]

Raymond Brown had expressed this deeper sense of Scripture in terms of *sensus plenior*. Brown explained *sensus plenior* as "additional, deeper meaning, intended by God but not clearly intended by the human author."[148] Joseph Ratzinger's preface to the *IBC* sums up canonical exegesis, *sensus plenior*, and what is expected in biblical interpretation:

> Accordingly, the text of the document inquires into how the meaning of Scripture might become known—this meaning in which the human word and God's word work together in the singularity of historical events and the eternity of the everlasting Word, which is contemporary in every age. The biblical word comes from a real past. It comes not only from the past, however, but at the same time from the eternity of God and it leads us into God's eternity, but again along the way through time, to which the past, the present and the future belong.[149]

---

147. Ratzinger, *Jesus of Nazareth*, xix–xx.
148. Raymond E. Brown, *The Sensus Plenior of Sacred Scripture* (St. Mary's University, 1955), cited in Wansbrough, "The Bible in the Church Since Vatican II," 11.
149. Joseph Ratzinger, preface to *IBC*, 2.

The Bible is read diachronically, historically, literally, synchronically, canonically, and theologically, in the light of the faith of the community of believers for whom the Bible is the word of God.[150] This is the theological reading of Scripture.[151] It is the interpretation of Scripture that while acknowledging the importance of the historical-critical method and interpreting the Bible using this modern critical method, does not negate the importance and role of Scripture in the life of the church. The emphasis of theologians, including Joseph Ratzinger, Stephen Fowl, Rowan Williams, Justin S. Ukpong, Musa W. Dube, Gerald O. West, Teresa Okure, and others, is that Christians read and interpret the Bible to deepen their communion with God and with one another as believers.[152] Theological interpretation of Scripture must not, however, ignore the historical-critical method. Theological interpretation should not be an opportunity to escape the rigor of critical method in favor of the simplistic, literalistic, proof-texting by cross-referencing similar texts in the Bible to prove the Bible's importance and use in the church or simply to justify church practices, doctrines, and beliefs.

CONCLUSION

The Dogmatic Constitution on Divine Revelation (*Dei Verbum*) of Vatican Council II and the Pontifical Biblical Commission document *The Interpretation of the Bible in the Church*, recognize the importance of holistic interpretation of the Bible that includes a diachronic, historical-critical method and synchronistic reading of the Bible as the word of God, as the literal sense of Scripture. Both documents extol the role of history in biblical exegesis but

---

150. Teresa Okure, an African theologian, expresses the community of believers as central to the nature of the Bible thus: "The Bible is essentially a community book, written for people living in communities of faith, and no passage of Scripture is subject to private interpretation (2 Pet. 1:19–21)." Teresa Okure, "What Is Truth?," 405.

151. Important texts in this regard include the IBC; *Dei Verbum* of Vatican II: *A Manifesto for Theological Interpretation*, ed. Craig G. Bartholomew and Heath A. Thomas (Baker Academic, 2016); John Webster, *Holy Scripture: A Dogmatic Sketch, Current Issues in Theology* (Cambridge University Press, 2003). See also John Webster, *The Domain of the Word: Scripture and Theological Reason* (T&T Clark, 2012); Stephen E. Fowl, *Theological Interpretation of Scripture* (Cascade, 2009); D. Christopher Spinks, *The Bible and the Crisis of Meaning: Debates on the Theological Interpretation of Scripture* (T&T Clark, 2007).

152. Nate Dawson, "Making the Shift to Theological Interpretation of Scripture," *Anglican Theological Review* 99, no. 4 (2017): 753–62.

are not ignorant of its limitations. The historical-biblical method must not be stuck in the past. It must be forward looking and read the historical events of the past in the light of the Bible as Scripture, as the word of God. Absence of integral, holistic, and biblical hermeneutics results in historicism, literalism, and fundamentalism. Historicism fails to recognize the Bible as a spiritual book. Literalism focuses only on the final form of the Bible and reads it as is, without accounting for the background of the various texts and the variety of literary genres of the Bible. Fundamentalism construes the inspiration of the Bible to imply a version of inerrancy in which the Bible is sufficient for every question or issue a Christian might have. In response to the inadequacies of historicism, literalism, and fundamentalism, *Dei Verbum* lays out biblical hermeneutics as requiring consideration of not only the diachronic, historical, and literal senses of Scripture but also the synchronic, spiritual, and allegorical senses as well. The point is to emphasize the unity of Scripture and the role of history and the Spirit in its interpretation and hence the reading of Scripture that is conscious of history and of its nature as the Word of God.

African biblical scholars agree on the limitations of historical-critical method but recognize its indispensability for critical study of the Bible. However, they insist the Bible must be read in the light of the conceptual frame of reference of each people. Hence, their emphasis of contextual biblical hermeneutics with a focus on inculturation and liberation motifs of African theology.

CHAPTER SIX

The Future of Bible Reading in Africa

INTRODUCTION

Bible reading in Africa is as old as Christianity itself. Early African theologians championed the development of unique methods of biblical interpretation that informed centuries of subsequent hermeneutics.[1] Later, Christian expansion in Africa was mediated by the various measures to bring the Bible home to the African people through translations into various African languages, with the collaboration of Western missionaries, African linguists, and Christian converts.[2] Because of the link between the missionary activities, colonialism, and the introduction of the Western education system, African Christians of the early colonial period saw the Bible not only as the word of God, the direct access to the white person's superior deity, but also as the gateway to the power and luxury enjoyed by the colonial administrators and the respect accorded to their missionaries.[3] The missionaries' disdain for African cultures, which were demonized, led to a peculiar missionary hermeneutic that sought to replace African religio-cultural life with "Biblical Christianity."[4]

---

1. Lynskey, *Tyconius' Book of Rules*.
2. Aloo Osotsi Mojola, "Bible Translation in Africa: A Brief Historical Overview," *Journal of African Christian Thought* 15, no. 2 (2012): 5–9; Nathan Esala, "Skopostheorie: A Functional Approach for the Future of Bible Translation in Africa?," *Journal of African Christian Thought* 15, no. 2 (2012): 26–32.
3. Achebe, *Things Fall Apart*; *Arrow of God* (Penguin Books, 1991); *No Longer at Ease* (Penguin Books, 1994).
4. James Amanze, "Conflict and Cooperation: The Interplay Between Christianity and African Traditional Religions in the Nineteenth and Twentieth Centuries," *Studies in World Christianity & Interreligious Relations* 48 (2014): 281–304; Ben Knighton, "The

With Christianity established as the true religion, and with the Bible associated with Western education, the Bible was read by all—the educated, semi-literate, illiterate (through public and liturgical recitations), and Africans trained as Bible scholars.[5] The ordinary people and the biblical scholars' joint reading of the Bible has deepened biblical interpretation in Africa.[6] The preferred biblical hermeneutics for Africa is an existential reading conscious of the reality of Africans. This is called the inculturation hermeneutics.[7] This form of reading is the gift of African biblical scholarship to world Christianity.[8]

But African reading of the Bible is not exotic, not disconnected from the readings of Christianities in other continents.[9] This is noteworthy because "not infrequently African culture and theological appropriations of the Bible and Christianity are idealized or romanticized,"[10] often in reaction to the colonialist suppression of African culture and refusal to engage African biblical studies by their European counterparts. Hence the tendency not to criticize elements of African culture by some scholars for fear of falling into the mistake of demeaning African culture as colonialism did to Africa. African readings of the Bible draw from the ecclesiological foundations of the various Christian traditions of the readers. For this reason, some Africans (Catholics) rely on the teaching authority of the church for the correct interpretation of the Bible. Others (Protestants) rely on the authority of the

---

Meaning of God in an African Traditional Religion and the Meaninglessness of Well-Meaning Mission: The Experience of Christian Enculturation in Karamoja, Uganda," *Transformation* 16, no. 4 (1999): 120–26.

5. Musimbi Kanyoro, "Reading the Bible from an African Perspective," *Ecumenical Review* 51, no. 1 (1999): 18–24.

6. Ukpong, "Popular Readings of the Bible in Africa, 582–94.

7. Dirk J. Smit, "A Story of Contextual Hermeneutics and the Integrity of New Testament Interpretation in South Africa," *Neotestamentica* 28, no. 2 (1994): 265–89.

8. Joseph Ogbonnaya, "Insight into Context: Systematic Theological Reading of the Bible in Africa: The Case of Nigeria," in *Watering the Garden: Studies in Honor of Deirdre Dempsey*, ed. Andre Orlov (Gorgias Press, 2023), 217–37; Draper, "Reading the Bible as Conversation, 12–24; Humphrey Mwangi Waweru, "Reading the Bible Contrapuntally: A Theory and Methodology for a Contextual Bible Interpretation in Africa," *Svensk Missionstidskrift* 94, no. 3 (2006): 333–48; Gerrie F. Snyman, "Hermeneutics, Contexts, Identity: A Critical Discussion of the Bible in Africa," *Religion & Theology* 10, nos. 3/4 (2003): 378–415.

9. Ngong, "Reading the Bible in Africa, 66–83.

10. Jeremy Punt, "Reading the Bible in Africa: Accounting for Some Trends Part I" *Scriptura* 68 (1999): 6.

Bible to interpret itself through the spirit. Most Pentecostals believe in the inspiration of the Holy Spirit to read the Bible. Not to be forgotten, of course, is the interpretation by the various AICs, which favor oral hermeneutics[11] and include the Bible as a tool for divination.[12] African Christians put together these interpretations and formulate distinct spiritualities unique to them and to their sociocultural beliefs and worldview.[13]

The African worldview is naturally spiritual or religious. All is sacred. And this worldview was obtained long before the Christian missionary era.[14] This pervasive religiosity is easily transferred to the Bible, which is regarded as the medium of communication between God and human beings. As aptly articulated by Nlelanya Onwu:

> African theologians are convinced that the Bible is more than the record of man's religious development from primitive beginnings. We do not see it aright unless we also see it as the only record of the redeeming love of God, able to speak the word of salvation in Christ to Africans in their present situations. This implies that in interpreting the Bible, approaching it with questions and problems relating to Africa's experience, the African theologians are forced to measure the answers they have received from the Euro-American counterparts against the African's own perceptions about the teaching of Christ.[15]

Africans apply the Bible to their various contexts and regard themselves as the recipients of the biblical messages.

According to Musimbi Kanyoro, "[African] spirituality is best illustrated in the way we read the Bible in Africa: we appropriate the words of the scriptures and assume that we are the intended audience."[16] Africans appropriate the word of God as a personal message because, for them, "the Bible is seen

---

11. Zablon Nthamburi, "Biblical Hermeneutics in the African Instituted Churches," *AICMAR Bulletin* 1 (2002): 15–30.

12. Jesse Davie-Kessler, "'Discover Your Destiny': Sensation, Time, and Bible Reading Among Nigerian Pentecostals," *Anthropologica* 58, no. 1 (2016): 3.

13. Fidon Mwombeki, "Reading the Bible in Contemporary Africa," *Word & World* 21, no. 2 (2001): 121–28.

14. Magesa, *What Is Not Sacred?*

15. Nlelanya Onwu, "The Current State of Biblical Studies in Africa," *Journal of Religious Thought* 42, no. 2 (1984/5): 37.

16. Kanyoro, "Reading the Bible from an African Perspective," 18.

as a symbol of God's presence and protection"[17] Fidon Mwombeki is right: "Africans read the Bible for practical utilization. It is a book of life, neither a book of fiction nor one of history. It is not read for curiosity or fun. In this book, the reader listens to God speaking: giving comfort, instruction, exhortation, even condemnation."[18] Because the Bible was used to justify slavery, colonialism, and the oppressive apartheid regime in South Africa, some Africans, especially African biblical scholars, regard the Bible as a tool of imperialism, which Africans must appropriate to subvert their oppressors and achieve freedom and equality as children of God. African women equally feel the Bible must be liberated from its patriarchal trappings by which women are degraded and treated as subhuman. Hence, they call for a gender-sensitive reading of the Bible.

This chapter aims to chart the future of African readings of the Bible and examines the form of Christianity in Africa engendered by the African reading of the Bible. It explores the influence of Pentecostalism, a so-called third stream of Christianity, and the impacts of prosperity gospel in worship, Bible reading, and Christian practice in Africa. It raises important questions concerning the Bible-in-Africa project. How is African contextual reading received across Christianity in other parts of the world? Is there a need to decolonize Christianity in Africa, to free it from Western cultural accoutrements? Considering the impact of modernity and the need for integral development in sub-Saharan Africa, the chapter will equally engage the question of fundamentalism and social gospel in Africa. What form of Bible reading enhances the people's well-being, progress, and development, both as individuals and as members of states in the pursuit of the common good?

RECEPTION OF AFRICAN CONTEXTUAL HERMENEUTICS

Biblical studies are dominated by a Western worldview drawn from the Enlightenment's emphasis on reason, literary studies, and critical study in its various forms. Reactions against the scientific study of the Scriptures gave rise to conservative positions like biblicism and literalism as alternative and novel forms of interpretation of Scripture. The various methods of biblical interpretation, though, even when opposed to each other, are predicated on

---

17. Mwombeki, "Reading the Bible in Contemporary Africa," 121.
18. Mwombeki, "Reading the Bible in Contemporary Africa," 122.

Western values through which the Bible is interpreted. According to Helen C. John,

"Western worldview" thus permeates biblical scholarship, grounding it in western presumptions, western ideological orientations, and (predominantly) Protestant confessional agendas. Furthermore, biblical scholarship takes a pronounced top-down approach, such that even when non-western worldviews are taken into account, they are usually mediated through western or western-educated scholarly voices. Underrepresented and undervalued, then, are diverse (yet particular) cultural perspectives and grassroots interpretative voices (that is, those without academic training in biblical criticism) from those diverse cultural settings.[19]

Some African biblical scholars, especially white South Africans, are skeptical of the Bible-in-Africa readings for many reasons, including their generality, lack of specificity, exaggerated positions, ignorance of the historical contexts of the texts, and particularly, their use of the Bible as liberative motif. Jeremy Punt argues along these lines, contending that care must be taken not to use culture to propagate continuity of oppression of some members of community. Punt is referring to the ideological use of culture as a tool of segregation of Blacks from whites and the subsequent marginalization of Black South Africans when "inculturation hermeneutics was all too easily confused with or coopted by apartheid uses of the Bible."[20] Every etic approach to culture must be accompanied by an emic example to avoid an overgeneralization of examples as representing Africa, which is broad, heterogenous, linguistically different, and culturally diverse. "There is an increasing need to concentrate on a particular African cultural group with its particular 'differences,' rather than to revert to generalized conceptions of things 'African.' There is also a need to realize that especially in Africa the 'Eurocentric' Stoic values of aloofness and disinterestedness should be pushed aside."[21]

---

19. Helen C. John, "Conversations in Context: Cross-Cultural (Grassroots) Biblical Interpretation Groups Challenging Western-Centric (Professional) Biblical Interpretation," *Biblical Interpretation* 27 (2019): 37.

20. John Riches, "Interpreting the Bible in African Contexts: Glasgow Consultation," *Semeia* 73 (1996): 185.

21. Jeremy Punt, "Reading the Bible in Africa: Accounting for Some Trends, Further Prolegomena for a Discussion," *Scriptura* 71 (1999): 322.

Acknowledging that most interpretations of Scripture are subjective, Punt critiques some possible misconceptions about African biblical studies. He notes that biblical interpretation is not a free-for-all relativism: "Some sort of 'ethics of reading/interpretation,' some kind of accountability and responsibility in the interpretive process is required. This responsibility in reading the Bible is an essential element lacking in the use of the Bible in the struggle against oppression, where there is frequently not enough consideration given to the biblical documents, their literary nature, their historical circumstances, and very important, the role of the reader and his/her community."[22] Punt gives the example of the Exodus event model often used by liberationist theologians, observing that they ignore the discriminatory, violent, and oppressive conquest of the land of Cannan. He disputes the similarity between the African and the biblical world, arguing that while there may be similar concepts of kinship, honor, and family, "the worldview or broader framework can be very different when the Bible and African life are compared, not only with reference to the New Testament but also (perhaps especially) in comparison to the Old Testament."[23]

Punt favors the development of African hermeneutics, one set within the African context and, at the same time, being conscious of the historical context of the texts of Scripture.[24] Christoph Stenschke agrees that the development of African biblical hermeneutics is the responsibility of Africans: "The quest for the reception of the Bible in Africa is and will remain a task for African biblical studies and other disciplines. This is also where the awareness and competence to do so lies. Some of this task has already been tackled by the several journals and countless monographs on the interpretation of the Bible in Africa."[25] Punt acknowledges the reception of the Bible in a variety of African contexts and warns of the dangers of restricting its historicity to the past and of narrow Afrocentricism:

> Let us also accept and rejoice that the Bible has been appropriated by African people, never to be relinquished again; the same Bible is not

---

22. Punt, "Reading the Bible in Africa, Part I," 9–10.
23. Jeremy Punt, "Reading the Bible in Africa: On Strategies and Ownership," *Religion &Theology* 14, no. 2 (1997): 126.
24. Punt, "Reading the Bible in Africa: On Strategies and Ownership," 139.
25. Christoph Stenschke, "Recent Contributions to the Study of the Reception of the Bible and Their Implications for Biblical Studies in Africa," *Religion and Theology* 22 (2015): 377.

only read but used in the lives of people in Africa in many different ways. The twin dangers which we should avoid is the one of viewing the Bible as uninterpretable locked up either in its "own" past or the past of the "history of its interpretation" and thus useless for Africa, and the other of assuming the aim of the Bible being to promulgate and promote Africanness, addressing us as an African document.[26]

African biblical studies are often referred to as the contextual subjective reading, as opposed to the Western supposedly "objective" reading presumed to have universal application. This is contrary to the postmodern deconstructionist view that all interpretation is contextual. For this reason, African biblical hermeneutics is not recognized in the European/North American academy and is thus "confined largely to the SBL's experimental journals (*Semeia*), European journals (e.g., *JSNT, BOTSA, NovT, VT, Exchange*), African journals (*AJET, AJBS, JABS, JAT, JTSA, Neot, OTE, Verb, et Eccl., Scriptura*), Asian journals (*ATA, AJT*), and essays in volumes (e.g., Dube 2001; Dube, Mbuvi and Mbuwayesango 2012)."[27] European ownership of academic biblical scholarship continues to be dominant while African biblical scholars work to establish their contextual hermeneutics in its various forms: inculturation, liberation, feminist, and so on. But now any dialogue between them must begin on the basis of equality. Can such a dialogue materialize? Knut Holter is pessimistic despite European biblical scholars becoming interested in the concerns of African biblical scholars. He attributes this to differences operating in economic worlds and the continued shadow of colonialism.[28]

As part of the conversations between European and African biblical scholars, a conference was held in Stellenbosch, South Africa, in 2016. The meeting highlighted areas of convergence and divergence between them. They converge in sharing the historical-critical method. They diverge in African biblical scholarship emphasizing context in addition to the critical method. The differences can be summed up historically in the relationship between the rational scientific methodology influenced by the European Enlightenment modernist focus on reason and critical analysis and the contextual, inculturation, and

---

26. Punt, "Reading the Bible in Africa: Accounting for Some Trends," 323.
27. Andrew M. Mbuvi, "African Biblical Studies: An Introduction to an Emerging Discipline," *Currents in Biblical Research* 15, no. 2 (2017): 156.
28. Knut Holter, "Does a Dialogue Between Africa and Europe Make Sense?," in de Wit and West, *African and European Readers of the Bible in Dialogue*, 69–80.

liberationist methodologies of the African scholars influenced by colonial, postcolonial, decolonial, liberationist, and feminist contexts.

Incidentally, both methodologies used to be part of one integrated reading of the Bible. The bifurcation was historic, arising from the need to control relativistic reductionistic readings by people, leading to the "exegesis/actualization or interpretation/application debate."[29] European and North American biblical scholars claim to focus on exegesis, while not excluding appropriation or relevance of the text to contemporary societies. African biblical scholars are said to privilege actualization or application of the Bible over the exegetical/critical method, but they equally make use of the historical-critical method because most of them were trained in Europe and North America. Gerald O. West notes that African biblical scholars distinguish between interpretive and life interests in reading the Bible. Interpretive interests refer to the various dimensions of the text, while life interests are the concerns that lead the reader to the Bible in the first place. Life interests are often sociological, political, economic, spiritual, and other issues of existence. "With regards to interpretive interests . . . African biblical scholarship has been strongly shaped by historical-critical interests of western biblical scholarship and this includes the full array of historical-critical methodology: text criticism, form criticism, source criticism, and redaction criticism."[30]

The sociohistorical interests of African biblical scholars allow them to concentrate on religious and cultural issues, especially the life interests of the readers. And here lies African interpretive distinctiveness. West argues that Ukpong's analysis of the methodology of African biblical studies clearly "demonstrates the exegetical dimensions of African biblical scholarship."[31] African biblical scholars do not simply stop at exegesis but advance toward "hermeneutics as the application of the meaning so recovered to a particular historical context."[32] West asserts that exegesis and application go together, that even those who deny it bring them together: "What is it that biblical scholars actually do? For it is evident that biblical scholars actually do what Gadamer indicates, namely, they interpret the bible out of and for a particular context. While some may stamp their feet and deny that they do so, they

---

29. Gerald O. West, "Interrogating the Comparative Paradigm in African Biblical Scholarship," in de Wit and West, *African and European Readers of the Bible in Dialogue*, 37.
30. West, "Interrogating the Comparative Paradigm," 39.
31. West, "Interrogating the Comparative Paradigm," 49.
32. West, "Interrogating the Comparative Paradigm," 49.

do."³³ West then sums up the engagement of African biblical scholars with the Bible as exegetical and contextual:

> What characterizes African biblical scholarship is that we are overt about why we come to the bible and what life interests drive our dialogue with it. In other words, we acknowledge the contexts out of which we interpret. This does not make African biblical scholarship uncritical or unexegetical, for both of these terms have been partially deconstructed.³⁴

Not every scholar is interested in collaboration. Hans de Witt opted for what he termed "living apart together," or noncollaboration with African biblical scholarship.³⁵ In a similar vein, Knut Holter concluded in a pessimistic tone that the relationship between European and African biblical scholarship "continue[s] to be influenced by power structures of the colonial past."³⁶ Holter regrets the lack of interest on the part of European biblical studies to interact with Africans because they feel they can do without it. "African biblical studies is still considered a rather exotic flower in the garden, a flower which Europeans can do without."³⁷

Nevertheless, differences in cultural contexts and relationships between ordinary reading and academic readings remain important factors in determining appropriate relationships between European/North American readings and African contextual biblical hermeneutics. John Riches came to a similar conclusion in his report on the consultations on ordinary and academic reading of the Bible. Riches reports: "What the survey also showed was that there were those who were seeking fresh ways of looking at the Bible as part of a wider search for personal growth and development; and that this was often related to attempts to relate personal faith to wider, public issues."³⁸ Riches sums up the fruit of the survey on the various readings of the Bible, between the popular and academic, European/North and African contextual biblical hermeneutic:

> One of the outcomes of the consultation was to underline the similarities between Western/Northern readings of the Bible and the goals of

---

33. West, "Interrogating the Comparative Paradigm," 51.
34. West, "Interrogating the Comparative Paradigm," 54.
35. De Wit, "Exegesis and Contextuality," 3–36.
36. Knut Holter, "Evaluation: Dialogue and Interpretative Power," in de Wit and West, *African and European Readers of the Bible in Dialogue*, 409.
37. Holter, "Evaluation," 414.
38. Riches, "Interpreting the Bible in African Contexts," 186.

African scholars engaged in inculturation hermeneutics. Both groups are engaged in cultural readings of the Bible. Nevertheless, these similarities remain on the theoretical level. Both try to read the Bible from their own perspective and to view it in the light of their own dominant concerns. The effect of this is, in turn, to point to the particularity of such local theologies and to raise the question of how far we can continue to speak of a universal theology, of any kind of commonality among the diversities of theology that will be produced once the cultural hegemony of Western/ Northern readings is broken.[39]

Both are contextual biblical interpretations: one (Western/Northern) is in denial because of centuries of claims to universality; the other (African) recognizes and professes its contextuality. Meanwhile, the spread of a peculiar form of Pentecostalism influenced by aspects of African cosmology paints African Christianity and its reading of the Bible in a particularly negative light to those other readings that have limited biblical interpretation to the criteria of Enlightenment reason.

AFRICAN PENTECOSTALISM

Pentecostalism is regarded as the third stream of Western Christianity, following Roman Catholicism and Protestantism. It takes various forms, but it is commonly recognizable by its deep respect of the Pentecost experience at the Upper Room when the Holy Spirit descended on the apostles in tongues of flame (Acts 2) and the belief in a direct encounter with God through the Holy Spirit, hence the need for each member to experience rebirth, renewal, Spirit-baptism, and so on.[40] Pentecostal Christianity also cuts across dominant Christian traditions in the modern expression of the faith, including the Catholic Church and Protestant Christianity.[41] Catholic and Protestant churches unofficially include Pentecostal charismatic formats in their devotional activities, with emphasis on encounters with the Holy Spirit as central to belief, worship, and prayer. In the Catholic Church, for instance, Charismatic

---

39. Riches, "Interpreting the Bible in African Contexts," 186–87.
40. Bankole Tokunbo, "'African Factors' in the Metamorphosis of Indigenous Pentecostalism in Ekitiland, Nigeria," *Black Theology* 17, no. 2 (2019): 150–62.
41. Paul Gifford, "African Catholicism's Vulnerability to Pentecostalism," *Concilium* 2023, no. 2 (2023): 36–45.

Renewal adopts Pentecostal common belief and stresses the gifts of the Holy Spirit, speaking in tongues, prophecy, healing, and exorcism.[42]

Pentecostals approach the Bible in different ways, consistent with their diverse expressions, based on their preunderstandings of the Bible and of the role of the Holy Spirit in direct encounter with God. All manners of hermeneutic can be found in Pentecostal interpretations of the Bible. Some predominantly ordinary people readers, including church leaders uneducated as biblical scholars, interpret the Bible in a biblicist and literalist way. Other Pentecostals read the Bible eschatologically, from the point of view of the end-times.[43] Some others adopt the historical critical view, looking for the world behind the text in search of the author's intended meaning while proposing an intercultural engagement acknowledging cross-cultural currents in biblical studies.[44] A few also employ postmodern and postcritical "approaches such as literary, reader-response, and advocacy hermeneutics."[45]

Pentecostalism emerged in various parts of Africa at different times, and its growth is fueled by various reasons. Some scholars trace its beginning to the transition from the African Independent Churches to the Pentecostal Charismatic churches and problematized the Africanization of Christianity.[46] The Charismatic churches are distinguished from the established Pentecostal churches, like the Assemblies of God.[47] In Nigeria, Ghana, and West Africa, where it is one of the fastest growing churches, dissatisfaction with the mainline churches' worship and religious fervor accompanied by claims of miracles attracted many into the Pentecostal churches.[48] Economic downturn and accompanying hardship[49] arising from the collapse of the expectations

---

42. Pious O. Abioje, "The Pentecostal Emphasis on Miracle in the Nigerian Perspective: A Theological Discourse," *The Nigerian Journal of Theology* 18 (2004): 53–67.

43. Margaret Mollett, "Apocalypticism and Popular Culture in South Africa: An Overview and Update," *Religion & Theology* 19 (2012): 219–36.

44. John, "Conversations in Context," 36–68.

45. Marius Nel, "Current Classical Pentecostal Bible Reading Methods: A Critical Perspective," *Theology Today* 80, no. 3 (2023): 285.

46. Meyer, "Christianity in Africa," 447–74.

47. Paul Gifford, "Ghana's Charismatic Churches," *Journal of Religion in Africa* 24, no. 3 (1994): 241.

48. Paul Gifford, "The Prosperity Gospel in Africa: Expecting Miracles," *The Christian Century* 124, no. 14 (2007): 20–24.

49. Boniface E. Nwigwe, "Language About God: A Case Study of Language Abuse in Contemporary Christian Religious Practice in Nigeria," *The Nigerian Journal of Theology* 18 (2004): 68–77.

of political independence, mismanagement of the oil boom and other natural resources, and corruption in politics, along with general dissatisfaction, pushed many more into Pentecostal churches, with their promises of vibrant worship, heartfelt conversion (in the sense of a deep turnaround of sinful lives), and prosperity.[50] According to Musa A. B. Gaiya, "The growth of the Pentecostal churches can be explained variously. Aside from the spiritual rebirth experience by those who were swayed to turn from their confessed evil ways, several others were enticed to Pentecostalism by the appealing and soothing messages that portrayed prosperity, holiness, and blissful living as attainable heights in Christendom."[51]

In response to challenging social malaise, "charismatic Pentecostalism in Nigeria currently is shifting from strictly spiritual solutions to sociopolitical problems to an emphasis on meeting social needs in practical ways."[52] Their scriptural interpretation leans toward biblicism and literalism, according to which the words of Scripture as the word of God is certain and true by virtue of the inspiration of Scripture and its inerrancy, its authority over every aspect of life, and of course, its being under the direction of the men and women of God. "The authority of the Bible as the word of God, and the experience of the Spirit form two of the most critical sources of Pentecostal theology."[53]

Pentecostalism affirms the Bible's healings, exorcisms, and miracles of Jesus as ongoing, continuing in the modern contemporary church because God's word is true and God is faithful to his promises (Acts 8:4–8; Acts 19:11–12).[54] Just like other Pentecostals, African Pentecostal churches engage in spiritual warfare to combat the forces of darkness, witches and wizards, the workings

---

50. Kate Bowler and Wen Reagan, "Bigger, Better, Louder: The Prosperity Gospel's Impact on Contemporary Christian Worship," *Religion and American Culture: A Journal of Interpretation* 24, no. 2 (2014): 186–230.

51. John Olushola Magbadelo, "Pentecostalism in Nigeria: Exploiting or Edifying the Masses?," *African Sociological Review/Revue Africaine de Sociologie* 8, no. 2 (2004): 17.

52. Musa A. B. Gaiya, "Charismatic and Pentecostal Social Orientations in Nigeria," *Nova Religio: The Journal of Alternative and Emergent Religions* 18, no. 3 (2015): 63–79.

53. J. Kwabena Asamoah-Gyadu, "Mission to 'Set the Captives Free': Healing, Deliverance, and Generational Curses in Ghanaian Pentecostalism," *International Review of Mission* 93, nos. 370–71 (2004): 390.

54. J. Kwabena Asamoah-Gyadu, "Pulling Down Strongholds: Evangelism, Principalities and Powers and the African Pentecostal Imagination," *International Review of Mission* 96, nos. 382–83 (2007): 306–17.

of the devil, the principalities and powers, and the wickedness of high places.[55] God's healing comes true for believers who in faith accept the fulfillment of divine promises. Because African cosmology is peopled with malevolent forces believed to be responsible for diseases, sicknesses, curses, and other afflictions, Christian hope of survival lies in freedom in Christ through radical prayers that confront the kingdoms of darkness, the abode of Lucifer and his wicked angels. As J. Kwabena Asamoah-Gyadu explains: "Obstacles that prevent people from realizing abundance of life in Jesus Christ, including sin, spiritual and physical afflictions, and other such negative influences, are in Pentecostal hermeneutics cast as 'strongholds.' Such strongholds must be pulled down by the authority of the risen Christ and in the power of the Holy Spirit as a validation of the gospel and not as an appendix to Christian ministry. This is one way in which Pentecostal/charismatic Christians understand the words of Jesus, 'You shall receive power when the Holy Ghost has come upon you' (Acts 1:8)."[56]

According to Kevin G. Smith, the success of Pentecostalism in Africa can be attributed to the way it takes African belief in the spirit world and its impacts on daily lives seriously. He writes: "Pentecostalism has prevailed in Africa precisely because it promises protection and freedom from the power of evil spirits. African Pentecostals differ from other Christian traditions not simply because they believe in 'speaking in tongues' but also because they emphasize the grace of the Holy Spirit in helping the believer overcome the debilitating influences of evil."[57] Healing in African Pentecostal churches consists of deliverance from generational and ancestral curses—"that is, events from the past that affect the present in negative ways"[58]—deliverance or exorcism as spiritual warfare against witches and wizards, and deliverance for healing from diseases often attested to by the beneficiaries.[59] Some of the

---

55. Primus M. Tazanu, "Practices and Narratives of Breakthrough: Pentecostal Representations, the Quest for Success, and Liberation from Bondage," *Journal of Religion in Africa* 46 (2016): 32–66.

56. Asamoah-Gyadu, "Pulling Down Strongholds," 307.

57. Kevin G. Smith, "Spiritual Warfare in African Pentecostalism in the Light of Ephesians," *Conspectus—The Journal of the South African Theological Seminary*, Special Edition (2018): 71–72.

58. Asamoah-Gyadu, "Mission to 'Set the Captives Free,'" 390.

59. Mookgo S. Kgatle, "'Go Deeper Papa, Prophesy, do Something': The Popularity and Commercialisation of Prophetic Deliverance in African Pentecostalism," *Verbum et Ecclesia* 43, no. 1 (2022): 1–7.

healing practices, like feeding the members with grass or live frogs, drinking gasoline, kissing, taking ritual baths involving intimate touching, and so on are unhealthy and quite concerning.[60]

Closely associated with its inclination to literalism, African Pentecostalism accepts and advances the "prosperity" gospel, according to which it is believed that God blesses faithful members with health and wealth. African Pentecostalism's success among the poor has been attributed to its promise of prosperity.[61] Church members are encouraged to "pray for and expect the spiritual delivery of health and wealth (packaged in a variety of products), and in return the church reaps significant material benefits. Even when health and wealth do not materialize, members are told to believe that all is well."[62] Through homilies, books, tapes, and other advertising strategies, members are led to believe that by sowing seeds (that is, giving money to God), a person of faith will be rewarded abundantly materially, will progress in their endeavors and businesses, and triumph over their enemies, including the devil, Lucifer.

Some tools go with prayer to effect divine favor—olive oils, handkerchiefs, blessed holy water, CDs, tapes, and books of the men and women of God, the founders of the churches—which are bought from the churches. These churches, for all intents and purposes, are full business ventures whereby the members as clients give money and other material gifts, including peddling influences for ease of business to the benefit of the founders. In return for all the money and other gifts they receive on God's behalf, these churches give tools for the realization of divine material favors, wealth, health, positions of power, and so on.

Debates on the impacts of the "prosperity" gospel in sub-Saharan Africa are inconclusive. Lovemore Togarasei, of the University of Botswana, struggles to explain how the prosperity gospel contributes to creating wealth by the encouragement of entrepreneurship, despite the lavish lifestyle of the pastors who benefit directly from the generous contribution of the members of the churches.[63] Because of the churches' concern with proximate (this worldly) rather than ultimate (eschatological) issues, Togarasei argues that

---

60. Zorodzai Dube, "Ritual Healing Theory and Mark's Healing Jesus: Implications for Healing Rituals Within African Pentecostal Churches," *Neotestamentica* 53, no. 3 (2019) 479–89.
61. Lovemore Togarasei, "The Pentecostal Gospel of Prosperity in African Contexts of Poverty: An Appraisal," *Exchange* 40 (2011): 336–50.
62. Gaiya, "Charismatic and Pentecostal Social Orientations in Nigeria," 64.
63. Togarasei, "The Pentecostal Gospel of Prosperity," 336–50.

Pentecostalism beliefs and practices are secular and that this is the pull factor of why people are drawn to them.[64] Other scholars point to the involvement of the "progressive Pentecostals" with social and political engagements.[65] Some question whether they are exploiting the masses,[66] especially since most of the wave of the prosperity gospel gained steam during the economically excruciating structural adjustment program (SAP) that robbed most Africans of their purchasing power as the state withdrew from the provision of social services as part of the implementation of the neoliberalism of the SAP. The coincidence of Pentecostalism—its prosperity gospel, wealth, and health— with these deprivations accounts for its appeal to Africans. Ebenezer Obadare explains the situation well: "Put differently, the promise of untold riches found a willing audience among subjects experiencing acute deprivation and general uncertainty, and for the first time, the message was insistently broadcast that one's chances of (material) success had less to do with social structures creating opportunities, and more with pernicious, ubiquitous spirits (e.g. 'the spirit of unemployment'), which can only be combated and brought to heel through faith in the power of prayer."[67] In the face of the deepening economic crisis, Pentecostal pastors position themselves as the authority in mediating between the people in the fight against spirit forces responsible for poverty, unemployment, and other ills of society. They become the beneficiaries of the ugly situation by cashing in on the religious gullibility of the masses.[68]

Paul Gifford reiterates the dangers of the prosperity gospel, especially the inhibiting of reforms for the transformation of society and social justice:

> By advocating the gospel of prosperity, it [born-again Christianity] dissuades adherents from evaluating the present economic order, merely persuading them to try to be amongst those who benefit from it. With its emphasis on personal healing, it diverts attention from social ills

---

64. Lovemore Togarasei, "Modern/Charismatic Pentecostalism as a Form of 'Religious' Secularism in Africa," *Studia Historiae Ecclesiasticae* 41, no. 1 (2015): 56–66.

65. Richard Burgess, "Pentecostalism and Democracy in Nigeria: Electoral Politics, Prophetic Practices, and Cultural Reformation," *Nova Religio: The Journal of Alternative and Emergent Religions* 18, no. 3 (2015): 38–62.

66. Magbadelo, "Pentecostalism in Nigeria," 15–29.

67. Ebenezer Obadare, "'Raising Righteous Billionaires': The Prosperity Gospel Reconsidered," *HTS Teologiese Studies/Theological Studies* 72, no. 4 (2016): 4.

68. Karen Lauterbach, "Fakery and Wealth in African Charismatic Christianity: Moving Beyond the Prosperity Gospel as Script," in *Faith in African Lived Christianity*, ed. Karen Lauterbach and Mika Vähäkangas (Brill, 2019).

that are crying out for remedy. Its stress on human wickedness and the fallen nature of "the world" is no incentive to social, economic and constitutional reform. By emphasizing personal morality so exclusively, it all but eliminates any interest in systemic or institutionalized injustice. By making everything so simple, it distracts attention from the very real contradictions in the lives of so many in Southern Africa.[69]

African Pentecostalism robs the human subject of agency in attainment of wealth. In the apt words of Obadare, "Wealth or success in the Pentecostal world is consistently advertised as something that happens 'accidentally' or miraculously, and not necessarily issuing from prior investment in terms of individual preparation. Things happen to the individual at the center of the Pentecostal prosperity gospel; the individual himself/herself, it seems, rarely makes them happen."[70] Even some Pentecostals are opposed to the prosperity gospel, especially the African variant's emphasis on "holistic spirituality which includes attaining health and prosperity by pacifying evil spirits and angry ancestors."[71] Marius Nel argues that African Pentecostalism is syncretistic and negates the gospel of Jesus Christ, which it describes in pantheistic terms. Its Christology distorts the divinity and humanity of Jesus, reducing Jesus to the merely human while elevating humans to the status of divinity. Finally, it destroys biblical revelation by equating extrabiblical revelation to the same status as biblical text.[72]

ENCHANTED CHRISTIANITY

Paul Gifford has highlighted the paucity of research on grassroots reading and reception of the Bible in Africa. He notes the contemporaneity of the Bible for African Pentecostals as divine power for success. He equally highlights its performative character by which one with authority can effect what is spoken by the word. Analyzing some homilies of some ordinary readers, Gifford notes

---

69. Cited in David Maxwell, "'Delivered from the Spirit of Poverty?': Pentecostalism, Prosperity and Modernity in Zimbabwe," *Journal of Religion in Africa* 28, fasc. 3 (1998): 351.
70. Obadare, "'Raising Righteous Billionaires,'" 6.
71. Marius Nel, "The Prosperity Message as a Syncretistic Deviation to the Gospel of Jesus," *Religions* 14, no. 346 (2023): 345.
72. Nel, "The Prosperity Message," 345.

that biblical texts are not read in the light of their historical contexts. On the contrary, the prophetic texts are understood performatively as addressed to Africans, with all the promised material blessings, the promises they believe become actualized in their lives by the words of the anointed men or women of God the people believe are sent by God to actualize divine blessings.[73]

Gifford attributes such performative and declarative reading to Africa's enchanted universe, characterized by the presence of the supreme being and divinities, each influencing for the good or bad events of life. In this enchanted religious imagination, Gifford argues that Pentecostal preachers and pastors are replacing the role of native doctors in "directing these spiritual forces"[74] through spiritual warfare. Thus, there is in Africa an enchanted Christianity, beliefs that fit African religious imagination, which is "concerned with explanation, prediction, and control of events in the world."[75] Enchanted Christianity refers to the belief of most Christians in the existence of various forms of evil spirits, marine spirits, spirit marriages, and spirit possession, including people not progressing in life because of generational and ancestral curses. "All Africa's Pentecostal churches originate from the same idea: a Christian is destined for victory in every aspect of life, which includes material prosperity. Among them are many that place enormous emphasis on material prosperity."[76]

But does African Pentecostalism and its prosperity gospel contribute to economic development through genuine entrepreneurship? According to Obadare, "Pentecostal spirituality offers no realistic path out of the economic crisis in Africa. To its identified critical blind spots—faux individuation, ethical sloppiness, susceptibility to being a regulatory valve for the state, neglect of structural barriers to upward mobility—may be added the fact that it has developed no cogent political economy to speak of. The prosperity gospel has no lever—historical or philosophical—on which it might be grounded."[77] This assessment validates Paul Gifford's concern about the potential for underdevelopment that the prosperity gospel poses for Africa. It is not built on the ethics of hard work, frugality, and continuous investment, which results in capital accumulation. Its prosperity is based on chance, luck, and trust in whimsical faith founded on platitudes rather than on the word of God.

---

73. Nel, "The Prosperity Message," 210.
74. Gifford, *Christianity* , 17.
75. Gifford, *Christianity*, 18.
76. Gifford, *Christianity*, 29.
77. Obadare, "'Raising Righteous Billionaires,'" 7.

Gifford thinks enchanted imagination and scientific rationality are irreconcilable, just as religion and science are radically different.[78] He further claims that Europe and the so-called civilized world have been freed of such enchanted religious imagination and hence Christianity for them is ruled by reason and measured by science. "It is true that in the West the existence of witches was not strictly disproved, but Western societies moved to operate on a totally different plane, where such postulates simply did not arise."[79] But is it so? Are these expressions of Christianity he termed enchanted not dispersed into Africa by Western Pentecostal preachers and occasionally funded by them? Even Gifford remains concerned about the presence of foreign elements in African Pentecostalism from the United States of America, which "has particular socio-political effects; this form of Christianity provides no incentive to economic analysis and socio-political involvement."[80] It is obvious that Gifford is concerned with aligning African Christianity with Western-style modernity, which for him, is perhaps the only valid expression of civilization, progress, and development.[81] African Pentecostalism, because of its emphasis on the prosperity gospel based on sowing in faith (giving money) and prophetic declaration, which it preaches, does not seem to align with Max Weber's Protestant work ethic "even though one can find elements in their message of motivation, entrepreneurship, practical morality and even organizational skills."[82] Thus, Gifford imposes "the hegemony of rationalism as the only way of interpreting the world and human life."[83]

While not endorsing enchanted Christianity uncritically, further study is needed on the link between the biblical world and cosmological worldviews. The issue is "that there are existential challenges and questions raised in Africa for which traditional Western forms of Christianity have no adequate answers."[84] According to Ogbu U. Kalu, the African worldview is characterized by "spiritual powers [that] control the gates of persons, families, villages,

---

78. Gifford, *Christianity*, 156.
79. Gifford, *Christianity*, 158.
80. Paul Gifford, "Prosperity: A New and Foreign Element in African Christianity," *Religion* 20 (1990): 373.
81. Gifford, *Christianity*, 159.
82. Paul Gifford and Trad Nogueira-Godsey, "The Protestant Ethic and African Pentecostalism: A Case Study," *Journal for the Study of Religion* 24, no. 1 (2011): 21.
83. Marius Nel, "The African Background of Pentecostal Theology: A Critical Perspective," *In die Skriflig* 53, no. 4 (2019): 1.
84. Nel, "The African Background," 2.

cities and countries"[85] and contrasts with the Western liberal theological, demythologized, and scientific worldviews. Kalu attributes the lingering difference, which often results in syncretism and disregard of Christianity as foreign, to years of weak missionary presence aided by "enervated theological traditions."[86] He asserts: "The gospel has not been preached with power, simplicity and direct confrontations with the powers in the African world. The Holy Spirit has been grieved and hindered. Thus the spiritual powers at the gates of individuals, family, communal and national lives have been left to operate untrammeled."[87]

Justin S. Ukpong affirms the findings of African scholars about the inadequacy of Western methods of biblical interpretation for Africa thus: "Today many African scholars who have been taught to read within a western context have experienced this, and have pointed to the inadequacy of the Western approaches and methods for the African context particularly in terms of answering typically African questions."[88] And as John S. Pobee and Gabriel Ositelu II observe, "It is an important role of religion to help free humanity from the tyranny of those forces of evil. *It is useless to debate the reality of such spirit beings*."[89] Pobee and Ositelu's view turns David T. Ngong's misunderstanding of inculturation biblical hermeneutics as a form of Bible reading that simply aims at perpetuating the enchanted African cosmology[90] on its head.

The African worldview is wrongly characterized as "enchanted" because it is not a magical worldview but one that integrates the spiritual and the material universe.[91] Inculturation biblical hermeneutics' reading according to an African conceptual frame does not shun the historical biblical method of reading but integrates it. The Bible is meaningful to a people in the light of their conceptual frame of reference. And an African conceptual frame of

---

85. Ogbu U. Kalu, "Unconquered Spiritual Gates: Inculturation Theology in Africa Revisited," *Journal of Inculturation Theology* 1, no. 1 (1994): 25.
86. Kalu, "Unconquered Spiritual Gates," 36.
87. Kalu, "Unconquered Spiritual Gates," 36.
88. Ukpong, "New Testament Hermeneutics in Africa," 149.
89. John S. Pobee and Gabriel Ositelu II, *African Initiatives in Christianity: The Growth, Gifts and Diversities of Indigenous African Churches: A Challenge to the Ecumenical Movement* (WCC Publications, 1998), 29. Emphasis added by Gifford in *Christianity*, 158.
90. Ngong, "Reading the Bible in Africa," 174–91.
91. Robert Falconer, *"Veni Sanctus Spiritus*: The Coming of the Holy Spirit in Inaugurated Eschatology and the Emergence of an Enchanted African Christian Society," *Conspectus—The Journal of the South African Theological Seminary* (2018): 95–114.

reference is not "enchanted." That categorization only reenacts the colonialist anthropological conception of the Afrocentric vision as magical. Humphrey Mwangi Waweru is right:

> At the most basic level, words themselves only have meaning in particular contexts, in relation to what the reader understands to be going on. We understand what is written if it agrees with what exists in our context, what is being read, and the conventions of oral traditions of a given community. So we understand what we read or hear from the Bible according to what we think is going on in the text and in our own culture, according to what we conceive or comprehend and what kind of writing it is.[92]

John S. Mbiti, whom Waweru cites, thought that it is within their frame of reference that Africans can make sense of the Christian message.[93] As has been noted "western theological education remains fairly sterile in addressing African concerns."[94] So, any interpretation of the Bible must be conscious of these thought forms or frame of reference because "in any successful interpretive process the context of the reader/listener must be considered in order to avoid running into a serious risk of self-deception."[95]

DECOLONIZING BIBLE READING

The debate over the activities of the European Christian missionaries to Africa has always been contentious. Unfortunately, colonialism defined mission practice, and the subsequent institutional Christianity remained colonialist, Western in all forms. Missionary Christianity is entrenched in the intricacies of power in colonialism. According to Chammah J. Kaunda and Roderick R. Hewitt, "The colonialist discourse is an explicit justification of colonialism and imperialism, whereas missionary discourse embedded and stabilized the hierarchical power relations generated by colonialism and imperialism without directly supporting them. The colonialist discourse had a significant influence

---

92. Waweru, "Reading the Bible Contrapuntally," 334–35.
93. Waweru, "Reading the Bible Contrapuntally," 335.
94. Mbuvi, "African Biblical Studies," 152.
95. Waweru, "Reading the Bible Contrapuntally," 337.

on Western/northern/European missionary education and its accompanying theological imagination."[96] One wonders whether much has changed, especially considering that the Enlightenment framework still undergirds Western Christianity and is foundational for global Christianity. Colonial, postcolonial, and decolonial studies and imagination agree on the use of the Bible both to justify the European presence in Africa and to pacify Africans religiously to keep them favorably disposed to colonial administration. It is well known that "Christianity played such a significant role in European colonialism that it can be difficult to find means of ecclesial organizing not tainted in some way by its habits."[97]

The disenchantment of African traditional religious symbols conceived as demonic and evil to pave way for Christianity and its symbols has been responsible for the genocide of African traditional religion in the minds of many Africans. This was followed by the destruction of African political institutions with the conquests of African ancient kingdoms and empires, including the decimation of egalitarian societies by the colonial army. "African thought—relations, values, ecological, economic, and spiritual practices—was reduced, ridiculed, and dismissed to pre-modern margins of irrelevance."[98] The subjugation and pacification of Africa following the scramble for, and partition of, Africa affected the psyche of the Africans, leading to the adoption of the language, lifestyle, and culture of the colonial masters, resulting in the African crisis of identity. As aptly expressed by Keith E. Eitel:

> The loss of traditional identity among Africans, before and after independence, was brought on by acculturation during colonial administration and economic dependence when colonial rule ended. European authorities replaced traditional African patterns for educational, economic, and political affairs with those typical in Europe. Even though Christian missionaries usually preceded colonial annexation and were generally motivated by religious rather than other stimuli, there was

---

96. Chammah J. Kaunda and Roderick R. Hewitt, "Toward Epistemic Decolonial Turn in Missio-Formation in African Christianity," *International Review of Mission* 104, no. 2 (2015): 383.

97. Ross Kane, "Political Ressourcement: Decolonizing Through Retrieval in African Political Theologies," *Political Theology* 24, no. 2 (2023): 148.

98. Kaunda and Hewitt, "Toward Epistemic Decolonial Turn in Missio-Formation in African Christianity," 379.

a social milieu during the colonial period which made missionary activity appear closely aligned with imperialism.[99]

The missionary hermeneutic gave rise to the adoption of the missionary ways of interpreting the Bible, according to which everything African is demonized. "The result was a systemic erosion and exorcising of African cultural and religious reality from among the early converts to Christianity, essentially forcing them to adopt European languages, cultures and values as a means of becoming Christians. In essence, the early African convert to Christianity could only read and interpret the Bible from the standpoint of the European colonizer, resulting in awkwardly Europeanized renditions of Bibles, hymnbooks, catechetical material, ecclesiastical groups and forms of worship."[100]

This of course does not mean that Africans condemn Christianity, that they do not accept the exclusive and the exceptional work of Christ in saving humankind, or that they do not need Christ. What is rejected is the Eurocentric cultural expression of Christianity as universal to humankind. What is objected to is the establishment of the one cultural ecclesial formula as applicable worldwide. The idea of church, liturgy, spirituality, Christology, ethics, eschatology, and theology followed the format found in the various European missionaries' homeland. The quest for alternative ecclesial forms to worship God and practice Christianity in accordance with the patterns of African thought gave rise to people leaving the mainline churches and led to the establishment of AICs in the quest for spiritual nutrition and satisfaction. World Christianity arising from the demographic change in the rise of Christianity in the Global South is leading positively to the recognition of the plurality of Christianity and the variety of contexts within which Christianity is practiced. It has also led to the gradual recognition of African biblical studies, with its emphasis on the contextuality of every interpretation of texts, including the Bible, even if grudgingly.

World Christianity emphasizes the autochthonocity of expression of Christianities in the light of the meaning-making processes of the recipients. Yet there are still concerns and fears of contextualization of Christianity in Africa, as possibly leading to a Christianity that is neither African nor Christian but at best syncretistic.[101] Yet one cannot be Christian, or religious, without

---

99. Keith E. Eitel, "Contextualization: Contrasting African Voices," *Criswell Theological Review* 2 (1988): 324.

100. Mbuvi, "African Biblical Studies: An Introduction to an Emerging Discipline," 159.

101. Byang H. Kato, "Theological Issues in Africa," *Bibliotheca Sacra* 133, no. 530 (1976): 143–52.

contextual appropriation in the light of one's conceptual frame of reference.[102] The same God revealed in the Bible is revealed in the African traditional religion. According to John S. Mbiti, "The God described in the Bible is none other than the God who is already known in the framework of our traditional African religiosity."[103]

Decolonization of the Bible is what African scholars and theologians are engaged in when they insist on and interpret the Bible using an African conceptual frame of reference. It is reading the Bible through African worldviews—that is, "reading the scripture from a premeditatedly Africentric perspective."[104] Such reading is an imperative because, contrary to the missionaries in Africa who tried to fix the meaning of the Bible over and above African oral cultures, the meaning of the Bible as Scripture cannot be fixed and applied to all cultures. As Waweru observes: "The Bible has no absolute or neutral meaning applicable from age to age in the same way. The same text will have a significantly different meaning depending on the reader's context. Even if the Bible remains the same, the change of context will result in a 'paradigm shift', small or great, depending on what the new context requires for interpretation. This is true for any reading for interpretation and not just the Bible."[105]

Decolonization of the Bible demands the joint engagement of ordinary readers with the biblical scholars. This is to ensure that the Bible is read in the light of the contextual realities of ordinary people and so that biblical scholars will shed light on social and political economic issues in the light of the Bible. It is also to avoid biblical relativism whereby the Bible is interpreted according to the whims of the interpreter without consideration of the historical background of the texts as well as the context of the reader or interpreter.

Waweru refers to this reading of the Bible as reading contrapuntally, following Edward W. Said.[106] Contrapuntal reading preserves the historicity of the text and its readers, the original audience, while reading it in new contexts in which it was not addressed initially. This implies reading biblical

---

102. Eitel, "Contextualization," 324–25.
103. J. S. Mbiti, "The Encounter of Christian Faith and African Religion," *Christian Century* 97 (1980): 818.
104. D. T. Adamo, *Reading and Interpreting the Bible in African Indigenous Churches* (Wipf and Stock Publishers, 2001), 2, cited in Gabriel Oludele Adeloye, "Decolonizing Biblical Interpretation and Its Effect on the Church in Africa," *Practical Theology* (Baptist College of Theology, Lagos) 9 (2016): 202.
105. Waweru, "Reading the Bible Contrapuntally," 334.
106. Edward W. Said, *Orientalism* (Vintage, 1979).

texts and a story from an African context together and comparing them for harmony. It requires attending to one's context, being ready for new interpretation without necessarily going through the context of the text through the historical-critical method and, finally, acceptance of the Bible as Scripture, as the word of God within a Christian tradition, making demands of change or repentance. In this reading, biblical texts, including the complicated stories about Christ, are concretized by relating them to one's own stories.

The alternative contextual hermeneutics of Gerald O. West, Teresa Okure, Musa W. Dube, Justin S. Ukpong, David Tuesday Adamo, Andrew W. Mbuvi, John S. Mbiti, John S. Pobee, and Kwesi Dickson, to mention but a few, have set in motion the decolonization of Bible reading. The various forms of contextual hermeneutics, inculturation, liberation, and feminism use biblical texts to dialogue with various situations of the readers, both to understand and to transform as well as to overcome oppressive situations and contexts, including patriarchal traditional cultures that marginalize women. Rather than focus on biblical criticism, contextual biblical studies make way for a cross-cultural biblical approach, one that champions Bible reading across a variety of cultures attentive to various contexts, to experiences of people, and to the contemporary relevance of the Bible in the existential struggles of humanity.

The recognition of ordinary people's reading of the Bible at the grassroots is another milestone toward decolonization of Bible reading. It is a move away from the formal scientific methods of reading of biblical scholars and from the point of view of Western Enlightenment frameworks. The criticisms of African biblical scholars have exposed the Western and Eurocentric biases of biblical studies. This includes how the Bible was used to prop up and perpetuate colonialism and its continued imperialism that ignores or dismisses the contextual Bible study approach. There is also the Eurocentric scholarship's promotion of methods of interpretation that do not make the biblical text relevant to the people and that is nonconfessional, fixated with defining biblical studies by European concerns.

In the reading of biblical scholars with ordinary readers, care must be taken to allow the ordinary people to speak and relate their readings to their experiences. Ordinary people, not biblical scholars, contribute a lot to the interpretation and dissemination of the Bible. Based on their acceptance of the Bible as the word of God, these readers challenge biblical studies to attend to the grassroots and to relate their interpretation to the existential concrete historical situations of the readers, of the nonbiblical scholars. They challenge the Eurocentric, Enlightenment, scientific, rationalistic biblical interpretation and expose its inadequacies.

Decolonization hermeneutics is not limited to drawing awareness to the use of the Bible to justify exclusion, oppression, segregation, and so forth, but it also draws attention to the ongoing structures of oppression toward African peoples. It exposes the internationalization of economics that excludes Africans on international trade, that diminishes African dignity in international politics, and that continues to disparage African cultural values as primitive. It questions how much freedom and sovereignty African countries have when their resources are controlled by former colonial masters and emerging international powers like China and Russia. "While African countries are now politically independent, postcolonial biblical studies points to the ever present reality of empire that casts a shadow on the former African colonies . . . This ubiquity of empire's shadow means postcolonial biblical studies must continue to grapple with the oppressive structures that still dominate the African continent economically, politically, militarily, psychologically."[107] Using the Bible as the word of God, it probes whether it is possible for Africa to be unaligned in the international proxy war between the superpowers—the United States of America and the rest of the G7 nations, China, and Russia. The Bible probes migration policies of nations that advocate for open European goods into Africa but prevent African goods and peoples from entering Europe and North America. African biblical studies are thus heavily dynamic, incorporating the economic, social, political, cultural, religious, and educational existential realities of Africans and their relations with varieties of international institutions and nations. Mbuvi captures the scope of African biblical studies with a focus on contemporary human experience vis-à-vis European biblical studies centered on philology, archeology, grammatical-historical methods, ancient languages, and so on:

> In this dynamism, the African biblical scholar can be perceived as a practitioner of a form of biblical interpretation that is socially engaged, politically active, decidedly non-European, unabashedly liberationist (against oppression in all its forms and imperialism more specifically), and for justice, equality, and fairness. There is a continual struggle to

---

107. Mbuvi, "African Biblical Studies," 164.

find a balance between commitment to African concerns and relevance in the wider spectrum of biblical studies.[108]

The battle over Christianity by Africans has always been establishing its indigeneity despite its spread by foreign European missionaries in the latter part of the nineteenth century, after the collapsed attempts in the fifteenth centuries and the early North African Christianity overrun by Islam and Arabic invasion of the seventh century. Christianity, and not just the Bible, must be decolonized and the vestiges of its foreignness removed by the cultures of Africa. M. A. C Warren's forward in John V. Taylor's *Christian Presence amid African Religion*, popularly known as *The Primal Vision*, clearly portrays the Christian expression in Africa that would make decolonization through contextualization and inculturation an imperative:

> For more than four centuries the expansion of the Christian Church has coincided with the economic, political, and cultural expansion of Western Europe. Viewed from the standpoint of the peoples of Asia, and to a growing extent from that of the peoples of Africa, this expansion has been an aggressive attack on their own way of life. Quite inevitably the Christian Faith has for many in these lands been inextricably bound up with this Western aggression. But it has also to be admitted quite frankly that during these centuries the missionaries of the Christian Church have commonly assumed that Western civilization and Christianity were two aspects of the same gift which they were commissioned to offer to the rest of humankind.[109]

Warren, characteristic of his time, defended the Westernization of human civilization, lionizing its achievements, including the scientific view of the world and the spread of Christianity worldwide. But faced with the possibility of the emergence of the plurality of Christianities different from its Western variant, he questions whether "to trust the Holy Spirit to lead the Christians of Asia and Africa, or must a controlling Western hand be permanently resting on the Ark of God?"[110] Taylor's *The Primal Vision* is a response to the fear held

---

108. Andrew M. Mbuvi, "An African Biblical Scholar Explores the Broadening of the Biblical Studies Landscape," *Journal of Theology for Southern Africa* 168 (2021): 42.

109. M. A. C. Warren, forward to *Christian Presence amid African Religion*, by John V. Taylor (Acton Publishers, 2001), v.

110. Warren, "Forward," vii.

at the Edinburgh Conference of 1910 about the possible collapse of Christianity in Africa with the end of colonialism, a project for which the Christian missionaries had evangelized Africa. "These missionaries were aided by the political fortunes of the European explorations/exploitation, political powers, the economic boom provided largely by colonies with their native workers and slaves in the new world, and the ability for faster maritime travels."[111]

Western Christianity, mistaken for civilization, spread to Africa but has now to be decolonized. The starting point was the colonial hermeneutics that fixed the meaning of the Bible to Western civilization, interpretation, and Enlightenment reason. The various Western-trained African biblical scholars knew upon return to Africa that biblical interpretation must be contextualized, removed from the Western European and North American context, and read within the African context within which it will be meaningful to the people.

CHARTING THE FUTURE OF READING THE BIBLE IN AFRICA

Justin S. Ukpong remarks that "the challenges that African biblical critics face arise from the contextual nature of African readings of the bible, the diversity of the African context and the ambivalence of the Bible."[112] Ukpong argues that the revolution in the reading of the Bible in Europe from going to the Scripture for ideas on issues of contemporary society to uncovering the past, from ecclesiocentric interpretation to the historical context, was a cultural revolution in Western Europe that happened when their meaning-making changed in the eighteenth century. In other words, the historical-critical method was a result of a cultural phenomenon. Ukpong also contends that another cultural revolution in relation to the reading of the Bible besides the literal approach is "the contextual approach practiced in the Third World... It is marked by a movement away from the context of the text and the text itself to the context of the readers. In this approach, the Bible is not seen as 'an aesthetic object of contemplation and study'... rather the concern of the contextual critic is the social role of the Bible in the present: the functioning

---

111. Andrew M. Mbuvi, "Missionary Acts, Things Fall Apart: Modeling Mission in Acts 17:15–34 and a Concern for Dialogue in Chinua Achebe's *Things Fall Apart*," *Ex auditu* 23 (2007): 141.

112. Ukpong, "New Testament Hermeneutics in Africa," 147.

of the Bible in the contemporary society."[113] The point of emphasis is that all readings are contextual; the shift in paradigms of reading the Bible are results of various contexts. The historical-critical method with its focus on the past of the text, the literal approach, and the contextual approach of the Global South came about by significant changes in the context of the people in question. Every reading is meaningful in the light of the conceptual frame of reference, of the patterns of thought of the people. The readings influence the other segments of society, including politics, economics, the environment, attitude to the Other, and other social issues.

Is the Bible itself a cultural text? Does it emanate from a variety of historical contexts? Can it be studied as a cultural text with applicability beyond its original context? If its meaning is beyond its immediate context, must its interpretation neglect its immediate context? We no doubt will agree that the interpretation of the Bible must be cognizant of its historical context. We also agree that its scope should not be limited to its immediate context if it is to be relevant to contemporary societies and valid for all times. We have noted the importance of methodologies of interpretation that recognize and respect the historical context of biblical texts. We have also emphasized the imperative of not neglecting the context of the reader. The efforts to study the cultural role of the Bible is aimed not only at its cultural role throughout history, its ideological dimensions, its influence on culture, and its appropriation by culture but also at the "mutual redefinition in which cultural appropriations constantly reinvent the Bible, which in turn constantly impels new appropriations."[114]

The constant interaction between the Bible and culture is central to the various methods of interpretation, as each is constructed to make sense of the biblical text in accordance with the prevailing meaning-making process. The Bible is appropriated and reappropriated, invented and reinvented, according to the prevailing ideological construct. And here ideology is not negative but is understood as the series of ideas that determine action and power relations. They are inventive just as they are biased, but they shape the way texts are understood. Ukpong illustrates the ideological bias of the various authors of biblical texts, the influence of culture on the authors and on the interpretation of the texts at various points in time thus:

---

113. Ukpong, "New Testament Hermeneutics in Africa," 148.
114. J. Cheryl Exum and Stephen D. Moore, "Biblical Studies/Cultural Studies," in Biblical Studies/Cultural Studies. The Third Sheffield Colloquium, cited in Gerald A. Klingbeil, "Cultural Criticism and Biblical Hermeneutics: Definition, Origins, Benefits, and Challenges," *Bulletin for Biblical Research* 15, no. 2 (2005), 265.

Every method arises from and is influenced by a certain ideology that can be linked to the intellectual cultural climate of a particular group and/or a particular time and space. For example, we cannot understand the typological and allegorical readings of the early Fathers of the church outside the Platonic world-view and the Greco-Roman classical intellectual culture in which the Fathers were reared, nor the historical critical method outside the Enlightenment culture, nor today's literary approaches outside the epistemological shift from a mechanistic to a holistic perception of reality in the Western culture that leads to seeking to understand the text in itself. Similarly, liberation, inculturation, feminist and other contextually based hermeneutics cannot be understood outside the contemporary post-modern intellectual culture that emphasizes identity and diversity.[115]

Ukpong's point and our emphasis on the cultural role of the Bible is the recognition of the contextuality of all interpretations, and the need to be conscious of the contextual position we take, because of the possible biases and the ideological influences of our contexts in our interpretations; hence the need for one to "consciously adopt reading methods and strategies that facilitate critical interaction of the biblical text with our contexts."[116]

Contextual hermeneutics fits perfectly with the African context that has suffered various forms of domination from the slave trade to colonialism, neocolonialism, other forms of segregation, marginalization of international trade, continued denigration, and coercion. The African context has been dominated by external forces compelling Africa to neglect its immediate context and adopt foreign frames of reference (hence the imperative of the contextual biblical interpretation) to at least be Christian in the light of its meaning-making process. However, adopting the contextual approach does not mean an abandonment of the scientific, critical, historical method or other approaches to biblical hermeneutics; they just are not central, objective, universally applicable methods of biblical interpretation. What needs to change is the move from the theory of contextualization to its actual practice so that contextual readings of the Bible participate in the transformation of the ethos of societies. Ukpong's words once more express the future of African reading of the Bible as lying on its contribution to the social order:

---

115. Ukpong, "New Testament Hermeneutics in Africa," 150.
116. Ukpong, "New Testament Hermeneutics in Africa," 150.

In Africa, in particular, where the worldview of most of the people does not dichotomize between the spiritual and the temporal, we must learn to read the Bible with holistic eyes and see our profession from a holistic perspective. We need to make a critical use of the Bible to build and mobilize public opinion and unmask the structures and mechanisms of the status quo of state and political arrangements that entrench practices and ways of existence that rest on oppression. We need to make our professional voices heard in the public and seek to influence political decision for the common good. We need to have in our individual and collective agendas a concern for the common good.[117]

Ukpong's suggestion is informed by the very nature of contextual hermeneutics, which cannot function authentically without African biblical scholars knowing the various dimensions of their context. This is also one of the reasons the nature of Christianity in Africa will always be a subject of critical analysis of the underlying ideological underpinnings, as well as the constant probing of the presuppositions of the readers of the Bible.

This position informed our brief study of African Pentecostalism and the prosperity gospel. Does the prosperity gospel contribute to the socio-economic, political development of Africa? Should contextual reading of the Bible in Africa imprint on African Christian witnesses the importance of hard work, frugal financial management, and charity to individual and community development rather than reliance on chance without any plan besides praying and sowing the seeds of faith by contributing certain percentages of one's meager income to men and women of God? In the light of Ukpong's inculturation hermeneutics of the parable of the shrewd manager in Luke 16:1–13,[118] "Christians of West Africa are challenged to reverse the oppressive structures imposed on the poor by the middlemen traders and the International Monetary Fund's Economic Structural Adjustment Program (ESAP)."[119] Contextual biblical hermeneutics challenges Africans to understand that integral development demands their involvement in the variety of contexts they belong—social, political, economic, religious, and so forth—to participate in the shaping of public policies that underpin wealth and health,

---

117. Ukpong, "New Testament Hermeneutics in Africa," 154.
118. Ukpong, "The Parable of the Shrewd Manager," 189–210.
119. Jean-Claude Loba-Mkole, "The New Testament and Intercultural Exegesis in Africa," *Journal for the Study of the New Testament* 30, no. 1 (2007): 13.

thus giving credibility to their religious faith's involvement and God's concern for human development.

African contextual hermeneutics would benefit from cultural criticism. As defined by Werner G. Jeanrond, cultural criticism is "the cultural role of the Bible."[120] Cultural criticism, Gerald A. Klingbeil notes, is focused on cultures and contexts; it is not so concerned with establishing texts in its original context but rather with meanings of texts in particular contexts.[121] This is akin to Bernard Lonergan's demand for critical culture, which he calls "cosmopolis," that demands particularity, is open to other traditions, and is critical of itself.[122] "For Lonergan, authentic cosmopolitanism does not impose a universal, totalizing metanarrative. Rather, it embraces the particularity of one's own cultural, religious, and intellectual traditions, while remaining radically open to dialogue with the other. By doing so, education for cosmopolis fosters both authentic appropriation and reflective critique of one's own traditions, as well as an appreciation for the authenticity of others."[123]

But what happens in the face of multiplicity of contexts, of cultures? How is a particular contextual interpretation to be saved from reductionistic interpretation and justification of some repressive practices and assumptions? What are the criteria for measuring the authentic plurality of biblical interpretations? Cultural criticism supplies the much-needed critical analysis of cultural contexts. This is even more important when one recalls the intriguing relation between the Bible and culture in African Christianity. African biblical studies focus on reading in the light of the African worldview or culture, or rereading from an Afrocentric perspective, all which leads back to the relation of the Bible and culture in Africa. The Bible is a sign of contradiction in Africa. It is accused of serving the purpose of European imperialism in Africa. But Bible translations also led to the formation of orthography for African languages, allowing the written word to both indigenize the Christian religion and mobilize decolonial social and political movements.

Contextual biblical hermeneutics must aggressively combat views that insist on a dialectical rather than a dialogical relationship between the Bible and African culture. A dialectical model of the encounter between the Bible

---

120. Werner G. Jeanrond, "Interpretation, History of," *ABD* 3, 442, cited in Klingbeil, "Cultural Criticism and Biblical Hermeneutics," 263.
121. Klingbeil, "Cultural Criticism and Biblical Hermeneutics," 268.
122. Lonergan, *Insight*, 263–67, 656, 712.
123. Dennis Gunn, "Teaching for Cosmopolis: Bernard Lonergan's Hopeful Vision for Education in a Globalized World," *Religious Education* 113, no. 1 (2018): 26.

and African culture considers the Bible as good and African culture as evil and so must be discarded. This view is the outcome of the militant nature of the European missionary's condemnation of all aspects of African culture and civilizations as demonic, which is to be destroyed to pave the way for European/North American civilization as Christianity. As Ezeogu clarifies, the Christian missionaries "were made to see themselves as 'Christian soldiers marching as to war' against demonic powers and the forces of darkness in order to liberate the land for Christ and save the hell-bound souls of its helpless inhabitants. Africa, together with all its cultures and religions, represented for them a kingdom controlled by Satan; a kingdom to be overthrown and brought to subjection under the cross of Jesus."[124] These fossilized views have stuck in the mentality of many Africans, including some educated ones, who depict their own African culture in the negative.

The dialogic model of the relationship of Christianity and culture recognizes that while the differences between both are contrary, they are not contradictory. Ezeogu paints a clear picture of such mutual coexistence between Christianity and culture: "Today, it is the unanimous conviction of all African Christian theologians that one can be fully Christian without compromising the essential values of African culture, just as one can be fully African without compromising the essentials of the biblical message. In other words, it is possible to be authentically Christian and authentically African at the same time. In fact, African theologians do not see this as merely a possibility but as an imperative that leaves no other option. They urge such a dialogue in clear terms."[125]

Contemporary missionaries, especially from conservative North American Christian sects, still disregard or condemn African cultures and distort the Bible. Their followers disdain every aspect of their own culture as opposed to the Bible, which is the word of God. Waweru notes, "In this context, the Bible and African culture are viewed as falling along bi-polar dimensions with both cultures as two polar opposites. Each answers the question of truth consistently in one direction. If one agrees with one religion or culture, then one would disagree with the other. This is the ideology the missionaries applied to imply that it was either Bible culture or African culture but not the two together because they cannot be both correct."[126]

---

124. Ernest M. Ezeogu, "Bible and Culture in African Christianity," *International Review of Mission* 87, no. 344 (1988): 29

125. Ezeogu, ""Bible and Culture in African Christianity," 32.

126. Humphrey Waweru, *The Bible and African Culture: Mapping Transactional Inroads* (Zapf Chancery, 2011), 12.

Fundamentalistic hermeneutics perpetuates this exclusivist view. According to Byang H. Kato, a prominent African evangelical theologian and secretary of the Association of Evangelicals of Africa and Madagascar (AEAM) until his untimely death in 1975, African culture and religion is reducible to the worship of idols. "Whatever rationalization we may try to make, the worship of gods in Africa is idolatry."[127] For Kato, there can be no Africanization of Christianity. The Bible must be the guide in the relationship of faith and culture: "It is God's will that Africans, on accepting Christ as their Savior, become Christian Africans. Africans who become Christians should therefore remain Africans wherever their culture does not conflict with the Bible. It is the Bible that must judge the culture. Where a conflict results, the cultural element must give way."[128] According to Kato, what the missionaries destroyed was not African culture but cultural idols, which Africans were worshipping even as they turned to Christianity. He asserts: "The defunct gods of African traditional religions are now rearing their heads."[129] "Culture as such can be baptized by Christianity. But once it is done the other way around; compromise has set in. Syncretism will be the end result and the unique salvation of Christ will be made non-effective."[130] Kato's views reject African theology as perpetuating syncretism and relativism.[131] Kato exhibits crass ignorance of the ideological underpinnings of the Western cultural Christianity catapulted as Christian culture and propagated by the European missionaries and which has solidified as Christianity in Africa.

Contextual biblical hermeneutics must work to conscientize Africans about reading the Bible through African eyes, in the light of African conceptual schemes and frames of thought. Reading the Bible with ordinary people is important to inculturation hermeneutics. According to Ukpong, "The primacy of the reading activity is located not among individual theologians working in isolation but among theologians working among communities of ordinary people—it is the ordinary people that are accorded the epistemological privilege."[132] West equally privileges ordinary people's thoughts

---

127. Byang H. Kato, "Christianity as an African Religion," *Evangelical Review of Theology* 4, no. 1 (1980): 19.
128. Kato, "Theological Issues in Africa," 146.
129. Byang H. Kato, "History Comes Full Circle," *Evangelical Review of Theology* 28, no. 2 (2004): 131.
130. Kato, "History Comes Full Circle," 133.
131. Eitel, "Contextualization," 323–34.
132. Ukpong, "Inculturation Hermeneutics: An African Approach to Biblical Interpretation," in *The Bible in a World context: An Experiment in Contextual Hermeneutics*, ed D. Walter and L. Ulrich (William B. Eerdmans, 2002), 20.

in the scholarly reading with them. Contextual hermeneutics' emphasis on the context of the readers—that is, the concerns of the readers of the Bible, including the ordinary readers—needs to be subject to critical analysis.

The presuppositions of ordinary readers need to be probed and corrected when their readings are fundamentalistic. This is important because even some educated ordinary readers might be operating on the one-dimensional dialectical model of Christianity and misconstrue African cultures as pagan (even idolatrous at times), think that biblical inspiration equates to its inerrancy, and often hold to the Bible being dictated from God word for word. In such instances, ordinary people's thoughts about the Bible should be challenged. In other words, the African biblical scholars should not just be neutral, not just accept obvious misinterpretations of the ordinary readers of the Bible. Such interventions do not deviate from the "reading with" approach emphasized as central to scholarly readings with ordinary people. As we mentioned, the relation of the biblical scholars with the ordinary people readings of the Bible is mutual self-mediation, benefiting both readers and the community as well as the contexts of the readers. African biblical scholars owe it to the ordinary readers, as a responsibility, to contribute to the higher viewpoint "reading with" is meant to foster.[133] This simply means inviting them to think of the Bible much more critically, in ways that would be starkly different from their perceptions of the Bible and its relation to contemporary issues of life and society.

But does contextual hermeneutics make God known? What is the basis of this hermeneutics: Is it faith which stems from spirituality? Does contextual hermeneutics serve as a bridge connecting God to His people? Does it enrich people's spirituality? Do people feel connected to God through reading the Bible in the light of their conceptual frame of reference? Or does it perpetuate the distance between biblical theology and dogma? Is it a form of reading that applies the Scripture to the various situations of the people and as such enables the people to find meaning and purpose in life through faith experience anchored in the presence of God in their lives? Faith leads to prayer; the Bible as the word of God should arouse love for God and a desire to communicate with God.[134] Does contextual hermeneutics advance prayer life, a yearning to be with and commune with God in acts of adoration? Or is contextual biblical hermeneutics merely intellectual, inhibiting faith and prayer?

---

133. Lonergan, *Insight*, 37–43, 258–59, 282, 398, 465.

134. Emmanuel Oyemomi, "Spirituality and Biblical Theology for Theological Education in Africa," *Ogbomoso Journal of Theology* 16, no. 2 (2011): 93–108.

Besides reading to know, to be informed, for academic purposes, biblical hermeneutics is primarily for spiritual purposes, for faith in God, for prayer and adoration of God, for guidance, for living as children of God, for being redeemed in Christ, and for bearing witness to the good news of salvation. Unlike other forms of literary analysis, African contextual biblical hermeneutics presupposes faith in God, in the Bible as the word of God. The Bible unveils God's self and God's relationship with creation, the universe, and humankind, all created by God out of love. This is the general belief of Christians who regard the Bible as Scripture, as the word of God addressed to humanity. According to Karl Rahner, "The Scriptures, of course, bear the individual stamp of the times in which they were written and the mental stamp of their human authors; they have quite definite designs and aims which have been partly influenced by the individual situation, both human and religious, of the author."[135]

And so, the business of scriptural interpretation is a spiritual one. Inspired authors of the Bible were moved to write about God's self-disclosure—that is, God's self-communication. In writing, the human authors made use of human symbols of communication, to mediate God's self-disclosure, and of God's involvement in human history. This means that the inspired authors "preserved and transmitted [divine revelation] to future generations in history by the mutual relationship between tradition and Scripture."[136] African contextual hermeneutics is therefore not a neutral detached interpretation of the Bible. It is an interpretation based on faith in the Bible as the word of God, a witness to divine revelation, as aimed at fostering faith experience of communion with God through the Bible.

CONCLUSION

African contextual biblical hermeneutics prioritizes the situation, the context of the reader, while equally advocating for the critical reading of the Bible. It stands against a particular form of reading deemed universally applicable and hence the only authentic way of interpreting the Bible. After decades of being

---

135. Karl Rahner, "On the Inspiration of the Bible," in *The Bible in New Age*, ed. Ludwig Klein (Sheed & Ward, 1965), 4–5.

136. Robert J. Hill, "Reading Symbols, and Writing Words. A Model for Biblical Inspiration," *New Blackfriars* 89, no. 1019 (2008): 32.

ignored by the mainstream theological and scholarly academy, the concerns of contextual hermeneutics are beginning to influence biblical interpretation worldwide, as the recognition of the contextuality of all hermeneutics and the importance of the context of the authors, the readers, and the relevance of biblical texts is being addressed in biblical interpretation.

The impact of biblicism and literalism on African readings of the Bible is gaining steam and is manifested in the growing influence of a particular brand of Pentecostalism in Africa characterized by the prosperity gospel influenced by African cosmology characterized by belief in spirits that could block human success. Prosperity gospels militate against the development of Africans who are exploited by the leadership of these churches into giving money to receive God's blessings in forms of health and wealth. The consequence is a brand of "enchanted" Christianity across Africa, even in the mainline churches. Despite its pretention, such enchantments remain artifacts of colonial assumptions and perspectives on both the meaning of Christianity and the authenticity of African culture.

The Bible must be decolonized to be relevant to Africans, to free Christianity from the cultural captivity of the European missionary legacy that is still entrenched in Africa. This calls for a dialogic relationship between Christianity and African culture that mutually enhances both Christianity and African cultures. We warned against the dialectical form of the relationship between Christianity and African culture, which demonizes African culture and seeks to enthrone European civilization under the guise of Christian culture. We argued that African contextual hermeneutics ought to engage in cultural criticism of its notion of culture, its values, and a variety of contexts to avoid reductionism, relativism, and subjectivism, which warrant the use of the Bible ideologically to benefit one's self-serving agendas. The future of African contextual hermeneutics lies in the recognition and faith in the Bible as the word of God. Hermeneutics is therefore a spiritual act leading to the experience of God, communion, prayer, and spirituality.

Conclusion

The way people read the Bible determines the face of Christianity in a particular area, church, or community. Contextual biblical hermeneutics is often dismissed as being unscientific, prioritizing the reader rather than the author of the texts of Scripture. Some argue it is local and lacks the universalizability of classical hermeneutics and exegesis, ignoring that all interpretation is local and contextual, influenced and arising from the conceptual frame of reference of a particular locality.

Because of the contextuality of all interpretation, African biblical hermeneutics is different from European/North American hermeneutics. And that is okay. Admitting the contextuality of biblical interpretation demands recognition of the cultures of various peoples as vehicles for the incarnation of the good news. It means inculturation of Christianity to allow for the autochthonocity of Christianity in a variety of contexts, in the light of the meaning-making process, in the culture of each people, and in a mutual self-mediation that benefits both Christianity and cultures. Contextual biblical hermeneutics in both its inculturation and liberation variants must prioritize the culture and liberation of the people as central to being Christian. It must engage the Bible in the pursuit of the solution to the identity crisis arising from the anthropological poverty occasioned by the ideologies that tried to destroy African cultures. These cultures are the springboard of the liberation of the people as they participate in politics, in economic emancipation, and in religious meaning through their conceptual frame of reference. European/North American missionaries condemning African cultures in the twenty-first century must not be allowed to succeed in making Africans feel inferior once again.

Inculturation contextual hermeneutics must take the center stage in biblical interpretation, especially in academic readings of the Bible with ordinary people. The missionary hermeneutics that pitted African traditional religions and cultural values against Christianity through fixed interpretations aimed at the promotion of Eurocentric cultural values as Christianity must be repudiated. It has been allowed for far too long; it now directs the attitude of the mass of ordinary readers of the Bible toward the religion and culture of Africans. A battleground is drawn where there ought to be harmony and better understanding. African Christians are made ignorant of their cultures and values. What ought to be a guide to life is ignored and castigated. For this reason, people live without guiding cultural values. Christianity destroyed without replacing the cultural values of the people. Thus, there is pervasive meaninglessness as the disenchantment of the sacred has led to creeping secularism amidst superficial religiosities. The outcome is various forms of get-rich-quick schemes, disregard for the sacredness of life, drug addiction, and purposelessness exacerbated by corrupt political systems.

Unless African traditional religion is understood and its relevance to the culture of the people appreciated, African Christianity will remain shallow and people will always regard it as a foreign religion, which it is not. Yet inculturation biblical hermeneutics has remained almost a secret in African Christianity. More study of African biblical scholars and intensification of community reading with ordinary people is imperative, not only for the future of reading the Bible through African eyes but also for a stronger, authentic, reliable, and autochthonous African Christianity.

Emphasis on inculturation hermeneutics segues to the liberation hermeneutics because it is not easy to shake off missionary hermeneutics that set the standard for the reading of and the meaning of the Bible in relation to African cultures and civilizations. The liberation of the people begins when Christianity is decolonized and made less foreign. Decolonization of the Bible is an aspect of the Bible not many people are aware of and hence is less attended to. The Bible as a tool of imperialism is a concept that would jar many Africans. One would find oneself questioning God in the eyes of some people. But a decolonized approach to the Bible sees through the various ideological underpinnings of the use of the Bible to support hate and the exclusion of others. Exposing Christians to such misinterpretations is an imperative so people will be on guard against the various forms of manipulative uses of the Bible to defraud them.

African contextual biblical hermeneutics must strike a balance between the specialized textual analysis of trained biblical scholars and the simpler reading of ordinary Africans. Ordinary readers have rediscovered the importance of reading from the conceptual frame of reference of Africans. They read the Bible as the word of God, designed to promote the love of God and neighbor. The faith-filled reading of the Bible can bring African academic biblical scholars closer to a sense of the Bible as socially and spiritually transformative. Ordinary people's deep regard for the authority of the Bible, at times bordering on biblicism, draw them to reverence the Bible by constant reading of the Bible as the word of God. What a change it would make if African biblical scholars and theologians would read the Bible faithfully as the word of God. They will be able to read "with" ordinary people, who through dialogue with scholars can learn to grasp the critical biblical reading that would enable them to understand the Bible better and guard against biblicism. Contextual biblical study between the experts and ordinary readers of the Bible must continue to be dialogic.

Decolonizing Africans' perception of the Bible in the missionary hermeneutics demands removal of the Eurocentric paddings in biblical interpretation that make Christianity appear as a foreign, imported religion. This implies injecting African perspectives, cultures, and meanings into the readings of the Bible so that the Bible becomes meaningful and addresses the problems of Africans. The relationship of African biblical hermeneuts with the ordinary readers of the Bible in Africa must be capable of achieving its original purpose by drawing closer to the ordinary readers and by introducing the African worldview into the understanding of the texts of Scripture.

African biblical hermeneutics must also constantly remind the reader of the context of the biblical texts so that the African cultural perspective is understood alongside the cultural context of the text, of the narrator, of the author, and of specific biblical texts. African biblical scholars must take seriously the criticism of not taking the context of the text seriously. Biblical hermeneutics must strike a balance between the context of the text, textual analysis, and the context of the reader. At the same time, African biblical scholars should not be stymied by Eurocentric/North American bias against their contextual biblical hermeneutics. African biblical scholars' vocation is toward Africans, to make the Bible meaningful to Africans, and contextual biblical hermeneutics does this well. What is important is not the view of hermeneuts from different conceptual frames of reference but development of strategies for making these contextual hermeneutics available to the majority of Africans, to enable all to be critical in their interpretation of biblical texts.

African biblical hermeneutics must attend to the double marginalization of women in church, society, and even in African biblical hermeneutics. The Bible is clearly patriarchal, emanating from patriarchal cultures with laws considered divine made against women, beginning with purity laws that marginalize women solely for biological reasons to the denial of the right to family inheritance, women as victims of laws mandating levirate marriage, exclusion from the sacrament of order, and so on. It is important to educate African people about these gender biases in the Bible so that people do not easily proof-text passages to justify injustices against women or invoke practices irrelevant to contemporary life. As women biblical scholars often observe, African biblical hermeneutics ignores the demands for gender neutrality to ensure gender equality for all in society. But male African biblical scholars must follow the lead of their female colleagues, joining alongside them in advocating for women's rights from the biblical perspective and using contextual African examples, like narratives, laws, institutions, customs, and traditions skewed against women.

African contextual biblical hermeneutics is not just reader focused, ignoring the context of the text of Scripture, or a self-confirming reading whereby the reader simply confirms what they think. That is not what African contextual biblical hermeneutics is about. It is a reading that is context based just as Eurocentric reading is context based. As emphasized earlier, each reading is through each people's conceptual frame of reference. No context or culture is superior to the other. Africans must appropriately read the Bible in the light of the patterns of their thought, just as every other culture (including European and North American) reads in the light of their experiences and concerns. The various allegations against African contextual biblical scholars to this effect is a gross misinterpretation and misrepresentation of their thoughts. The aim of contextual biblical hermeneutics is to showcase the relationship between God and humans, in the context of a people's frame of reference. Contextual biblical hermeneutics relates the God-human relationship to the African context—that is, African cultural, sociopolitical, and economic situations—to foster deeper love of God and neighbor. I do not see any other way of doing this outside the culture, the context, the history, the stories, and the narratives of each people.

Despite criticisms, the concerns of African contextual biblical hermeneutics are gaining traction in biblical hermeneutics with the growing recognition of the validity of the existential needs of the reader in biblical exegesis and hermeneutics. Diachronic, synchronic, and reader-response analyses are now greatly appreciated because of the role contexts play in biblical interpretation. In African contextual hermeneutics, African biblical scholars interpret and understand the texts of Scripture, bearing in mind African sociopolitical, economic, and religious contexts; engage in critical analysis of the texts of Scripture, in recognition of the various contexts of the emergence of these texts; and apply the biblical texts to the dynamic sociocultural contexts of Africa's existential realities.

Bibliography

Abbott, Walter M., S.J. *The Documents of Vatican II*. Guild Press, 1966.

Abioje, Pious O. "The Pentecostal Emphasis on Miracle in the Nigerian Perspective: A Theological Discourse." *The Nigerian Journal of Theology* 18 (2004): 53–67.

Achebe, Chinua. *Arrow of God*. Penguin Books, 1991.

Achebe, Chinua. *No Longer at Ease*. Penguin Books, 1994.

Achebe, Chinua. *Things Fall Apart*. Penguin Books, 1994.

Adamah, Jackson Nii Sabaah. "Food Insecurity, Eucharist, and Community: Reading Jean-Marc Éla's "Shade-Tree" Theology in Light of Balthasar's Ecclesiology." *Review and Expositor* 117, no. 4 (2020): 536–46.

Adamo, D. T. *Reading and Interpreting the Bible in African Indigenous Churches*. Wipf and Stock Publishers, 2001.

Adeloye, Gabriel Oludele. "Decolonizing Biblical Interpretation and Its Effect on the Church in Africa." *Practical Theology* 9 (2016): 198–208.

Ajani, Ezekiel Oladapo Aremu. "The Kingdom of God and Its Missiological Imperatives for the Contemporary African Christian Mission." *Ogbomoso Journal of Theology* 12 (2007): 117–35.

Akper, Godwin I. "The Role of the 'Ordinary Reader' in Gerald O. West's Hermeneutics." *Scriptura* 88 (2005): 1–13.

Alexis-Baker, Andy. "*Ad Quirinum* Book Three and Cyprian's Catechumenate." *Journal of Early Christian Studies* 17, no. 3 (2009): 357–80.

Alfsvag, Knut. "These Things Took Place as Examples for Us: On the Theological and Ecumenical Significance of the Lutheran *Sola Scriptura*." *Dialog: A Journal of Theology* 55, no. 3 (2016): 202–9.

Amanze, James. "Conflict and Cooperation: The Interplay between Christianity and African Traditional Religions in the Nineteenth and Twentieth

Centuries." *Studies in World Christianity & Interreligious Relations* 48 (2014): 281–304.

An, Keon-Sang. "Ethiopian Contextualization: The Tradition of the Ethiopian Orthodox Tewahido Church." *Mission Studies* 33, no. 2 (2016): 147–62.

Anderson, Allan. "Spreading Fires: The Globalization of Pentecostalism in the Twentieth Century." *International Bulletin of Missionary Research* 31, no. 1 (2007): 8–12.

Andrei, Cristina, and Decebal Nedu. "The Campaign of Marcus Atilius Regulus in Africa. Military Operations by Sea and by Land (256–255 B.C.)." *Annals* (Constanța Maritime University), 11, no. 13 (2010): 206–9.

Andrews, James A. *Hermeneutics and the Church*. University of Notre Dame Press, 2012.

Andrews, James A. "Why Theological Hermeneutics Needs Rhetoric: Augustine's *De doctrina Christiana*." *International Journal of Systematic Theology* 12, no. 2 (2010): 184–200.

Anum, Eric. "Comparative Readings of the Bible in Africa: Some Concerns." In *The Bible in Africa: Transactions, Trajectories, and Trends*, edited by Gerald O. West and Musa W. Dube. Brill, 2001.

Anum, Eric. "The Usage of The Bible in African Missionary History: The Legacy of New Testament Usage in Africa." *Ghana Journal of Religion and Theology* 1 (2006): 69–82.

Anum, Eric. "Ye Ma Wo Mo! African Hermeneuts, You Have Spoken at Last: Reflections on Semeia 73 (1996)." In *Reading Other-Wise Socially Engaged Biblical Scholars Reading with their Local Communities*, edited by Gerald O. West. Society of Biblical Literature, 2007, 7–19.

Antwi, Emmanuel Kojo Ennin. "Assessing the Mode of Biblical Interpretation in the Light of African Biblical Hermeneutics: The Case of the Mother-Tongue Biblical Interpretation in Ghana." *Religions* 15, no. 2 (2024): 1–13.

Asale, Bruk A. "The Ethiopian Orthodox Tewahedo Church Canon of the Scriptures: 'Neither Open nor Closed.'" *The Bible Translator* 67, no. 2 (2016): 202–22.

Asamoah-Gyadu, J. Kwabena. "Mission to 'Set the Captives Free" Healing, Deliverance, and Generational Curses in Ghanaian Pentecostalism." *International Review of Mission* 93, nos. 370–71 (2004): 389–406.

Asamoah-Gyadu, J. Kwabena. "Pulling Down Strongholds: Evangelism, Principalities and Powers and the African Pentecostal Imagination." *International Review of Mission* 96, no. 382–83 (2007): 306–17.

Avotri, Solomon K. "The Vernacularization of Scripture and African Beliefs: The Story of the Gerasene Demoniac Among the Ewe of West Africa." In *The Bible in Africa: Transactions, Trajectories, and Trends*, edited by Gerald O. West and Musa W. Dube. Brill, 2001.
Azikiwe, Nnamdi. "Respect for Human Dignity." *Negro History Bulletin* 24, no. 6 (1961): 123–29.
Barnes, Michael, SJ. "Opening Up a Dialogue: *Dei Verbum* and the Religions." *Modern Theology* 29, no. 4 (2013): 10–31.
Barolín, Dario. "Popular Reading of the Bible in Revolutionary and Imperial Times." *Exchange* 44, no. 1 (2015): 27–44.
Barr, James. *The Bible in the Modern World*. SCM Press, 1973.
Barr, James. *Fundamentalism*. Westminster Press, 1977.
Barr, James. *Old and New in Interpretation*. SCM Press, 1982.
Barr, James. *The Scope and Authority of the Bible*. Westminster Press, 1980.
Barrett, David B. *Schism and Renewal in Africa*. Oxford University Press, 1968.
Bartholomew, Craig G., and Heath A. Thomas, eds. Dei Verbum *of Vatican II, A Manifesto for Theological Interpretation*. Baker Academic, 2016.
Bartkowski, John. "Beyond Biblical Literalism and Inerrancy: Conservative Protestants and the Hermeneutic Interpretation of Scripture." *Sociology of Religion* 57, no. 3 (1996): 259–72.
Baur, John. *2000 Years of Christianity in Africa*. Daughters of St. Paul, 1994.
Beckman, Peter. "The Interpretation of the Bible in the Church and the Fundamentalist Interpretation." *Theoforum* 50 (2020): 71–80.
Bediako, Kwame. *Christianity in Africa: The Renewal of Non-Western Religion*. Orbis Books, 1997.
Bediako, Kwame. *Jesus and the Gospel in Africa: History and Experience*. Orbis Books, 2004.
Begant, Diane. "Fundamentalism and Biblical Commission." *Chicago Studies* 34, no. 3 (1995): 209–21.
Belay, Yimenu Adimass. "Scripture and Context in Conversation: The Ethiopian Andəmta Interpretative Tradition." *Conspectus* 34 (2022): 41–49.
Beuken, Wim, Sean Freyne, and Anton Weiler, eds. *The Bible and Its Readers. Concilium* 1995/1. SCM Press, 1991.
Bigalke, Ron J. Jr. "The Revival of Futurist Interpretation Following the Reformation." *Journal of Dispensational Theology* 13, no. 38 (2009): 43–56.
Bính, Philiphe, and Prince Dom João. "Invoking the Padroado." In *Vietnamese Moses: Philiphe Binh and the Geographies of Early Modern Catholicism*, edited by George E. Dutton. University of California Press, 2017.

Bishara, Azmi. "Can We Speak of a 'Coptic Question' in Egypt?" *Arab Center for Research & Policy Studies* (2011): 1–39.
Bowler, Kate, and Wen Reagan. "Bigger, Better, Louder: The Prosperity Gospel's Impact on Contemporary Christian Worship." *Religion and American Culture: A Journal of Interpretation* 24, no. 2 (2014): 186–230.
Bray, Gerald. Review of *The Sufficiency of Scripture*, by Noel Weeks." *Churchman* 102, no. 3 (1988): 262.
Bright, Pamela. *The Book of Rules of Tyconius: Its Purpose and Inner Logic*. University of Notre Dame Press, 1988.
Brown, R. E. *The* Sensus Plenior *of Sacred Scripture*. St. Mary's University, 1955.
Buhlmann, Walbert. *The Coming of the Third Church: An Analysis of the Present and Future of the Church*. Orbis Books, 1977.
Bujo, Bénézet. *Foundations of an African Ethic: Beyond the Universal Claims of Western Morality*. Translated by Brian McNeil. Crossroad Publishing Company, 2001.
Burgess, Richard. "Pentecostalism and Democracy in Nigeria: Electoral Politics, Prophetic Practices, and Cultural Reformation." *Nova Religio: The Journal of Alternative and Emergent Religions* 18, no. 3 (2015): 38–62.
Burk, Denny R. "Is Inerrancy Sufficient? A Plea to Biblical Scholars Concerning the Authority and Sufficiency of Scripture." *Southwestern Journal of Theology* 50, no. 1 (2007): 76–91.
Burk, Denny R. "Why Nashville and Why Now?" *Eikon: A Journal for Biblical Anthropology* 4, no. 2 (2002): 7–23.
Burnham, S. "The Value of the Old Testament for a Correct Knowledge of the New." *The Old Testament Student* 5, no. 4 (1885): 157–61.
Burns, J. Patout. "Cyprian of Carthage." *Expository Times* 120, no. 10 (2009): 469–77.
Cannon, Katie Geneva. "Christian Imperialism and the Transatlantic Slave Trade." *Journal of Feminist Studies in Religion* 24, no. 1 (2008): 127–34.
Celarent, Barbara. "*Facing Mount Kenya* by Jomo Kenyatta." *American Journal of Sociology* 116, no. 2 (2010): 722–28.
Clifford, Richard J. "The Achievements and Challenges of Vatican II on Scripture: The Gift of the Word." *America* 209, no. 14 (2013): 14–19.
Comaroff, J., and Jean Comaroff. *Ethnography and the Historical Imagination*. Westerview, 1992.

Culbertson, Philip. "Known, Knower, and Knowing: The Authority of Scripture in the Episcopal Church." *Anglican Theological Reviewer* 74, no. 2 (1992): 144–74.

Da Costa, Emilia Viotti. "The Portuguese-African Slave Trade: A Lesson in Colonialism." *Latin American Perspectives* 12, no. 1 (1985): 41–61.

Da Silva, José Antunes. da "African Independent Churches Origin and Development." *Anthropos* Bd. 88, H. 4/6 (1993): 393–402.

Davie-Kessler, Jesse. "'Discover Your Destiny': Sensation, Time, and Bible Reading Among Nigerian Pentecostals." *Anthropologica* 58, no. 1 (2016): 226–47.

Dawson, Nate. "Making the Shift to Theological Interpretation of Scripture." *Anglican Theological Review* 99, no. 4 (2017): 753–62.

Delitzsch, Franz. "Must We Follow the New Testament Interpretation of Old Testament Texts?" *The Old Testament Student* 6, no. 3 (1886): 77–78.

De Lubac, Henri, SJ, *Medieval Exegesis*. Vol. 1, *The Four Senses of Scripture*. William B. Eerdmans, 1998.

Denzinger, Heinrich, ed. *Compendium of Creeds, Definitions, and Declarations on Matters of Faith and Morals*. 43rd ed. Ignatius Press, 2012.

De Wit, Hans. "Exegesis and Contextuality: Happy Marriage, Divorce or Living (Apart) Together?" In *African and European Readers of the Bible in Dialogue: In Quest of a Shared Meaning*, edited by Hans (J.H.) de Wit and Gerald West. Brill, 2008.

Dickson, Kwesi A. "Continuity and Discontinuity Between the Old Testament and African Life and Thought." In *African Theology En Route*, edited by Kofi Appiah-Kubi and Sergio Torres. Orbis Books, 1979.

Dobbs-Allsopp, F. W. "Rethinking Historical Criticism." *Biblical Interpretation* 7, no. 3 (1999): 235–71.

Dockery, David S. "The History of Pre-Critical Biblical Interpretation." *Faith and Mission* 10, no. 1 (1992): 3–18.

Dolamo, Ramathate. "Botho/Ubuntu: The Heart of African Ethics." *Scriptura* 112 (2013): 1–10.

Dores, Hugo Gonçalves. "The Road to an Agreement on Missions: The Quarrel Between Portugal and the Holy See Regarding the Missionary Policy for the Portuguese Empire in Africa (c.1880–1910)." *Journal of Religion in Africa* 51, nos. 1–2 (2021): 86–110.

Draper, Jonathan A. "Reading the Bible as Conversation: A Theory and Methodology for Contextual Interpretation of the Bible in Africa." *Grace and Truth* 19, no. 2 (2002): 12–24.
Dube, Musa W. "'And God Saw that it was Very Good': An Earth-Friendly Theatrical Reading of Genesis 1." *Black Theology* 13, no. 3 (2015): 230–46.
Dube, Musa W. "Boleo: A Postcolonial Feminist Reading." *HTS Teologiese Studies/Theological Studies* 76, no. 3 (2020): 1–8.
Dube, Musa W. "Consuming a Colonial Cultural Bomb: Translating Badimo into 'Demons' in the Setswana Bible (Matthew 8.28–34; 15.22; 10.8)." *Journal for the Study of the New Testament* 21, no. 73 (1999): 33–59.
Dube, Musa W. "'God Never Opened the Bible to Me': Women Church Leaders in Botswana." *Studies in World Christianity & Interreligious Relations* 48 (2014): 317–40.
Dube, Musa W. "Go Tla Slama. O Tla Fola: Doing Biblical Studies in an HIV and AIDS Context." *Black Theology: An International Journal* 8, no. 2 (2010): 212–41.
Dube, Musa W. "Let There Be Light! Birthing Ecumenical Theology in the HIV and AIDS Apocalypse." *The Ecumenical Review* 67, no. 4 (2015): 531–42.
Dube, Musa W. "A Luta Continua: Toward Trickster Intellectuals and Communities." *Journal of Biblical Literature* 134, no. 4 (2015): 890–902.
Dube, Musa W. "On Becoming a Change Agent: Journeys of Teaching Gender and Health in an African Crisis Context." *Journal for Interdisciplinary Biblical Studies* 21 (2020): 13–28.
Dube, Musa W. *Postcolonial Feminist Interpretation of the Bible*. Chalice Press, 2000.
Dube, Musa W. "Readings of Semoya: Batswana Women's Interpretations of Matt 15:21–28." *Semeia* 73 (1996): 111–29.
Dube, Musa W. "The Scramble for Africa as the Biblical Scramble for Africa: Postcolonial Perspectives." In *Postcolonial Perspectives in African Biblical Interpretations*, edited by Musa W. Dube. The Society of Biblical Literature, 2012.
Dube, Musa W. "The Subaltern Can Speak: Reading the Mmutle (Hare) Way." *Journal of Africana Religions* 4, no. 1 (2016): 54–75.
Dube, Musa W. "Theological Challenges: Proclaiming the Fullness of Life in the HIV/AIDS & Global Economic Era." *International Review of Missions* 91 no. 363 (2002): 535–49.

Dube, Musa W. "Toward a Post-Colonial Feminist Interpretation of the Bible." *Semeia* 78 (1997): 11–26.

Dube, Musa W. "Twenty-Two Years of Bleeding and Still the Princess Sings!" In *Grant Me Justice!*, edited by Musa W. Dube and Musimbi Kanyoro. Cluster Publications, 2004.

Dube, Musa W. "Villagizing, Globalizing, and Biblical Studies." In *Reading the Bible in the Global Village: Cape Town*, edited by Justin S. Ukpong, Musa W. Dube, Gerald O. West, and Alpheus Masoga. Brill, 2002.

Dube, Musa W. "Who Do You Say That I Am?" *Feminist Theology* 15, no. 3 (2007): 346–67.

Dube, Zorodzai. "Ritual Healing Theory and Mark's Healing Jesus: Implications for Healing Rituals Within African Pentecostal Churches." *Neotestamentica* 53, no. 3 (2019) 479–89.

Dunn, Geoffrey D. "Rhetoric and Tertullian's *De Virginibus Velandis*." *Vigiliae Christianae* 59, no. 1 (2005): 1–30.

Dunn, Geoffrey D. *Tertullian*. Routledge, 2004.

Dunn, Geoffrey D. "Tertullian's Scriptural Exegesis in *de praescriptione haereticorum*." *Journal of Early Christian Studies* 14, no. 2 (2006): 141–55.

East, Brad. "What Are the Standards of Excellence for Theological Interpretation of Scripture." *Journal of Theological Interpretation* 14, no. 2 (2020): 149–79.

Eden, Kathy. "The Rhetorical Tradition and Augustinian Hermeneutics in *De Doctrina Christiana*." *Rhetorica: A Journal of the History of Rhetoric* 8, no. 1 (1990): 45–63.

Eitel, Keith E. "Contextualization: Contrasting African Voices." *Criswell Theological Review* 2 (1988): 323–34.

Éla, Jean-Marc. *African Cry*. Orbis, 1986.

Emerson, Michael O., and David Hartman. "The Rise of Religious Fundamentalism." *Annual Review of Sociology* 32 (2006): 127–44.

Esala, Nathan. "Skopostheorie: A Functional Approach for the Future of Bible Translation in Africa?" *Journal of African Christian Thought* 15, no. 2 (2012): 26–32.

Ezeogu, Ernest M., CSSP. "Bible and Culture in African Christianity." *International Review of Mission* 87, no. 344 (1998): 25–38.

Fahey, Michael Andrew. *Cyprian and the Bible: A Study of Third-Century Exegesis*. J.C.B. Mohr [Paul Siebeck], 1971.

Falconer, Robert. "*Veni Sanctus Spiritus*: The Coming of the Holy Spirit in Inaugurated Eschatology and the Emergence of an Enchanted African Christian Society." *Conspectus—The Journal of the South African Theological Seminary* (2018): 95–114.

Farley, Edward. "Fundamentalism: A Theory." *Cross Currents* 55, no. 3 (2005): 378–403.

Farmer, Craig S. Review of *Introducing Medieval Biblical Interpretation: The Senses of Scripture in Premodern Exegesis*, by Ian Christopher Levy. *Review of Biblical Literature* 24 (2022): 494–97.

Fashole-Luke, Edward. "The Quest for African Christian Theologies." In *Mission Trends No 3: Third World Theologies*, edited by G. H. Anderson and T. F. Stransky. Eerdmans, 1976.

Fashole-Luke, Edward, Richard Gray, Adrian Hastings, and Godwin Tasie, eds. *Christianity in Independent Africa*. Indiana University Press, 1978.

Favazza, A. "Chaos Contained: The Construction of Religion in Cyprian of Carthage." *Questions liturgiques* 80, no. 2 (1999) 81–90.

Fishbane, Michael. "The Teacher and the Hermeneutical Task: A Reinterpretation of Medieval Exegesis." *Journal of the American Academy of Religion* 43, no. 4 (1975): 709–21.

Fitzmyer, Joseph A., SJ, ed. *The Biblical Commission's Document*. Subsidia Biblica 18Pontificio Istituto Biblico, 1995.

Fitzmyer, Joseph A. "Catholic Principles for Interpreting Scripture: A Study of the Pontifical Biblical Commission's *The Interpretation of the Bible in the Church*." *Biblica* 83, no. 3 (2002): 437.

Fitzmyer, Joseph A. *The Interpretation of Scripture: In Defense of the Historical-Critical Method*. Paulist Press, 2020.

Fitzmyer, Joseph A. *Scripture, The Soul of Theology*. Paulist Press, 1994.

Foster, Lewis. "Realgeschichte: Old and New in Interpretation." *Journal of the Evangelical Theological Society* 28, no. 2 (1985): 153–68.

Fowl, Stephen. *Theological Interpretation of Scripture*. Cascade, 2009.

Fowl, Stephen. "Theological Interpretation of Scripture and Its Future." *Anglican Theological Review* 99, no. 4 (2017): 671–90.

Froehlich, Karlfried. *Biblical Interpretation in the Early Church*. Fortress Press, 1984.

Fulford, Ben. "An Igbo Esperanto: A History of the Union Igbo Bible 1900–1950." *Journal of Religion in Africa* 32, no. 4 (2002): 457–501.

Gaiya, Musa A. B. "Charismatic and Pentecostal Social Orientations in Nigeria." *Nova Religio: The Journal of Alternative and Emergent Religions* 18, no. 3 (2015): 63–79.

Gathogo, Julius, and John Kennedy Kinyua. "Afro-Biblical Hermeneutics in Africa Today." *Churchman* 124, no. 3 (2010): 254–55.

Gerlach, Matthew Thomas. "*Lex Orandi, Lex Legendi*: A Correlation of the Roman Canon and the Fourfold Sense of Scripture." PhD diss., Marquette University, 2011. https://epublications.marquette.edu/dissertations_mu/122.

Greer, Rowan A. "The Christian Bible and Its Interpretation." In *Early Biblical Interpretation*, edited by James L. Kugel and Rowan A. Greer. Westminster, 1986.

Grogan, Geoffrey W. "The New Testament Interpretation of the Old Testament: A Comparative Study." *Tyndale Bulletin* 18 (1967): 54–76.

Gifford, Paul. "African Catholicism's Vulnerability to Pentecostalism." *Concilium* 2023, no. 2 (2023): 36–45.

Gifford, Paul. "The Bible in Africa: A Novel Usage in Africa's New Churches." *Bulletin of SOAS* 71, no. 2 (2008): 203–19.

Gifford, Paul. *Christianity, Development and Modernity in Africa*. Oxford University Press, 2016.

Gifford, Paul. "Ghana's Charismatic Churches." *Journal of Religion in Africa* 24, no. 3 (1994): 241–65.

Gifford, Paul. Introduction to *New Dimensions in African Christianity*. Edited by Paul Gifford. All African Conference of Churches, 1992.

Gifford, Paul. "Prosperity: A New and Foreign Element in African Christianity." *Religion* 20 (1990): 373–88.

Gifford, Paul. "The Prosperity Gospel in Africa: Expecting Miracles." *The Christian Century* 124, no. 14 (2007): 20–24.

Gifford, Paul, and Trad Nogueira-Godsey. "The Protestant Ethic and African Pentecostalism: A Case Study." *Journal for the Study of Religion* 24, no. 1 (2011): 5–22.

Gray, Richard. "Christianity and Religious Change in Africa." *African Affairs* 77, no. 306 (1978): 89–100.

Griffin, Joseph A. "The Sacred Congregation De Propaganda Fide Its Foundation and Historical Antecedents." *Records of the American Catholic Historical Society of Philadelphia* 41, no. 4 (1930): 289–27.

Gunn, Dennis. "Teaching for Cosmopolis: Bernard Lonergan's Hopeful Vision for Education in a Globalized World." *Religious Education* 113, no. 1 (2018): 26–37.

Habets, Myk. "Theological Interpretation of Scripture." *International Journal of Systematic Theology* 23, no. 2 (2021): 235–58.Hall, Stuart G. "The Versions of Cyprian, De Unitate, 4–5. Bévenot's Dating Revisited." *Journal of Theological Studies* 55, no. 1 (2004): 138–46.

Hanson, R. P. C. *Allegory and Event: A Study of the Sources and Significance of Origen's Interpretation of Scripture*. SCM Press, 1959.

Hanson, R. P. C. "Biblical Exegesis in the Early Church." In *The Cambridge History of the Bible. Vol. 1, From the Beginnings to Jerome*, edited by P. R. Ackroyd and C. F. Evans. Cambridge University Press, 1970.

Hanson, R. P. C. "Notes on Tertullian's Interpretation of Scripture." *The Journal of Theological Studies* 12, no. 2 (1961): 273–79.

Harrison, Carol. "*De Doctrina Christiana*." *New Blackfriars* 87, no. 1008 (2006): 121–31.

Heijke, Jan. "Thinking in the Scene of Disaster: Theology of Jean-Marc Ela from Cameroon" *Exchange* 29, no. 1 (2000): 61–88.

Helleman, Wendy Elgersma. "New Horizons in the Study of Early African Christianity." *Vox Patrum* 81 (2022): 127–56.

Hendricks, William L. Review of *The Battle for the Bible*, by Harold Lindsell. *Southwestern Journal of Theology* 19, no. 1 (1976): 113.Henriksen, Thomas. "Portugal in Africa: A Noneconomic Interpretation." *African Studies Review* 16, no. 3 (1973): 405–16.

Herbert, Eugenia W. "Portuguese Adaptation to Trade Patterns Guinea to Angola (1443–1640)." *African Studies Review*. 17, no. 2 (1974): 411–23.

Hiebert, Terry G. Review of *The Sufficiency of Scripture*, by Noel Weeks. *Journal of the Evangelical Theological Society* 33, no. 2 (1990): 249.

Hill, Robert J. "Reading Symbols, and Writing Words. A Model for Biblical Inspiration." *New Blackfriars* 89, no. 1019 (2008): 22–38.

Hollingworth, Miles. *St. Augustine of Hippo: An Intellectual Biography*. Oxford University Press, 2013.

Holter, Knut. "Does a Dialogue Between Africa and Europe Make Sense?" In *African and European Readers of the Bible in Dialogue: in Quest of a Shared Meaning*, edited by Hans de Wit and Gerald O. West. Brill, 2008.

Holter, Knut. "Evaluation: Dialogue and Interpretative Power." In *African and European Readers of the Bible in Dialogue: In Quest of a Shared Meaning*, edited by Hans de Wit and Gerald O. West. Brill, 2008.

Hoover, Dwight W. "The New Historicism." *The History Teacher* 25, no. 3 (1992): 355–66.
Hughes, Kyle R. "The Spirit and the Scriptures: Revisiting Cyprian's Use of Prosopological Exegesis." *Journal of Early Christian History* 8, no. 2 (2018): 35–48.
Igenoza, Andrew Olu. "Contextual Balancing of Scripture with Scripture: Scripture Union in Nigeria and Ghana." In *The Bible in Africa: Transactions, Trajectories and Trends*, edited by Gerald O. West and Musa W. Dube. Brill, 2001.
Ijoma, J. O. "Portuguese Activities in West Africa Before 1600: The Consequences." *Transafrican Journal of History* 11 (1982): 136–46.
Isaacman, Allen, and Jennifer Davis. "United States Policy Toward Mozambique Since 1945: 'The Defense of Colonialism and Regional Stability.'" *Africa Today* 25, no. 1 (1978): 29–55.
Jackon, Bernard S. "Why the Name New Testament" *Melilah: Journal of Jewish Studies* 9 (2012): 50–100.
James, A. Lloyd. "Phonetics and African Languages." *Africa: Journal of the International African Institute* 1, no. 3 (1928): 358–71.
James, A. Lloyd. "The Practical Orthography of African Languages." *Africa: Journal of the International African Institute* 1, no. 1 (1928): 125–29.
Jenkins, Philip. *The Lost History of Christianity*. Oxford University Press, 2009.
Jenkins, Philip. *The New Faces of Christianity: Believing the Bible in the Global South*. Oxford University Press, 2006.
Jenkins, Philip. *The Next Christendom*. 3rd ed. Oxford University Press, 2011.
Jewett, Paul K. "Concerning the Allegorical Interpretation of Scripture." *The Westminster Theological Journal* 17, no. 1 (1954): 1–20.
John, Helen C. "Conversations in Context: Cross-Cultural (Grassroots) Biblical Interpretation Groups Challenging Western-Centric (Professional) Biblical Interpretation." *Biblical Interpretation* 27 (2019): 36–68.
Johnson, Wendell G. "'Out of Egypt Have I Called My Son': A Bibliographic Essay on Egyptian Christianity from Its Origins to the Arab Conquest." *Journal of Religious & Theological Information* 18, nos. 2–3 (2019): 45–54.
Jowers, Dennis W. "The Sufficiency of Scripture and the Biblical Canon." *Trinity Journal* 30, no. 1 (2009): 49–65.
Kabamba, J. *Kiboko, Divining the Woman of Endor African Culture, Postcolonial Hermeneutics, and the Politics of Biblical Translation*. T&T Clark, 2017.

Kalu, Ogbu U., ed. *African Christianity: An African Story*. Africa World Press, 2007.
Kalu, Ogbu U. "Unconquered Spiritual Gates: Inculturation Theology in Africa Revisited." *Journal of Inculturation Theology* 1, no. 1 (1994): 25–37.
Kane, Ross. "Political Ressourcement: Decolonizing Through Retrieval in African Political Theologies." *Political Theology* 24, no. 2 (2023): 148–63.
Kannengiesser, Charles. "Biblical Interpretation in the Early Church." In *Historical Handbook of Major Biblical Interpreters*, edited by Donald K. McKim. InterVasity Press, 1998.
Kannengiesser, Charles. "A Conflict of Christian Hermeneutics in Roman Africa: Tyconius and Augustine." In *Protocol of the Colloquy of the Center for Hermeneutical Studies in Hellenistic and Modern Culture*, edited by Charles Kannengiesser and Pamela Bright. Center for Hermeneutical Studies in Hellenistic and Modern Culture, 1989.Kanyoro, Musimbi. "Reading the Bible from an African Perspective." *Ecumenical Review* 51, no. 1 (1999): 18–24.
Kato, Byang H. "Christianity as an African Religion" *Evangelical Review of Theology* 4, no . 1 (1980): 18–23.
Kato, Byang H. "History Comes Full Circle." *Evangelical Review of Theology* 28, no. 2 (2004): 130–39.
Kato, Byang H. "Theological Issues in Africa." *Bibliotheca Sacra* 133, no. 530 (1976): 143–52.
Katoke, Israel K. "Christianity and Culture: An African Experience." *Transformation* 1, no. 4 (1984): 7–10.
Kaunda, Chammah J., and Roderick R. Hewitt. "Toward Epistemic Decolonial Turn in Missio-Formation in African Christianity." *International Review of Mission* 104, no. 2 (2015): 378–92.
Kearsley, R. "Tertullian (fl. 200)." In *Historical Handbook of Major Biblical Interpreters*, edited by Donald K. McKim. InterVarsity Press, 1998.
Kendall, R. Elliot. "The Missionary Factor in Africa." In *Christianity in Independent Africa*, edited by Edward Fashole-Luke, Richard Gray, Adrian Hastings, and Godwin Tasie. Indiana University Press, 1978.
Kenyatta, Jomo. *Facing Mount Kenya: The Tribal Life of the Gikuyu*. Secker and Warburg, 1953.
Kevane, Eugene. "Augustine's *De Doctrina Christiana* in World-Historical Perspective." *Augustiniana* 41, nos. 1–4 (1991): 1011–31.

Kgatle, Mookgo S. "'Go Deeper Papa, Prophesy, do Something': The Popularity and Commercialisation of Prophetic Deliverance in African Pentecostalism." *Verbum et Ecclesia* 43, no. 1 (2022): 1–7.

Kĩnyua, Johnson Kĩriakũ. *Introducing Ordinary African Readers' Hermeneutics: A Case Study of the Agĩkũyũ Encounter with the Bible*. Peter Lang, 2011.

Kĩnyua, Johnson Kĩriakũ. "A Postcolonial Analysis of Bible Translation and Its Effectiveness in Shaping and Enhancing the Discourse of Colonialism and the Discourse of Resistance: The Gĩkûyû New Testament—A Case Study." *Black Theology* 11, no. 1 (2013): 58–95.

Klingbeil, Gerald A. "Cultural Criticism and Biblical Hermeneutics: Definition, Origins, Benefits, and Challenges." *Bulletin for Biblical Research* 15, no. 2 (2005): 261–77.

Knighton, Ben. "The Meaning of God in an African Traditional Religion and the Meaninglessness of Well-Meaning Mission: The Experience of Christian Enculturation in Karamoja, Uganda." *Transformation* 16, no. 4 (1999): 120–26.

Kurz, William. "*Dei Verbum*: Sacred Scripture Since Vatican II," in *After Forty Years: Vatican Council II's Diverse Legacy*, edited by Kenneth D. Whitehead. St. Augustine's Press, 2007.

Kurz, William. Review of *Catholic Principles for Interpreting Scripture: A Study of the Pontifical Biblical Commission's* The Interpretation of the Bible in the Church, by Peter S. Williamson. *Theological Studies* 64, no. 1 (2003): 155–57.

Latourette, Kenneth Scott. *Christianity in a Revolutionary Age: A History of Christianity in the Nineteenth and Twentieth Centuries*. Vol. 5, *The Twentieth Century Outside Europe*. Zondervan Publishing House, 1969.

Laurance, John D. "The Eucharist as the Imitation of Christ." *Theological Studies* 47, no. 2 (1986): 286–96.

Lauro, Elizabeth Ann Dively. *The Soul and Spirit of Scripture Within Origen's Exegesis*. Brill, 2005.

Lauterbach, Karen. "Fakery and Wealth in African Charismatic Christianity: Moving Beyond the Prosperity Gospel as Script." In *Faith in African Lived Christianity*, edited by Karen Lauterbach and Mika Vähäkangas. Brill, 2019.

Lee, Ralph. "Symbolic Interpretations in Ethiopic and Ephremic Literature." PhD diss., University of London, 2011.

Lerner, Laurence. "Against Historicism." *New Literary History* 24, no. 2, (1993): 273–92.

Lindsell, Harold. *The Battle for the Bible*. Zondervan Publishing House, 1976.
Loba-Mkole, Jean-Claude. "The New Testament and Intercultural Exegesis in Africa." *Journal for the Study of the New Testament* 30, no. 1 (2007): 7–28.
Lonergan, Bernard. "The Transition from a Classicist World-View to Historical-Mindedness." In *A Second Collection*, edited by William F. J. Ryan and Bernard J. Tyrrell. Westminster Press, 1975.
Lonergan, Bernard J. F. *Insight: A Study of Human Understanding*. CWL 3, edited by Frederick E. Crowe and Robert M. Doran. University of Toronto Press, 1992.
Lonergan, Bernard J. F. "The Mediation of Christ in Prayer." In *Philosophical and Theological Papers, 1958–1964*. CWL 6, edited by Robert C. Croken, Frederick E. Crowe, and Robert M. Doran. University of Toronto, 1996.
Lonergan, Bernard J. F. *Method in Theology*. CWL 14, edited by Robert M. Doran and John D. Dadosky University of Toronto Press, 2017.
Lonergan, Bernard J. F. "The Transition from a Classicist Worldview to Historical Mindedness." In *A Second Collection*. CWL 13, edited by Robert M. Doran and John D. Dadosky. University of Toronto Press, 2016.
Lugard, Frederick D. "The International Institute of African Languages and Cultures." *Africa: Journal of the International African Institute* 1, no. 1 (1928): 1–12.
Lynskey, Matthew R. *Tyconius' Book of Rules: An Ancient Invitation to Ecclesial Hermeneutics*. Brill, 2021.
MacArthur, John. "The Sufficiency of Scripture." *The Master's Seminary Journal* 15, no. 2 (2004): 165–74.
MacArthur, Julie. "The Making and Unmaking of African Languages: Oral Communities and Competitive Linguistic Work in Western Kenya." *The Journal of African History* 53, no. 2 (2012): 151–72.
Magalhães, Joaquim Romero. "Africans, Indians, and Slavery in Portugal." *Portuguese Studies* 13 (1997): 143–51.
Magbadelo, John Olushola. "Pentecostalism in Nigeria: Exploiting or Edifying the Masses?" *African Sociological Review/Revue Africaine de Sociologie* 8, no. 2 (2004): 15–29.
Magesa, Laurenti. *Anatomy of Inculturation: Transforming the Church in Africa*. Paulines Publications Africa, 2005.
Magesa, Laurenti. *What Is Not Sacred? African Spirituality*. Orbis Books, 2014.
Malekandathil, Pius. "Cross, Sword and Conflicts: A Study of the Political Meanings of the Struggle Between the Padroado Real and the Propaganda Fide." *Studies in History* 27, no. 2 (2011): 251–67.

Maluleke, Tinyiko S. "Of Lions and Rabbits: The Role of the Church in Reconciliation in South Africa." *International Review of Mission* 96, nos. 380–81 (2007): 41–55.

Marshall, Ruth. "Pentecostalism in Southern Nigeria: An Overview." In *New Dimensions in African Christianity*, edited by Paul Gifford. All African Conference of Churches, 1992.

Martens, Peter W. "Origen Against History? Reconsidering the Critique of Allegory." *Modern Theology* 28, no. 4 (2012): 635–56.

Martens, Peter W. *Origen and Scripture: The Contours of the Exegetical Life*. Oxford University Press, 2012.

Martin, John Hilary, OP. "The Four Senses of Scripture: Lessons from the Thirteenth Century." *Pacifica* 2 (1989): 87–106.

Masondo, Sibusiso. "The History of African Indigenous Churches in Scholarship." *Journal for the Study of Religion* 18, no. 2 (2005): 89–103.

Massaad, May. "The Copts of Egypt: State Discrimination and Exclusion." *Arab Center for Research & Policy Studies* (2011): 1–19.

Maxwell, David. "'Delivered from the Spirit of Poverty?': Pentecostalism, Prosperity and Modernity in Zimbabwe." *Journal of Religion in Africa* 28, no. 3 (1998): 350–73.

Mayhue, Richard L. "The Authority of Scripture." *The Master's Seminary Journal* 15, no. 2 (2004): 227–36.

Mbiti, John S. "The Encounter of Christian Faith and African Religion." *Christian Century* 97 (1980): 817–20.

Mbiti, John S. *New Testament Eschatology in an African Background: A Study of the Encounter Between New Testament Theology and African Traditional Concepts*. Oxford University Press, 1971.

Mbiti, John S. "The Role of the Jewish Bible in African Independent Churches." *International Review of Mission* 93, no. 369 (2004): 219–37.

Mbuvi, Andrew M. "An African Biblical Scholar Explores the Broadening of the Biblical Studies Landscape." *Journal of Theology for Southern Africa* 168 (2021): 40–62.

Mbuvi, Andrew M. "African Biblical Studies: An Introduction to an Emerging Discipline." *Currents in Biblical Research* 15, no. 2 (2017): 149–78.

Mbuvi, Andrew M. "Missionary Acts, Things Fall Apart: Modeling Mission in Acts 17:15–34 and a Concern for Dialogue in Chinua Achebe's *Things Fall Apart*." *Ex auditu* 23 (2007): 140–56.

McGill, Alan Bernard. "Reading the Bible Through Stained Glass: Postliberal Resistance to the Historical-Critical Method." *New Theology Review* 30, no. 2 (2018): 31–42.

McLean, B. H. "The Crisis of Historicism: And the Problem of Historical Meaning in New Testament Studies." *Heythrop Journal* 52, no. 2 (2012): 217–40.

McNally, Robert Edwin. "Medieval Exegesis." *Theological Studies* 22, no. 3 (1961): 445–54.

Meinhof, Carl, and Daniel Jones. "Principles of Practical Orthography for African Languages." *Africa: Journal of the International African Institute* 1, no. 2 (1928): 228–39.

Meyer, Birgit. "Christianity in Africa: From African Independent to Pentecostal-Charismatic Churches." *Annual Review of Anthropology* 33 (2004): 447–74.

Mitchell, Margaret M. "Christian Martyrdom and the 'Dialect of the Holy Scriptures': The Literal, the Allegorical, the Martyrological." *Biblical Interpretation* 17 (2009): 177–206.

Moberly, R. W. L. "Christ in All the Scriptures? The Challenge of Reading the Old Testament as Christian Scripture." *Journal of Theological Interpretation* 1, no. 1 (2007): 79–100.

Mojola, Aloo Osotsi. "Bible Translation in Africa: A Brief Historical Overview." *Journal of African Christian Thought* 15, no. 2 (2012): 5–9.

Mollett, Margaret. "Apocalypticism and Popular Culture in South Africa: An Overview and Update." *Religion & Theology* 19 (2012): 219–36.

Mosala, Itumeleng. *Biblical Hermeneutics and Black Theology in South Africa.* William B. Eerdmans, 1989.

Mosala, Itumeleng. "Race, Class, and Gender as Hermeneutical Factors in the African Independent Churches' Appropriation of the Bible." *Semeia* 73 (1996): 43–57.

Murphy, Edwina. *The Bishop and the Apostle: Cyprian's Pastoral Exegesis of Paul.* De Gruyter, 2018.

Murphy, Edwina. "Divine Ordinances and Life-Giving Remedies: Galatians in the Writings of Cyprian of Carthage." *Journal of Theological Interpretation* 8, no. 1 (2014): 81–101.

Mveng, Engelbert. "Impoverishment and Liberation: A Theological Approach for Africa and the Third World." In *Paths of African Theology*, edited by Rosino Gibellini. Orbis Books, 1994.

Mwombeki, Fidon. "Reading the Bible in Contemporary Africa." *Word & World* 21, no. 2 (2001): 121–28.

Ndiokwere, Nathaniel I. *Prophecy and Revolution: The Role of Prophets in the Independent African Churches and in Biblical Tradition*. SPCK, 1981.

Ndung'u, Nahashon W. "The Role of the Bible in the Rise of African Instituted Churches: The Case of the Akurinu Churches in Kenya." In *The Bible in Africa: Transactions, Trajectories and Trends*, edited by Gerald O. West and Musa W. Dube. Brill, 2001.

Nel, Marius. "The African Background of Pentecostal Theology: A Critical Perspective." *In die Skriflig* 53, no. 4 (2019): 1–8.

Nel, Marius. "Current Classical Pentecostal Bible Reading Methods: A Critical Perspective." *Theology Today* 80, no. 3 (2023): 285–96.

Nel, Marius. "The Prosperity Message as a Syncretistic Deviation to the Gospel of Jesus." *Religions* 14, no. 346 (2023): 1–12.

Nel, Marius. "A South African View of Pentecostalism as Another Response to Modernism." *In die Skriflig* 54, no. 1 (2000): 1–7.

Ney, Stephen. "Samuel Ajayi Crowther and the Age of Literature." *Research in African Literatures* 46, no. 1 (2015): 37–52.

Ngong, David T. "Reading the Bible in Africa: A Critique of Enchanted Bible Reading." *Exchange* 43 (2014): 66–83.

Ngong, David T. "The Theologian as Missionary: The Legacy of Jean-Marc Ela." *Journal of Theology for South Africa* 136 (2010): 4–19.

Njoku, Chukwudi A. "The Missionary Factor in African Christianity," In *African Christianity: An African Story*, edited by Ogbu U. Kalu. Africa World Press, 2007.

Nthamburi, Zablon. "Biblical Hermeneutics in the African Instituted Churches." *AICMAR Bulletin* 1 (2002): 15–30.

Nwigwe, Boniface E. "Language About God: A Case Study of Language Abuse in Contemporary Christian Religious Practice in Nigeria." *The Nigerian Journal of Theology* 18 (2004): 68–77.

Nyamiti, Charles. "African Christologies Today." In *Jesus in African Christianity: Experimentation and Diversity in African Christology*, edited by J. N. K. Mugambi and Laurenti Magesa. Acton Publishers, 2003.

Obadare, Ebenezer. "'Raising Righteous Billionaires': The Prosperity Gospel Reconsidered." *HTS Teologiese Studies/Theological Studies* 72, no. 4 (2016): 1–8.

Ocker, Christopher. "Medieval Exegesis and the Origin of Hermeneutics." *Scottish Journal of Theology* 52, no. 3 (1999): 328–45.
Ogbonnaya, Joseph. "African Liberative Theologies." In *Introducing Liberative Theologies*, edited by Miguel A. De La Torre. Orbis Books, 2015.
Ogbonnaya, Joseph. "Insight into Context: Systematic Theological Reading of the Bible in Africa: The Case of Nigeria." In *Watering the Garden: Studies in Honor of Deirdre Dempsey*, edited by Andre Orlov. Gorgias Press, 2023.
Ogunbiyi, Isaac Adejoju. "The Search for a Yoruba Orthography Since the 1840s: Obstacles to the Choice of the Arabic Script." *Sudanic Africa* 14 (2003): 77–102.
Ojo, Matthew A. "Eschatology and the African Society: The Critical Point of Disjunction." *Ogbomoso Journal of Theology* 11 (2006): 93–100.
Okoye, James. "The Pontifical Biblical Commission, the Old Testament, and Christ as the Key to All Sacred Scripture." *Catholic Biblical Quarterly* 80, no. 4 (2018): 670–86.
Okumu, Bishop John Henry. *Church and Politics in East Africa*. Uzima Press, 1974.
Okure, Teresa, SHCJ. "Africa: Globalization and the Loss of Cultural Identity." In *Globalization and Its Victims*, edited by Jon Sobrino and Felix Wilfred, *Concilium* 2001/5. SCM Press, 2001.
Okure, Teresa, SHCJ. "Conversion, Commitment: An African Perspective." *Mission Studies* 10, nos. 1–2 (1993): 109–133.
Okure, Teresa, SHCJ. "Guest Editorial: Ecclesiology in Africa." *International Journal for the Study of the Christian Church* 8, no. 4 (2008): 271–74.
Okure, Teresa, SHCJ. "In Him All Things Hold Together:" A Missiological Reading of Colossians 1:15–20." *International Review of Mission* 91, no. 360 (2002): 62–72.
Okure, Teresa, SHCJ. "'I will open my mouth in parables' (Matt 15.55): A Case for a Gospel-Based Biblical Hermeneutics." *New Testament Studies* 46, no. 3 (2000): 445–63.
Okure, Teresa, SHCJ. "Jesus and the Samaritan Woman (Jn 4:1–42) in Africa." *Theological Studies* 70 (2009): 401–18.
Okure, Teresa, SHCJ. "The Life-Giving Spirituality of the Syro-Phoenician Woman (Matt 15:21–28 and Mark 7:24–30)." *Grace & Truth* 37, no. 2 (2021): 40–51.
Okure, Teresa, SHCJ. "The Ministry of Reconciliation" (2 Cor 5:14–21): Paul's Key to the Problem of 'the Other' in Corinth." *Mission Studies* 23, no. 1 (2006): 105–21.

Okure, Teresa, SHCJ. "The Significance Today of Jesus' Commission to Mary Magdalene." *International Review of Mission* 81 no. 322 (1992): 17-31.
Okure, Teresa, SHCJ. "The Use of Scripture in *Laudato Si'*." *Grace & Truth* 37, no. 1 (2021): 6-15.
Okure, Teresa, SHCJ. "What is Truth?" *Anglican Theological Review* 93, no. 3 (2011): 405-22.
O'Malley, T. P., SJ. *Tertullian and the Bible: Language—Imagery—Exegesis*. Dekker & Van DeVegt, 1967.
Omenka, Nicolas. "The Role of the Catholic Mission in the Development of the Vernacular Literature in Eastern Nigeria." *Journal of Religion in Africa* 16, no. 2 (1986): 121-37.
Onwu, Nlelanya. "The Current State of Biblical Studies in Africa." *Journal of Religious Thought* 42, no. 2 (1984-85): 35-46.
Origen. "On First Principles: Book Four." In *Biblical Interpretation in the Early Church*, translated by Karlfried Froehlich. Fortress Press, 1984.
Oyali, Uchenna. "Bible Translation and Language Elaboration: The Igbo Experience." PhD diss., Universität Bayreuth, 2018. https://epub.uni-bayreuth.de/4298/1/Bible%20Translation%20and%20Language%20Elaboration%20%E2%80%93%20The%20Igbo%20Experience.pdf.
Oyemomi, Emmanuel. "Spirituality and Biblical Theology for Theological Education in Africa." *Ogbomoso Journal of Theology*. 16, no. 2 (2011): 93-108.
Orobator, Agbonkhianmeghe E. "Ethics Brewed in an African Pot." *Journal of the Society of Christian Ethics* 31, no. 1 (2011): 3-16.
Ottuh, John Arierhi. "The Urhobo Traditional Theologumenon on Afterlife and Christian Theology of Eschatology: A Comparative Study." *Africology: The Journal of Pan African Studies* 10, no. 3 (2017): 203-20.
Pachuau, Lalsangkima. *World Christianity: A Historical and Theological Introduction*. Abingdon Press, 2018.
Pascoe, Louis B. "The Council of Trent and Bible Study: Humanism and Scripture." *The Catholic Historical Review* 52, no. 1 (1966): 18-38.
Pauw, C. M. "African Independent Churches as a 'People's Response' to the Christian Message." *Journal for the Study of Religion* 8, no. 1 (1995): 3-25.
Phipps, William E. "Christianity and Nationalism in Tropical Africa." *Civilisations* 22, no. 1 (1972): 92-100.
Pickering, J. *Turn Neither Right Nor Left*. Wipf & Stock, 2019.
Pobee, John S., and Gabriel Ositelu II. *African Initiatives in Christianity: The Growth, Gifts and Diversities of Indigenous African Churches: A Challenge to the Ecumenical Movement*. WCC Publications, 1998.

Pontifical Biblical Commission, *The Interpretation of the Bible in the Church (1993)*. The Holy See. https://www.vatican.va/roman_curia/congregations/cfaith/pcb_documents/rc_con_cfaith_doc_19930415_interpretazione_sw.html.

Prabhu, Wilfred Prakash D'Souza. "Padroado Versus Propaganda Fide': The Jurisdictional Conflict Between Portugal and Rome: State—Church Relations in Sixteenth-Seventeenth—Eighteenth Century Indo-Portuguese History, Its Repercussion on Konkani Roman Catholics of Coastal Karnataka." *Proceedings of the Indian History Congress* 66 (2005-06): 974-98.

Prior, Michael, C. M. "The Bible and the Redeeming Idea of Colonialism." *Studies in World Christianity* 5, no. 2 (1999): 129-55.

Punt, Jeremy. "Reading the Bible in Africa: Accounting for Some Trends, Further Prolegomena for a Discussion." *Scriptura* 71 (1999): 313-29.

Punt, Jeremy. "Reading the Bible in Africa: Accounting for Some Trends Part I." *Scriptura* 68 (1999): 1-11.

Punt, Jeremy. "Reading the Bible in Africa: On Strategies and Ownership." *Religion &Theology* 14, no. 2 (1997): 124-54.

Rahner, Karl. "On the Inspiration of the Bible." In *The Bible in New Age*, edited by Ludwig Klein. Sheed & Ward, 1965.

Ramelli, Ilaria L. E. "Philo as One of the Main Inspirers of Early Christian Hermeneutics and Apophatic Theology." *Adamantius* 24 (2018): 276-92.

Ranger, Terence. "African Initiated Churches." *Transformation* 24, no. 2 (2007): 65-71.

Ratzinger, Joseph. *Eschatology: Death and Eternal Life*. 2nd ed. Translated by Michael Waldstein. Translated and edited by Aidan Nichols, OP. Catholic University of America Press, 1988.

Ratzinger, Joseph. Introduction to *The Interpretation of the Bible in the Church (1993)*, by Pontifical Biblical Commission. The Holy See, https://www.vatican.va/roman_curia/congregations/cfaith/pcb_documents/rc_con_cfaith_doc_19930415_interpretazione_sw.html.

Ratzinger, Joseph. *Jesus of Nazareth II*. Translated by Adrian J. Walker. Doubleday, 2007.

Rée, Jonathan. "The Vanity of Historicism." *New Literary History* 22, no. 4 (1991): 961-83.

Reid, George W. "Missionaries and West African Nationalism." *Phylon* 39, no. 3 (1978): 225-33.

Richard, Ramesh E. "Methodological Proposals for Scripture Relevance, Pt 1: Selected Issues in Theoretical Hermeneutics." *Bibliotheca sacra* 143, no. 569 (1986): 14-25.

Richard, Ramesh E. "Methodological Proposals for Scripture Relevance, Pt 2: Levels of Meaning." *Bibliotheca Sacra* 143, no. 570 (1986): 123–33.
Richard, Ramesh E. "Methodological Proposals for Scripture Relevance, Pt 4: Application Theory in Relation to the Old Testament." *Bibliotheca Sacra* 143, no. 572 (1986): 302–13.
Riches, John. "Interpreting the Bible in African Contexts: Glasgow Consultation." *Semeia* 73 (1996): 181–88.
Runyon, Jacob. "A Spiritual Application of the Historical-Critical Method." *Assembly: A Journal of Liturgical Theology* 37, no. 1 (2011): 10–13.
Ryrie, Charles Caldwell. Review of *The Battle for the Bible*, by Harold Lindsell. *Bibliotheca Sacra* 133, no. 532 (1976): 356.
Said, Edward W. *Orientalism*. Vintage, 1979.
Saint Augustine, *On Christian Doctrine*. Translated by D. W. Robertson. Library of Liberal Arts, 1958.
Sanders, James A. *From Sacred Story to Sacred Text*. Fortress Press, 1987.
Sanders, James A. "Scripture as Canon for Post-Modern Times." *Biblical Theology Bulletin* 25, no. 2 (1995): 56–63.
Sanneh, Lamin. *Disciples of All Nations: Pillars of World Christianity*. Oxford University Press, 2008.
Sanneh, Lamin. "Post-Western Wine, Post-Christian Wineskins? The Bible and the Third Wave Awakening." In *Understanding World Christianity: The Vision and Work of Andrew F. Walls*, edited by William R. Burrows, Mark R. Gornik, and Janice A. McLean. Orbis Books, 2011.
Sanneh, Lamin. *Translating the Message: The Missionary Impact on Culture*. 2nd ed. Orbis Books, 2009.
Sanneh, Lamin. *West African Christianity: The Religious Impact*. George Allen & Unwin, 1983.
Sanneh, Lamin. *Whose Religion Is Christianity? The Gospel Beyond the West*. William B. Eerdmans, 2003.
Sanneh, Lamin, and Michael J. McClymond. Introduction to *World Christianity*, edited by Lamin Sanneh and Michael J. McClymond. Wiley & Sons, 2016.
Sargent, Benjamin. "One Meaning or Many? A Study in New Testament Interpretation of Old Testament Texts." *Churchman* 124, no. 4 (2010): 357–65.
Sarisky, Darren. *Scriptural Interpretation: A Theological Exploration*. Wiley & Sons, 2013.

Schaaf, Ype. *On Their Way Rejoicing: The History and the Role of the Bible in Africa*. Paternoster Press, 1994.

Schaeffer, John D. "The Dialectic of Orality and Literacy: The Case of Book 4 of Augustine's *De Doctrina Christiana*." *PMLA* 111, no. 5 (1996): 1133–45.

Schmidt, Daved Anthony. "Scripture Beyond Common Sense: Sentimental Bible Study and the Evangelical Practice of 'the Bible Reading.'" *Journal of Religious History* 41, no. 1 (2017): 60–80.

Schnackenburg, Rudolf. "The Position in the Theology of the New Testament." In *The Bible in the New Age*, edited by Ludwig Klein. Sheed & Ward, 1965, 35–58.

Shomanah, Musa W. Dube. "Fifty Years of Bleeding: A Storytelling Feminist Reading of Mark 5:24–43." *The Ecumenical Review* 51, no. 1 (1999): 11–17.

Shomanah, Musa W. Dube. "Praying the Lord's Prayer in a Global Economic Era." *The Ecumenical Review* 49, no. 4 (1997): 439–50.

Shorter, Aylward. "Eschatology in the Ethnic Religions of Africa." *Studia Missionalia* 32 (1983): 1–24.

Shutte, Augustine. "Ubuntu as the African Ethical Vision." In *African Ethics: An Anthology of Comparative and Applied Ethics*, edited by Munyaradzi FelixMurove. University of KwaZulu-Natal Press, 2009.

Sithole, Ndabaningi. "African Nationalism and Christianity." *Transition*, no. 10 (1963): 37–39.

Smit, Dirk J. "A Story of Contextual Hermeneutics and the Integrity of New Testament Interpretation in South Africa." *Neotestamentica* 28, no. 2 (1994): 265–89.

Smith, Kevin G. "Spiritual Warfare in African Pentecostalism in the Light of Ephesians." *Conspectus—The Journal of the South African Theological Seminary*, Special Edition (2018): 70–80.

Snyman, Gerrie F. "Hermeneutics, Contexts, Identity: A Critical Discussion of the Bible in Africa." *Religion & Theology* 10, nos. 3–4 (2003): 378–415.

Spinks, D. Christopher. *The Bible and the Crisis of Meaning: Debates on the Theological Interpretation of Scripture*. T&T Clark, 2007.

Spinks, D. Christopher. "Catching Up on a Conversation: Recent Voices on Theological Interpretation of Scripture." *Anglican Theological Review* 99, no. 4 (2017): 769–86.

Stanley, Brian. *Christianity in the Twentieth Century: A World History*. Princeton University Press, 2018.

Stanley, Brian. *The Bible and the Flag*. Apollos, 1990.

Stenschke, Christoph. "Recent Contributions to the Study of the Reception of the Bible and Their Implications for Biblical Studies in Africa." *Religion and Theology* 22 (2015): 329–83.

Stevenson, Ian. "The Belief in Reincarnation Among the Igbo of Nigeria." *Journal of Asian and African Studies* 20, no. 1 (1985): 13–30.

Sundkler, Bengt G.M. *Bantu Prophet in South Africa*. Lutterworth Press, 1948.

Sundkler, Bengt G.M. *The Christian Ministry in Africa*. SCM Press, 1960.

Sugirtharajah, Rasiah S. *The Bible and the Third World*. Cambridge University Press, 2011.

Tabbernee, William. Review of *The Bible in Christian North Africa: The Donatist World*, by Maureen A. Tilley. *Church History* 67, no. 4 (2009): 748–51.

Tàrrech, Armand Puig i. "Interpreting the Scripture from A Catholic Point of View." *Sacra Scripta* 15, nos. 1–2 (2017): 30–50.

Tazanu, Primus M. "Practices and Narratives of Breakthrough: Pentecostal Representations, the Quest for Success, and Liberation from Bondage." *Journal of Religion in Africa* 46 (2016): 32–66.

Taylor, John V. *The Primal Vision: Christian Presence Amid African Religion*. SCM Press, 1963.

Tilley, Maureen A. *The Bible in Christian North Africa: The Donatist World*. Fortress, 1997.

Tilley, Maureen A. "The Collapse of a Collegial Church: North African Christianity on the Eve of Islam." *Theological Studies* 62 (2001): 3–22.

Togarasei, Lovemore. "Modern/Charismatic Pentecostalism as a Form of 'Religious' Secularism in Africa." *Studia Historiae Ecclesiasticae* 41, no. 1 (2015): 56–66.

Togarasei, Lovemore. "The Pentecostal Gospel of Prosperity in African Contexts of Poverty: An Appraisal." *Exchange* 40 (2011): 336–50.

Togarasei, Lovemore. "The Shona Bible and the Politics of Bible Translation." *Studies in World Christianity* 15, no. 1 (2009): 51–64.

Tokunbo, Bankole. "'African Factors' in the Metamorphosis of Indigenous Pentecostalism in Ekitiland, Nigeria." *Black Theology* 17, no. 2 (2019): 150–62.

Towey, Anthony. "*Dei Verbum*: Fit for Purpose?" *New Blackfriars* 90, no. 1026, (2009): 206–18.

Trigg, Joseph Wilson. *Origen: The Bible and Philosophy in the Third-century Church*. John Knox Press, 1949/1983.

Trout, Bradley M. "The (Mis)interpretation of the Bible in South Africa: Towards a Better Hermeneutic." *In die Skriflig* 55, no. 3 (2021): 1–8.
Ukpong, Justin S. "Can African Old Testament Scholarship Escape the Historical Critical Approach?" *Newsletter on African Old Testament Scholarship* 7 (1999): 2–5.
Ukpong, Justin S. "Contextualisation: A Historical Survey." *AFER* 29, no. 5 (1987): 278–86.
Ukpong, Justin S. "Current Theology: The Emergence of African Theologies." *Theological Studies* 45 (1984): 501–36.
Ukpong, Justin S. "Developments in Biblical Interpretation in Africa: Historical and Hermeneutical Directions." In *The Bible in Africa: Transactions, Trajectories and Trends*, edited by Gerald O. West and Musa W. Dube. Brill, 2001.
Ukpong, Justin S. "Inculturation: A Major Challenge to the Church in Africa Today." *AFER* 38, no. 5 (1996): 258–67.
Ukpong, Justin S. "Inculturation Hermeneutics: An African Approach to Biblical Interpretation." In *The Bible in a World Context: An Experiment in Contextual Hermeneutics*, edited by D. Walter and L. Ulrich. William B. Eerdmans, 2002.
Ukpong, Justin S. "New Testament Hermeneutics in Africa: Challenges and Possibilities." *Neotestamentica* 35, nos. 1–2 (2001): 147–67.
Ukpong, Justin S. "The Parable of the Shrewd Manager (Luke 16:1–13): An Essay in Inculturation Biblical Hermeneutic." *Semeia* 73 (1996): 189–210.
Ukpong, Justin S. "Popular Readings of the Bible in Africa and Implications for Academic Readings." In *The Bible in Africa: Transactions, Trajectories, and Trends*, edited by Gerald O. West and Musa W. Dube. Brill, 2001.
Ukpong, Justin S. "Reading the Bible in a Global Village: Issues and Challenges from African Readings." In *Reading the Bible in the Global Village: Cape Town*, edited by Justin S. Ukpong, Musa W. Dube, Gerald O. West, and Alpheus Masoga. Society of Biblical Literature, 2002.
Ukpong, Justin S. "Rereading the Bible with African Eyes." *Journal of Theology for South Africa* 91 (1995): 3–14.
Ukpong, Justin S. "Towards a Holistic Approach to Inculturation Theology." *Mission Studies* 16, no. 2 (1999): 100–24.
Uzukwu, Elochukwu, CSSp. *Memorializing the Unsung: Slaves of the Church and the Making of Kongo Catholicism*. Penn State University Press, 2024.

Van der Bersselaar, Demitiri. "Creating 'Union Igbo': Missionary and the Igbo Language." *Africa: Journal of the International African Institute* 67, no. 2 (1977): 273–95.

Van der Waal, C. "The Continuity Between the Old and New Testaments." *Neotestamentica* 14 (1980): 1–20.

Vanhoozer, Kevin J. *Biblical Authority After Babel: Retrieving the Solas in the Spirit of Mere Protestant Christianity*. Brazos Press, 2016.

Vanhoozer, Kevin J. "The Sufficiency of Scripture: A Critical and Constructive Account." *Journal of Psychology and Theology* 49, no. 3 (2021): 218–34.

Vercruysse, Jean-Marc. "Tyconius Hermeneutics: The Way the Holy Spirit Expresses Itself Through Scripture." In *Patristic Theories of Biblical Interpretation*, edited by Tarmo Toom. Cambridge University Press, 2015.

Vos, Nienke. "A Universe of Meaning: Cyprian's Use of Scripture in Letter 58." In *Cyprian of Carthage: Studies in His Life, Language, and Thought*, edited by Henk Bakker, Paul van Geest, and Hans van Loon. Peeters, 2010.

Vosté, James M. "Medieval Exegesis." *The Catholic Biblical Quarterly* 10, no. 3 (1948): 229–46.

Wacker, Grant. "Reckoning with History: Richard Bushman, George Marsden, and the Art of Biography." *Journal of Mormon History* 43, no. 2 (2017): 21–45.

Walden, Justine. "Capuchins, Missionaries, and Slave Trading in Precolonial Kongo-Angola, West Central Africa (17th Century)." *Journal of Early Modern History* 26, nos. 1–2 (2022): 38–58.

Wallace, Anthony F. C., and Timothy B. Powell. "How to Buy a Continent: The Protocol of Indian Treaties as Developed by Benjamin Franklin and Other Members of the American Philosophical Society." *Proceedings of the American Philosophical Society* 159, no. 3 (2015): 262–63.

Walls, Andrew F. *The Cross-Cultural Process in Christian History: Studies in the Transmission and Appropriation of Faith*. Orbis Books, 2002.

Wansbrough, Henry, OSB. "The Bible in the Church Since Vatican II." *Scripture Bulletin* 43, no. 1 (2013): 10.

Warren, M. A. C. Forward to *Christian Presence amid African Religion*, by John V. Taylor. Acton Publishers, 2001.Waweru, Humphrey Mwangi. *The Bible and African Culture: Mapping Transactional Inroads*. Zapf Chancery, 2011.

Waweru, Humphrey Mwangi. "Reading the Bible Contrapuntally: A Theory and Methodology for a Contextual Bible Interpretation in Africa." *Svensk Missionstidskrift* 94, 3 (2006): 333–48.

Webster, John. *The Domain of the Word: Scripture and Theological Reason.* T&T Clark, 2012.
Webster, John. *Holy Scripture: A Dogmatic Sketch, Current Issues in Theology.* Cambridge University Press, 2003.
Weeks, Noel. *The Sufficiency of Scripture.* Banner of Truth Trust, 1988.
Welch, Sharon D. *A Feminist Ethic of Risk.* Fortress, 1990.
Wendland, Ernst R. "The Challenge of Bible Translation in Africa Today." *Wisconsin Lutheran Quarterly* 80, no. 4 (1983): 284–92.
West, Gerald O. *The Academy of the Poor: Toward a Dialogical Reading of the Bible.* Sheffield Academic Press, 2003.
West, Gerald O. "(Ac)claiming the (Extra)ordinary African 'Reader' of the Bible." In *Reading Other-Wise Socially Engaged Biblical Scholars Reading with Their Local Communities,* edited by Gerald O. West. Society of Biblical Literature, 2007.
West, Gerald O. *Biblical Hermeneutics of Liberation: Models of Reading the Bible in the South African Context.* 2nd rev. ed. Orbis Books, 1995.
West, Gerald O. "Contextual Bible Study: Creating Sacred (and Safe) Space for Social Transformation." *Grace & Truth* 16, no. 2 (1999): 51–63.
West, Gerald O. "Facilitating Interpretive Resilience: The Joseph Story (Genesis 37–50) as a Site of Struggle." *Acta Theologica* 26 (2018): 17–37.
West, Gerald O. "The Historicity of Myth and the Myth of Historicity: Locating the Ordinary African 'Reader' of the Bible in the Debate." *Neotestamentica* 38, no. 1 (2004): 127–44.
West, Gerald O. "Interrogating the Comparative Paradigm in African Biblical Scholarship." In *African and European Readers of the Bible in Dialogue: In Quest of a Shared Meaning,* edited by Hans de Wit and Gerald O. West. Brill, 2008.
West, Gerald O. Introduction to *Reading Other-Wise Socially Engaged Biblical Scholars Reading with Their Local Communities,* edited by Gerald O. West. Society of Biblical Literature, 2007.
West, Gerald O. "Locating 'Contextual Bible Study' Within Biblical Liberation Hermeneutics and Intercultural Biblical Hermeneutics." *HTS Teologiese Studies/Theological Studies* 70, no. 1 (2014): 1–10.
West, Gerald O. "On the Eve of an African Biblical Studies: Trajectories and Trends." *Journal of Theology for Southern Africa* 99 (1997): 99–115.
West, Gerald O. "Reading the Bible with the Marginalised: The Value/s of Contextual Bible Reading." *Stellenbosch Theological Journal* 1, no. 2 (2015): 235–61.

West, Gerald O. *Reading Other-Wise Socially Engaged Biblical Scholars Reading with Their Local Communities*. Society of Biblical Literature, 2007.
West, Gerald O. "Redaction Criticism as a Resource for the Bible as 'a Site of Struggle.'" *Old Testament Essays* 30, no. 2 (2017): 525–45.
West, Gerald O. "The Relationship between the Different Modes of Reading (the Bible) and the Ordinary Reader." *Scriptura* 9 (1991): 90–96.
West, Gerald O. "Some Parameters of the Hermeneutic Debate in the South African Context." *Journal of Theology for Southern Africa* 80 (1992): 3–13.
West, Gerald O. "Towards an Inclusive and Collaborative African Biblical Hermeneutics of Reception and Production: A Distinctively South African Contribution." *Scriptura* 119, no. 3 (2020): 1–18.
West, Gerald O., and Sithembiso Zwane. "Re-Reading 1 Kings 21:1–16 Between Community-Based Activism and University-Based Pedagogy." *Journal for Interdisciplinary Biblical Studies* 2, no. 1 (2020): 179–207.
Wete, Pothin. "The Popular Reading of the Bible." *The Pacific Journal of Theology* 6 (1991): 107–10.
Wielenga, Bob. "Bible Reading in Africa: The Shaping of a Reformed Perspective." *In die Skriflig* 44, nos. 3–4 (2010): 699–721.
Wilhite, David. *Tertullian the African: An Anthropological Reading of Tertullian's Context and Identities*. Walter de Gruyter, 2007.
Williams, Rowan. "The Literal Sense of Scripture." *Modern Theology* 7, no. 2 (1991): 121–34.
Williamson, Peter S. "Catholic Principles for Interpreting Scripture." *The Catholic Biblical Quarterly* 65, no. 3 (2003): 327–49.
Witvliet, Theo. "Response to Lamin Sanneh, 'Domesticating the Transcendent: The African Transformation of Christianity.'" In *Bible Translation on the Threshold of the Twenty-First Century: Authority, Reception, Culture and Religion*, edited by Athalya Brenner and Jan Willem van Henten. Sheffield, 2002.
Wood, Susan K. *Spiritual Exegesis and the Church in the Theology of Henri De Lubac*. William B. Eerdmans, 1998.
Woodard-Lehman, Derek Alan. "Through a Prism Darkly: Reading with Musa Dube." *Cultural Encounters* 4, no. 2 (2008): 37–60.
Yorke, Gosnell. "Bible Translation in Anglophone Africa and Her Diaspora: A Postcolonialist Agenda." *Black Theology* 2, no. 2 (2004): 153–66.
Young, F. Lionel III. *World Christianity and the Unfinished Task: A Very Short Introduction*. Cascade Books, 2021.

Youmans, Peter J. "The Hermeneutical Method of Origen: The Influences upon Him and the View of Inspiration He Developed." *Journal of Dispensational Theology.* 14 (2010): 7–20.

Zarwan, John. "William Wade Harris: The Genesis of an African Religious Movement." *Missiology* 3, no. 4 (1975): 431–50.

Zogbo, Lynell. "Issues in Bible Translation in Africa." *Review and Expositor* 108 (2011): 279–96.

Index

academic biblical scholarship, 93, 101, 104, 178
Africae Munus, 130
African Christianity, 1, 39, 55, 63, 81, 87, 102, 105
African Indigenous Churches, 57, 94
African theology, 3, 96, 172, 205
African traditional religion, 60, 77, 112, 193, 210
African worldview, 59, 68, 97
allegory, 73, 75, 164
Amharic, 37, 38
anagogy, 73, 165
ancestors, 80, 119, 188
apartheid, 95, 99, 105, 107, 121, 130, 175
appropriation, 107, 112, 130, 174, 180, 195
Augustine of Hippo, 1, 13
authorship, 9, 30, 135, 141, 149, 151, 153

biblicism, 28, 85, 154, 157, 160, 176, 184, 208

Christology, 28, 75, 112, 188
colonial hermeneutics, 96, 108
colonialism, 55, 59, 62
conceptual frame of reference, 96, 97, 200, 206, 209, 212
contextual hermeneutics, 201, 203, 206, 207, 208, 209, 213

contextualization, 97, 194, 201
Coptic, 2, 12, 34, 35
cosmology, 58, 146, 182, 185, 191, 208
culture, 208, 209, 210, 212

decolonization, 115, 120, 131, 195, 197, 210
Dei Verbum, 133, 135, 138, 139, 151, 166, 169, 172
deliverance, 67, 99, 185
devil, 17, 22, 24, 74, 86, 88, 119, 185
diachronic, 93, 110, 131, 139, 142, 144, 163, 171, 213
discourse, 117, 145, 192
discrimination, 34, 55, 117, 121, 129

ecclesiology, 21, 23, 113, 124
education, 56, 63, 72, 94, 126, 130, 173, 193, 197, 203
encounter, 41, 48, 82, 91, 99, 105, 121, 139, 182, 203
Enlightenment, 81, 105, 138, 147, 159, 199
eschatology, 23, 78, 79, 89
ethics, 77, 116, 178, 189, 194
Ethiopian Orthodox Tewahedo Church, 37
Eurocentric, 81, 97, 102, 177, 194, 196, 197, 210, 211
evangelicals, 71, 156, 205

INDEX

exegesis, 1, 4, 8, 19, 39, 73, 131, 164, 169, 171, 180, 209, 212
exorcism, 72, 184, 185

faith, 12, 72, 74, 83, 87, 138, 141, 149, 155, 166, 190, 206, 208
feminist, 15, 113, 114, 115, 118, 121, 130
Foreign Bible Society, 45, 50, 51
frame of reference, 96, 97, 172, 191, 195, 209, 212
freedom, 28, 55, 56, 86, 103, 120
fuga mundi spirituality, 88
fundamentalism, 139, 146, 147, 148, 151, 160, 172
futurism, 78, 90, 139

Geʻez, 37, 38

Hanson, R. P. C, 6, 18
health, 77, 186, 187, 188, 202
hermeneutics of suspicion, 111, 115
historical sense, 73, 144
historical-critical method, 93, 95, 137, 141, 143n32, 145, 151, 159, 162, 171, 179, 180
historicism, 137, 151, 161, 162, 172
HIV/AIDS, 87, 122, 130
Holy Spirit, 135, 138, 153, 159, 175, 182, 185, 191

identity, 3, 12, 27, 51, 54, 60, 118, 120
ideological, 95, 96, 100, 126, 177, 200, 201, 205, 210
imperialism, 111, 112, 114, 121, 130, 176, 192, 196, 203, 210
inclusion, 27, 36, 102, 103, 112, 157
inculturation, 58, 62, 93, 96, 98, 102, 104, 112, 129, 130, 174, 191, 205, 209
indigenous, 3, 35, 43, 57, 61, 82, 94, 105, 120

inerrancy, 1, 39, 76, 83, 139, 146, 149, 151, 153, 155, 157, 172, 184, 206
injustice, 95, 114, 116, 125, 128, 212
inspiration, 1, 9, 14, 23, 30, 39, 52, 74, 83, 133, 147, 149, 153, 154, 156, 172, 175, 184, 206
intercultural, 124, 183
interest, 41, 49, 51, 70, 88, 107

liberation, 46, 96, 100, 106, 113, 116, 121, 124, 130, 179, 201, 208, 210
literalism, 6, 72, 139, 172
Lonergan, Bernard F., 61, 65, 104, 203
love of God, 1, 21, 25, 28, 32, 39, 154, 168, 211
Lucifer, 184, 186

Mbiti, John S., 75, 78, 89, 192, 195, 196
missionaries, 41, 43, 46, 54, 56, 58, 62, 82, 120, 173, 193, 197, 199, 204, 209
modernity, 71, 147, 176, 190
mutual self-mediation, 104, 206, 209

neighbor, 25, 28, 31, 211, 212

Okure, Teresa, 93, 124, 131, 142, 171
oppression, 35, 71, 100, 107, 112, 122, 177, 197, 202
ordinary readers, 74, 76, 80, 86, 90, 105, 132, 195, 206
Origen, 1, 13, 17, 19, 20

patriarchal, 113, 117, 121, 130, 176, 196, 211
Pentecostalism, 183, 184, 202
philology, 143n32, 197
postcolonial, 2, 44, 95, 105, 111, 117, 119, 121, 193
praxis, 8, 103, 108

prosperity gospel, 69, 176, 186, 189, 202, 208
Protestantism, 148, 153, 157

reception, 91, 138, 178, 188
redaction criticism, 95, 145
relativism, 155, 178, 195, 205, 208
rereading, 100, 116, 120, 131, 169, 203
resistance, 112, 115, 118, 120
revelation, 5, 8, 9, 74, 100, 133, 135, 138, 158, 163, 167, 171, 188, 207

Sanneh, Lamin, 43, 51, 57, 61, 81
segregation, 130, 177, 201
senses of Scripture, 1, 16, 39, 90, 142, 163, 165, 172
sola scriptura, 45, 151, 158, 160
solidarity, 111, 113, 114, 124
spiritual warfare, 72, 184, 185, 189
spirituality, 1, 8, 39, 46, 58, 87, 90, 128, 175, 189, 194, 206, 208
structures, 53, 60, 101, 113, 120, 131, 181, 187, 197, 202
subjugation, 81, 112, 117, 193
sufficiency of Scripture, 152, 155, 157, 158n97
survival, 66, 112, 114
symbols, 30, 48, 78, 89, 120, 193, 207

synchronic, 93, 110, 132, 141, 143, 146, 163, 172, 213

Tertullian, 2, 4, 6, 33
transcendence, 124, 159, 160
translation, 31, 36, 38, 47, 50, 54, 59, 61, 81, 119, 173, 203
tropology, 165, 166
Tyconius, 21, 22, 24, 27, 28

ubuntu, 77, 114
Ukpong, Justin S., 67, 94, 97, 101, 104, 130, 162, 180, 191, 199
universality, 23, 105, 112, 125, 131, 182

values, 46, 76, 91, 97, 120, 162, 193, 204, 210
vulnerable, 26, 87, 92, 113

wealth, 186, 188, 202, 208
West, Gerald O., 83, 94, 104, 130, 180
western education, 56, 94, 173
witches, 67, 87, 91, 185, 190
word of God, 100, 109, 121, 130, 133
world Christianity, 44, 61, 92, 174, 194
worldview, 175, 178, 190, 191, 195, 203, 211
worship, 8, 13, 59, 85, 118, 194, 205